Peter Robinson's Settlers

Carol Bennett

Dedicated to
Sister St.Donald of Mount St.Joseph;
a loving heart and a generous spirit.

The support of the Ontario Arts Council in providing
research funding for this book is gratefully
acknowledged by the author.

Juniper Books *Limited*

R.R.2, Renfrew, Ontario, K7V 3Z5, Canada.

ISBN 0-919137-16-4

Printed and bound in Canada.

Canadian Cataloguing in Publication Data

Bennett, Carol, date
Peter Robinson's Settlers.
Includes index.
Bibliography: p.
ISBN 0-919137-16-4

1. Irish Canadians- Ottawa River Valley (Quebec and Ont.) - History. 2. Irish Canadians- Ontario- Peterborough, Region- History. 3. Ottawa River Valley (Quebec and Ont.) - History. 4. Peterborough Region (Ont.) - History. I. Title.

FC3100. 16B46 1987 971.3'8 C87-090188-5
F1059.7.16B46 1987.

Cover photo: D.W.McCuaig.
Historian Simon J. Connell surveys the ancient tombstones in St. Luke's cemetery, Emily Township. Mr Connell is a descendant of John Connell who sailed on the ship Regulus in 1825. The tombstone to the right is that of another 1825 settler, William Fitzgerald. It is no longer readable, but Mr Connell has given his permission for the inscription to be copied from his booklet, Some Facts From St. Luke's Past. It reads:
Fitzgerald.
In memory of William Fitzgerald
Better known as Daddy Bill. (A native of Liscarrol, Ireland.)
Not Dead Yet.
and whose age at this date Nov 10, 1857 is 80 years.
Here lies Daddy Bill
In this cold grave laid
Forsaken by all his friends.
May the Lord have mercy on him.

Preface

In the 1820s, impoverished Irish families were brought to Upper Canada by the British government under an experimental emigration scheme. The plan was implemented by a Canadian, the Hon. Peter Robinson, and the new arrivals were taken to the District of Bathurst in the Ottawa Valley, and to the Newcastle District, in the area surrounding Peterborough.

The latter group, the settlers of 1825, have been given more prominence than the former, due in part to the fact that, in 1975, Peterborough celebrated its 150th anniversary. Mr Howard Pammett's M.A. thesis, completed some fifty years earlier, ably explored the Peter Robinson settlement of 1825, while other historians, such as Bill LaBranche who prepared a booklet which was sold in conjunction with the celebrations of 1975, have publicized the group in more recent years.

The writers of local histories in both districts have often mentioned the Peter Robinson families in their work, usually confining themselves to mention of the immigrants in their own locale. Primary research materials are easily available to the researcher through various archives in Ottawa, Peterborough and Toronto, which makes possible an indepth study of Robinson's settlers.

Why, then, write a new book on the subject? My main reason for doing so is that nobody has yet undertaken a study which looks at both the Bathurst and Newcastle settlements together. When Robinson was travelling in the south of Ireland to promote the scheme in 1823, he noted that many people asked if they could bring out their relatives later, if they themselves went to Upper Canada initially. This made me wonder whether there were any ties of kinship between the 1823 and 1825 groups. Did any come from the same communities? Did any of the latter group travel to the Ottawa Valley to join families there?

In an earlier book, Valley Irish, I touched on the story of the 1823 settlers in the Bathurst District. Space did not permit a lengthy treatment of the subject, yet I knew that I wanted to do further research. I asked descendants of the original settlers to contact me, and I was surprised by the enthusiastic response.

Although Valley Irish deals only with the old Bathurst District, some readers were disappointed that the Robinson settlers of the Newcastle District were not included. This convinced me that a book on the subject must include material from both areas.

Next came the question of what to include in the book. I wanted the human side of the story, rather than using these people as statistics. What sort of people were they? What happened to them? Were they the music-hall Irish, rowdy and carefree, or were they solid citizens who helped to build Ontario into the prosperous province that it is today?

I wanted to dispel some of the myths which have grown up around the settlers. Some years ago, one historian touched on this migration to the Bathurst District, calling it "an experiment which failed." All I can say is that the writer must not have visited the Ottawa Valley, to see the churches built by these people, to see some of the farms which have remained in family hands for generations, and to hear of the exploits of those pioneers.

I wanted to list all the families, with their place of origin in Ireland and their location here. Should I list the groups according to their year of arrival, I wondered, or keep them grouped according to the ships' passenger lists? It seemed best, for the genealogists who will be using this book as a reference tool, to list families alphabetically by surname. Once I had done this, I was quite excited to find that there were a number of connections between families in the two groups. More links were discovered after I had contacted individual descendants who knew something of their history.

What I wanted most of all was to seek out information which might help to turn these faceless people into fellow human beings with a story of their own. While I knew that it would be impossible to contact descendants of all the families, I felt that enough stories might be tracked down to enable me to give readers an overview of what became of these immigrants. The most enjoyable part of the research has been in corresponding or meeting with descendants of these people.

Some people have pointed out that by now there must be many thousands of people who are descendants of these settlers, and that it is a matter of pride to be counted among this group. It is indeed! Some ask whether there is any society or association which would entitle members to put certain letters after their name, as do the United Empire Loyalists. As far as I know, there is no such thing, but it certainly sounds like a great idea. Some of my correspondents have fallen quite naturally into the habit of writing PR after their names to identify themselves, so who knows what the future may hold? In some cases I have used this device in the genealogical section, quite unofficially, to denote the fact that someone married a member of another family who came with the Peter Robinson group.

I hope that readers will enjoy this book, whether they are "PR" people or not. It has certainly been a joy to compile.

Carol Bennett, 1987.

The background

The government-sponsored emigration scheme whereby impoverished Irish families were transported to Upper Canada under the leadership of Peter Robinson was an experimental venture. The terrible famine years, which would greatly reduce the population of Ireland, either by death or by emigration, were still a quarter of a century in the future.

However, the economic situation in the early 1820s was grim. The Napoleonic wars had only recently come to a close, and as the war industry came to a halt, the price of grain fell sharply throughout Britain, of which Ireland at that time was a part. In addition to this there was a decline in world markets for goods which Ireland produced, for American entrepreneurs, newly freed from their own war with the British, were stepping in with cheaper goods. Their cotton began to replace Irish linen, a factor which put many weavers out of work, and they also cut into the market with salt beef, another staple. While the city of Cork had been an important trading centre in the eighteenth century, its wealth was now declining.

In 1821, the potato crop failed. The cause was a disease known as curl, or dry rot, quite different from the fungus which led to widespread famine in the 1840s. This 1821 failure caused great distress among the poor, who subsisted mainly on a diet of potatoes and buttermilk. Observers who travelled in Ireland at that time have given us a graphic account of the conditions which resulted. Many people, unable to find work and thus deprived of the means of livelihood, starved to death, with whole families huddled together in primitive, earth-floored dwellings which contained little or no furniture.

Unfortunately, these economic and agricultural problems coincided with a dramatic increase in the size of the population, the cause of which has never been satisfactorily explained by demographers. In 1767 the population had stood at two and a half million; by the turn of the century it was five million.

This trend continued at an alarming rate, and at the time of the famine years of the 1840s there were some eight million people in Ireland. By what strikes us as a horrible trick of nature, these figures were drastically reduced by 1850 because of the famine, both by death and by emigration. It is only in recent years that the population of Ireland has once again reached pre-famine levels.

The British government saw that emigration was one way to relieve the distress of the 1820s. They decided to try an experiment in which they would underwrite the cost of sending carefully selected families from the south of Ireland to Upper Canada, giving them free land (subject to the successful completion of settlement duties) and supplying them with tools and a year's supply of rations.

The idea of placing in Canada large groups of families, loyal to the Crown, would also give the government many more members for the militia which had been formed in Upper Canada following the war of 1812-14. Such men could quickly be called to service if the Americans should attempt to invade Canada, whereas it would take some months to import British regular soldiers in the event of trouble.

As we shall see in another chapter, Peter Robinson, a Canadian, was sent to Ireland to promote the scheme, and it was his duty to line up volunteers, who had to be induced to leave for the New World within a matter of weeks. Although only a limited number could be accomodated, many thousands applied. This was in spite of the fact that Robinson was plied with anxious questions concerning the presence of bears, wolves and marauding Indians.

Economic problems were not the only reason that so many people were willing to try their luck in a strange country. To understand this point, we have to know something about social conditions at that time. The vast majority of the poorer people in the south of Ireland were Roman Catholic. For many years, people of this faith had been severely restricted by the Penal Laws which had been introduced after the war in the latter part of the seventeenth century in which the army of William of Orange had defeated that of King James II.

This war, which included the famous battles of Aughrim and the Boyne, had been fought between the two kings for religious reasons. While it is over-simplifying matters to say that the English wanted a Protestant ruler rather than a Catholic regime, it is true that William, the Princess Mary's Protestant husband, was invited to drive out his Catholic father-in-law and to become co-ruler of England and her possessions.

After the defeat of the Jacobite forces in Ireland, most of the Catholic nobility of Ireland were permitted to leave the country. These defeated men, who had fought for King James, were given refuge in France, where many served in the King's army there. They have gone down into history under yet another nickname, "the wild geese."

The British parliament then devised a plan which would limit the power of those Catholic aristocrats who remained, and which would severely limit the lives of other classes of Catholic society.

4

These Penal Laws were designed to eliminate the threat of a Stuart revival, although this threat fell away to nothing after the defeat of Charles Stuart (the Young Pretender) in Scotland in 1745. After that time, some of the laws were allowed to lapse.

When these harsh laws were first enacted, the wealthier Catholics found that their lands were confiscated unless they took an Oath of Allegiance to the Crown, a pledge which included the forsaking of some of their religious beliefs. At that time, some families became Protestant in order to save their estates.

Smaller land owners were forced to follow the ancient system of gavelkind, a system of land inheritance in which a farm had to be equally divided among all the heirs on the death of an owner. After a few generations the plots of land became quite small and it was impossible to support a family on them. If, on the death of his father, the eldest son became Protestant, he could inherit the land and his siblings would get nothing.

Catholics could not buy land, and when they rented it they could not obtain a lease longer than 31 years. Inter-faith marriage was discouraged, and if a Protestant land owner married a Catholic girl, he forfeited all lands and titles. Among the Peter Robinson settlers there were a number of couples who ran away to this country because their families disapproved of a mixed marriage, and this may have been not simply because of bigotry, as one might expect, but because of the Penal Laws which were still being enacted within living memory.

It was difficult for those outside the Church of Ireland to practice their religion. Catholics, Presbyterians and other nonconformists had to pay tithes to the established Church. All Catholic priests had to register with the government, and, although they were permitted to minister to their flock, no new priests were to be ordained. The bishops were forbidden to remain in Ireland for this reason. At various periods, the Mass was proscribed.

The result was that the Catholic Church went underground. Mass was conducted in barns or in de-roofed churches, or in the open air. Sentries were posted on these occasions in case of discovery. Priests were trained and ordained on the continent and smuggled into Ireland, where they risked their lives to keep the faith alive.

In that period, no Catholic was allowed to run a school, and neither was he allowed to send his children out of the country for an education. Not wanting to send their children to state schools, where they would be open to Protestant dogma, thousands of parents sent them to the hedge schools, secret institutions where Latin and Greek might be taught in the shadow of a hedge, or in private homes. Some of the Peter Robinson settlers were products of the hedge schools, and we can see from some of their surviving letters and petitions just how literate they were. Those settlers might have been poor in worldly goods, but they were well educated.

The hedge schools continued in rural parts of southern Ireland well beyond the 1820s and so many of those who came to Upper Canada as children in 1823 and 1825 may well have been the product of that system; their parents almost certainly were.

Other laws forebade Catholics to vote in elections, to enter the legal profession, to hold a commission in the armed forces or to hold any government office. That is to say, these professions were open to anyone who would take the Oath of Allegiance, but since that included the denial of those doctrines most essential to the Catholic Church, no devout person could consider it.

By the 1790s, some of these laws had been relaxed to the extent where Catholics could buy land and practice their religion, and those who could meet a property qualification could vote. The seminary at Maynooth was founded in 1795, which meant that young men could train for the priesthood without fear of reprisal. However, Catholic emancipation would not come until 1829, and many ambitious young men were prevented from earning a living as they chose. Furthermore, no Catholic could take a seat in Parliament.

Among those who came to Upper Canada with the Peter Robinson settlers in 1823, the average age of the heads of families (and I am excluding the young bachelors) was 35 years. This means that a number of those men had been born in the 1770s and 1780s and had either experienced the effects of the Penal Laws at first hand, or had heard about them from their parents.Change is always slow to come in rural areas, and country folk have long memories. The idea of living under a system with more relaxed rules may have appealed to such men, and so played a role in their decision to come to Upper Canada.

The Province was under the thumb of the Family Compact, and although the Penal Laws did not extend to Canada, the established church did have the upper hand in terms of privilege. One wonders if this was made plain to the prospective settlers at the time.

It would be wrong, too, to assume that the Penal Laws were the main reason that the people wished to leave Ireland. Many of the restrictions affected only the middle class, not the mass of poor people who were the majority in the Catholic Church at that time. They were more concerned with survival than in getting the vote, and they were too poor to hope to make professional men out of their sons. There was a desperate competition for land, and the small acreages,combined with declining markets and failing crops, meant that small farmers could no longer afford to employ labourers, and the labourers could no longer support their families.

When we examine the list of occupations followed by the Peter Robinson settlers, we find that many are described as "reduced farmers," a title which could well be applied to some Canadians today. It is hard to imagine who felt the more desperate, the unemployed labourer who was used to a sub-marginal existence, or the respectable farmers who had been reduced to penury through no fault of their own. Some descendants of the Peter Robinson settlers feel embarrassed because their ancestors were "poor" or "impoverished." I hasten to point out that these were, for the greater part, hard-working people who had been overtaken by circumstances outside their control. There is no suggestion that they were penniless as a result of their own mismanagement.

Such was the backdrop to the scene when Peter Robinson entered the stage in 1822. Before we go on to other things, it should be pointed out that, reprehensible though the Penal Laws were, we must not view the situation out of context. These laws were passed because the English were afraid that Ireland would be used as a springboard for invasion by supporters of the Stuart cause, arriving from France and mustering an army which would then head across the Irish Sea.

Today, we quite properly view any kind of bigotry with abhorrence, yet it is not so many years since brawls took place in Canada between different factions on March 17 or July 12. This chapter is not meant as an editorial judgement for either side. It is an attempt to portray life as it was when the Peter Robinson settlers came to Canada.

Similarly, we must look at the tragic living conditions of Ireland's poor in context. While their problems were compounded by the complexities of the Penal era, we must remind ourselves that the English, Welsh and Scots were also suffering economic deprivation following the Napoleonic wars, as were the citizens of other European countries.

The important thing from the point of view of this book is that British politicians of the 1820s were aware of the distress in Ireland and knew that it must be alleviated. They decided to conduct an experimental emigration project, with the idea that it might be expanded later. This did not happen, partly because people began to emigrate under their own steam, but their findings present an excellent opportunity for the historian to take a closer look at the life and times of settlement in Upper Canada in the 1820s. Everything was well documented, and the settlers received a number of follow-up visits from government officials so that their progress could be checked.

PR PR PR PR PR PR PR PR PR PR PR

The plan takes shape

As we have said, the British government had decided by 1822 to undertake an experimental emigration scheme, designed to alleviate distress in the south of Ireland. Ireland had been part of Britain since the Act of Union of 1800. This move was altruistic in part, but it may also have been thought of in self defence. After all, it was not many years since the French Revolution had taken place and Ireland was a likely spot for a similar outbreak. A crime wave had struck the country, particularly in the urban areas; overcrowded conditions, hunger and unemployment are not conducive to good behaviour. The upright members of the population were sometimes preyed upon by the desperate.

It was believed that if people were removed from these conditions and given the means to support themselves, everyone would be better off, and the difficult element might settle down. Accordingly, Robert Wilmot Horton, who was Britain's Under Secretary of Colonial Affairs, contacted Sir John Beverley Robinson, who was Attorney General for Upper Canada, and directed him to find a suitable man who could oversee the experiment. This had to be a Canadian because he was to accompany them into the bush and assist them in getting settled.

Sir John approached his elder brother, the Hon. Peter Robinson, who at that time was MPP for York. The pair travelled to England to work out the details with the government officials there, and by the spring of 1823 they were ready to put the plan into action. Peter left Liverpool in May of that year, arriving in Fermoy, County Cork, on the twentieth.

"Being a stranger in Ireland," he later wrote to Wilmot Horton, "I was ordered to act under the office of Lord Ennismore and the magistrates and in order to receive the full benefit of their assistance I made Fermoy my principal place of residence." He was happy to find that the scheme met with the "cordial approbation" of the Irish authorities, noting that the clergy, members of parliament and Lords Ennismore, Kingston and Doneraile were all ready to give any help that they could.

On the second of June, Robinson received authorization from England to proceed with recruitment, and by this time his Irish contacts had persuaded him to take as many people as possible from County Cork, which was in "a very distressed state."

A memorandum was printed and several hundred copies were distributed in the towns of Fermoy, Mitchelstown, Doneraile, Charleville, Kanturk, Mallow and Newmarket, and in the villages within that circle. The nobleman and magistrates consented to act as agents, receiving the applications of the would-be emigrants, the idea being that all applicants would be interviewed by these men and a final selection made, based on their recommendations. Only decent citizens, who showed a likelihood of being able to take proper advantage of the opportunity, were supposed to be selected. There is evidence,however, that the officials slipped in a few troublemakers, seizing the chance to get rid of them.

The memorandum set down the terms under which the settlers were to be taken from Ireland and located in Upper Canada. Nobody above the age of 45 years could be taken out at public expense, or given land, "unless under particular circumstances." Such circumstances might include a widowed mother who wished to accompany her grown children, for example. Every male between the ages of 18 and 45 years would receive a ticket for seventy acres of land, in return for which he was expected to perform "duties of settlement and cultivation" on his farm. When these were completed he could obtain a patent to the land for a small fee,and he would also become eligible to purchase an adjoining thirty acres for the sum of ten pounds sterling , if he could do so within a ten year period. As long as the land remained Crown property, the settler had to pay an annual rent of two pence, but this would not take effect until 1828.

At this time, not everyone could read, and not everyone was able to view a copy of the memorandum, so Robinson toured the area, speaking to as many people as possible. Religious differences seemed to be set aside in this effort to relieve human suffering,and Robinson noted that "the whole business was conducted in the true spirit of conciliation, for in every town or village from which emigrants might be expected I called upon the Roman Catholic priest as well as the more respectable inhabitants,to afford them the opportunity of asking any questions they chose to put."

"Several priests entered into the matter with much zeal and one of them promised to read the memorandum from the pulpit and to explain to his parishioners the great advantages to themselves which must accrue from emigrating in such liberal conditions."

Robinson's family was firmly allied with the Family Compact in Canada, and "I had been frequently told that much opposition might be expected from the Roman Catholic priests," he wrote, "as the plan if successful would lessen their congregations and circumscribe their influence but so far was this from being the case that in many parishes which I visited I found them on the best of terms with the Protestant clergymen, and instead of giving unfavourable impressions of the plan they most liberally gave it their support."

Naturally, the people had many fears and questions to put to Robinson, and he made sure that answers were provided. "I made myself accessible to all people, and entered patiently into their fears and feelings, answering their enquiries and affording them

as true a description of the country as I was capable of giving. On these occasions it was that I found the benefit of being well acquainted with Upper Canada,the place of their destination."

He was able to describe the hazards of the overland journey once Upper Canada was reached, and he could talk knowledgeably of farming methods over here. He "dissipated their apprehensions concerning wild beasts and the danger of being lost in the woods."

Many people wished to know whether friends and relatives might join them at a later date, and if they,too, would receive land grants. Robinson replied honestly, saying that he could not say what the government might decide to do in the future, but that in any case they could probably travel out at their own expense, for "there was room enough in Upper Canada for more than could ever come from Ireland."

The people must have liked his answers for the applications soon exceeded fifty thousand. Officials were then given the difficult task of whittling down the number of candidates to a mere five hundred, that is, to one per cent of the total. This led to some "difference of opinion among many intelligent persons... with regard to the description of persons that ought to be received."

Some believed that "a few respectable persons" should be included as an example to the rest, while the scheme should be mainly for the relief of the poor. Others pointed out that taking those who were better off was not giving the experiment a fair trial. The plan was to see if paupers might do well in new surroundings; those with a little capital could afford to take themselves off to Canada. Furthermore, the government might drop the idea of assisted emigration if the system was abused.

The final concensus was that they should go along with the government plan to make "a fair experiment of an emigration confined to paupers," based on the ideal that the scheme was "calculated to promote the permanent comfort and happiness of the persons sent out."

Robinson then decided to confine himself "strictly to the selection of persons who had no capital whatsoever, and who might properly be called paupers, satisfied that if such succeeded in Canada, persons disposed to emigrate having some property would be sufficiently encouraged, since they would have the fullest evidence before them that industry and prudence without their advantage would in time ensure success."

He also decided not to look too closely into the past conduct of the applicants, as he believed that a change of circumstances would cause malcontents to turn over a new leaf, "removed from the influence of the turbulent, the selfish and the designing."   The local noblemen who were assisting him also suggested that if "some of the more fiery spirits could be removed from a troubled district, "those left behind might be induced to live in greater tranquillity."

Once the wheels were set in motion, Robinson distributed embarkation tickets in a manner that was strangely reminiscent of modern airlines. "I had distributed six hundred tickets," he noted, "a greater number than I could have taken out, but I acted in the presumption that some would keep back from sickness or imaginary fears and apprehensions, on the advice of friends. The event proved that I was right, for on the first of July four hundred and sixty were embarked."

Note that the embarkation date was less than one month from the day that Robinson had received the go-ahead from England. It was probably only two or three weeks since some of the emigrants had first heard of the scheme. This called for a hasty decision on the part of those who were to leave home and family. Small wonder that such a large number had second thoughts! Those who did go may have suffered even more. In many cases settlers went out leaving behind wives, parents or children, planning to send for them when they had become established in the new country.

This may have indicated prudence. "I'll go out first and take a look around. There's no point in uprooting us all immediately." "Tickets are hard to get with so many folk applying. I'll have a better chance to get a passage than ten of us would. They won't turn you down next time if I'm already out there."

Prudence aside, it must have been hard on those who stayed behind, wondering if they would ever see their loved ones again. In many cases they did not. There was a high mortality rate among the settlers, who died from accident or disease. This was not unusual in the 1820s, when there were many more fatal diseases than we have today. Those who stayed at home were in just as much danger of dying young.

Robinson himself marvelled at the fact that the plan had been carried out so quickly. "Thus in rather less than a month's time from the time of issuing the proposals the emigrants were on board and the ships ready to sail, such was the promptness of government in making arrangements, and the active exertions of the magistrates and nobility in enabling me to select the requisite number. For their kindness in thus forwarding the object of my journey to Ireland as well as their attentions to myself I feel exceedingly grateful."

To the 460 persons who arrived on the dock at Cork, Robinson was able to add another 108 the next day from among the waiting hopeful, whose applications had been previously refused. One can imagine the stress under which those families prepared to leave, having been on "standby" as we would say today.

A total of 568 people were placed on board two ships, the Hebe and the Stakesby, English vessels of about 500 tons, which had been sent from London for the purpose of transporting the settlers to Quebec. The travellers were well looked after, compared with the usual shipboard conditions of that era, and they were certainly much better off than those who were later to leave Ireland in the famine days of the 1840s, when the term "coffin ship" was a grim reality.

The two ships were well provisioned with food, much better than the subsistence diet which the majority of these people had known at home, and there was a ship's surgeon on each vessel, who would not only care for the people aboard, but who would also escort them to Upper Canada.

Ironically enough, the passengers had complaints about the food. Robinson wrote in his letters that "the rations were abundant and comfortable. The men were allowed cocoa for breakfast and nearly half a pint of spirits, which was perhaps not too much. The women and children were allowed tea and sugar... it is maybe worth remarking, as it is so characteristic of the fondness of the Irish people for potatoes, that the men preferred them to the cocoa, which they refused for several days to take till they saw the officers of the ship repeatedly breakfasting upon it. The children during sickness called repeatedly for potatoes, refusing arrowroot or any other aliment more congenial to their situation, and nothing could prevail on man, woman or child to eat plum pudding, which, as is usual on shipboard, was part of Sunday's dinner. Few of them would eat the best English cheese and when it was served out as part of their ration it was commonly thrown overboard."

This seems strange to us. Surely people who had been near to starvation would be glad to get anything edible, particularly if it was free! This must be taken in context, however. The poorer people in Ireland at that time were used to a diet which consisted almost exclusively of potatoes and buttermilk, other items of produce being earmarked for sale in order to pay the rent. It has been suggested by sociologists that this potato-milk diet was "almost perfect," and it has been pointed out that the health and development of the Irish was vastly improved, following the introduction of the potato to Ireland in Elizabethan times. A theory has also been put forward that this diet is a possible explanation of the population explosion which began late in the eighteenth century there.

Anyway, the Peter Robinson settlers had to learn to develop a taste for such delicacies as cheese, cocoa and plum pudding! (When the author of this book first came to Canada from the old country, she had trouble coping with two new taste sensations, weiners and corn on the cob. The latter, which was known in Britain as maize, was then fed only to livestock. Corn on the cob has since become a delicacy over there.)

The ships arrived safely at Quebec after a voyage of eight weeks,the Hebe getting in on August 31,1823 and the Stakesby on the second of September. Robinson recorded that the voyage had been uneventful, "nothing happened of importance." The fact that nine people had died in the interim was taken as a matter for congratulation because the number was so small; this was attributed to good management.

"One woman and eight children died in the passage, and those from smallpox, which had unfortunately got into both ships, and not from any cause that could be attributed to their change of circumstances or situation." These unfortunates included Bridget Ahern and her three-month-old baby,Jane, who died within a week of each other, leaving behind a 28 year-old husband and a three -year-old boy. Others, who survived the Atlantic crossing, were probably unfit to face the journey to Upper Canada; some died soon after their arrival in the Ottawa Valley. Several pregnant women gave birth at,or en route to, their new homes. They at least had medical aid as far as Prescott in the form of the two surgeons, Mr Hamilton and Mr Dixon (In Britain, surgeons were, and still are, referred to as Mr rather than doctor. This also applies to dentists and veterinarians.)

Robinson praised the two surgeons, "whose indefatigable attention to the emigrants and kind benevolent treatment cannot be sufficiently praised. Such was their zeal and anxiety for the success of the emigration that they volunteered their services from Quebec to Prescott, a distance of more than three hundred miles, and were of great service in preserving the health of the emigrants while passing up the river in boats, which was the most difficult and tedious part of the journey."

At Quebec City, the settlers were transferred from the ships to steamboats, without setting foot on land. They left on the fourth of September, arriving at Montreal two days later. Here they touched land for the first time in two months, but they were marched to Lachine without delay, a distance of ten miles. They camped there for two days, and then came the adventure which was possibly more frightening than the ocean voyage.

The people were shepherded onto flat bottomed boats, with various male settlers being selected as crew members under the direction of "two Canadians to guide and steer." Few of the Irish had even been in a boat before and the speed of the current was terrifying.

Prescott was reached on September 15, and a commissary from Montreal was waiting for the new arrivals with rations. The people camped out while they enjoyed a welcome break, before leaving on September 18 for their final destination, the Bathurst District. (The old District of Bathurst was made up of parts of the present-day counties of Lanark, Renfrew and Carleton. The settlers were heading for the Mississippi River, for Robinson intended to settle them in Ramsay Township, close to the modern towns of Almonte and Carleton Place.

The sixty mile trip by wagon took four days. Robinson was pleased to find that Sir Peregrine Maitland had provided "many articles useful to settlers, which remained in the King's Stores." This storehouse was at Franktown; it had initially been established for the military settlements of the 1816-1818 period, which included Perth and Richmond. However, it was dismaying to find that much of the land in Ramsay Township, where Robinson had proposed to located his people, was in fact already settled.

"More than half had been settled by Scotchmen from the neighbourhood of Glasgow," he wrote. "The adjacent townships of Huntley, Goulbourn and Pakenham were also partially settled by disbanded soldiers and others. Being anxious to settle the people as near each other as possible I determined to examine carefully what land remained in these townships at the disposal of the government and fortunately I found a sufficient number of vacant lots for settlement."

"I therefore located in the Township of Ramsay 82 heads of families, in Pakenham 29, in Bathurst, one, in Lanark,two, Beckwith five, Goulbourn 26, in Darling, three and in Huntley 34, making in all 182. As there were no barracks or government buildings in the neighbourhood and the whole party without shelter, my first care was to provide log houses for them, and that on their prospective lots. Fortunately the autumn was unusually dry and warm and I completed this object by the first of November."

Today, when we have good roads, mechanized transport and power tools, we may have difficulty in understanding the magnitude of this task. Most of the settlers were located on their land during October,and since few of the settlers were experienced in the use of the axes with which they had been provided, they were aghast when confronted with dense bush and told that they had to cut down trees with which to build a log shanty. Accordingly, Robinson had to hire local men, some of whom had already been on their farms for two or three years,to help with the work.

Not long afterwards, the new arrivals were left to face their first Canadian winter and their first taste of solitude in the bush. They may have been homesick for Ireland and slow to grasp new ways, but they were extremely grateful for their chance, as some of their surviving letters show. They wrote to friends and family back home, urging them to come to Canada, and they were thrilled with the security given them

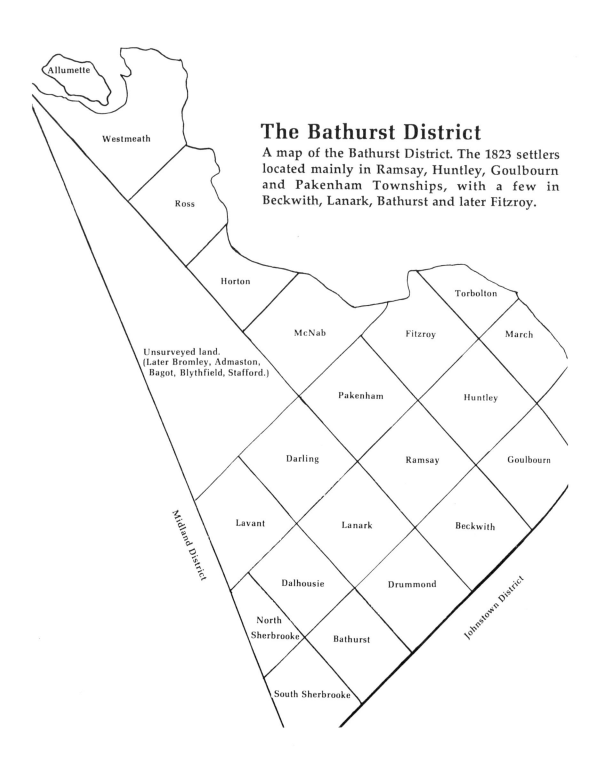

The Bathurst District

A map of the Bathurst District. The 1823 settlers located mainly in Ramsay, Huntley, Goulbourn and Pakenham Townships, with a few in Beckwith, Lanark, Bathurst and later Fitzroy.

Allumette

Westmeath

Ross

Horton

McNab

Torbolton

Fitzroy

March

Unsurveyed land.
(Later Bromley, Admaston,
Bagot, Blythfield, Stafford.)

Pakenham

Huntley

Darling

Ramsay

Goulbourn

Midland District

Lavant

Lanark

Beckwith

Dalhousie

Drummond

Johnstown District

North
Sherbrooke

Bathurst

South Sherbrooke

by free rations and ownership of their own land.

Inevitably, disillusionment would set in the following summer, when they were faced with the task of planting the crop which would keep them alive the following winter. Some families had drawn land which was rocky or swampy, and so unfit for farming. Within a few years, such people would trade lots, or even leave the district.

A head count of these families, taken in March,1826,showed that eight heads of families had died in the interim. Many children had been born, but some lived for only a short time. The cold may have been responsible for some of these deaths; some families received only one blanket, a poor protection against an Ottawa Valley winter.

Some of the men were skilled tradesmen,who managed to accumulate some money by working in the embryo villages of the area,such as Richmond, Shipman's Mills and Perth. Others were recruited for work on the canal which was then under construction at Kingston. Most later returned to their land, where families were waiting.

In order for Robinson to assess the success of his scheme it was necessary to keep track of the settlers, because one of the conditions they had agreed to was that they would remain on the land.

"If the person locating on any lot under the present system shall before receiving his Patent for the same, withdraw from Upper Canada, and remain absent for the space of six months ,without sufficient cause to be allowed by the Lieutenant Governor of the Province, the land so assigned to such person shall be given to another applicant."

Given this understanding, why did men leave their land? In the case of the tradesmen , it seems logical that they would seize the chance to make some money which would buy much needed clothing and furniture for their families.. After all,they did have ten years in which to improve their land. There is evidence, also, that the officials approved this temporary employment, as letters carried to Ireland by Robinson often mentioned that men were working here, and the wages received.

In any event, the majority of the settlers stayed on. In some cases, their farms are still held by their descendants. In 1824, most managed to clear a few acres of land, and the list of crops raised in the summers of 1824 and 1825 shows that these Irish people were prepared to work hard. They were beginning to fulfill the promise which the emigration scheme had held out.

Michael Corkery of Ramsay was among the most successful at that point, no doubt because he had several grown children to assist him. In two years, this family cleared thirty acres of land and produced 300 bushels of grain, 1200 bushels of potatoes and 900 bushels of turnips. They soon owned ten head of cattle and 20 hogs.

Martin Ryan of Ramsay had a similar success; he,too, had teen-aged sons to assist them. Others with a lot to show for their labour included Thomas Madden, Patrick Healey and John Phelan in Ramsay and Richard Forrest in Huntley. By 1826, Forrest, head of another large family, had cleared 26 acres and raised 1000 bushels of potatoes, among other things. Obviously the most fortunate families were those who had a good number of adult or teenaged children to help with the work.

By 1826, a total of 298 cattle were to be found among the settlers; some were oxen, stolid creatures which were indispensible for farm work. Only two horses were owned by the group; these were the property of the Mansells of Huntley. Robinson had been responsible for obtaining the nucleus of these herds as another service to the settlers.

Religion.

Many of the new arrivals , particularly the Roman Catholic majority, took care to begin the practice of their religion in the new land. We know this because at the time of the Ballyghiblin riots, which will be mentioned later, the Catholics were gathered at Shipman's Mills for an eleven o'clock mass. This was on May second, 1824. Most of the Catholics at that time were cared for by a missionary priest, Father John MacDonald, who was stationed at Perth. Those who settled in Huntley and Goulbourn Townships soon came under the care of the priest from Richmond.

St Mary's church,Almonte, was not built until 1842 but before that, Mass was celebrated in private homes. The Corkery, Slattery, O'Brien and Dowling families hosted the priest on these occasions in Ramsay Township, while the Meehans and the Kennedys were among those so honoured in Huntley. The Manions of Huntley were the first to offer their home as a "station" but they were in the township before the arrival of the Peter Robinson settlers, with whom they later inter-married.

Although, as we shall see later, Robinson had some anxious moments over the problem of the Ballyghiblin riots, the scheme was considered to have been a success, and the British government authorized a second wave of emigration of people who would belocated in the Newcastle District, which was part of the present counties of Victoria and Peterborough.

The Ballyghiblin Riots

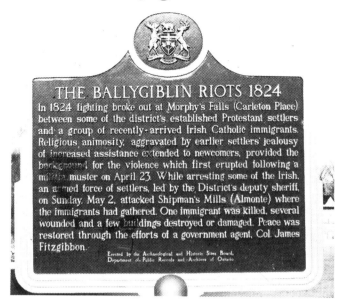

This plaque at Carleton Place, erected on a bridge over the Mississippi, commemorates the riots of 1824 in which Peter Robinson settlers took part.

In 1824, an unpleasant affray occurred in Ramsay Township which could well have blocked the 1825 migration to the Newcastle District, had matters been unresolved. This affair has gone down in local history as "the Ballyghiblin Riots", although at least one writer has glorified it by calling it "the battle of Morphy's Falls", that being an old name for Carleton Place.

When Robinson settled many of his Irish families in Ramsay Township, part of the district was already settled by Scots. Naturally enough, the people who had settled there without the benefit of the tools and rations given to the Irish group were envious of their superior lifestyle and there must have been much talk among themselves of the unfairness of their own situation.

Now at that time, the war of 1812-14 was still a recent memory, and it was mandatory for all able-bodied men to meet periodically for militia training. Accordingly, the men of the district, who formed part of the 4th Carleton Militia, mustered at Morphy's Falls on April 23, 1824. It may have been the first time that the Scots and the Irish met formally, en masse, for by and large they were of different religious persuasions and so would not have met through at church. So, on that occasion, there were the old settlers, primarily Scottish Presbyterians, and the Peter Robinson settlers, largely Roman Catholic, and privileged by virtue of their government aid.

Unfortunately, some of the participants met at William Morris's tavern, there to drink the king's health, a diversion that was not supposed to be part of the proceedings, despite the fact that it was the king's birthday. It appears that, for some time past, this Morris had been complaining bitterly to all and sundry about the preferential treatment given to Robinson's settlers. The sight of so many Irishmen gathered in one place must have lent fuel to the fire. As the liquor flowed, matters came to a head.

As to who struck the first blow; this is by no means clear. The Montreal Herald of May 5 contained a colourful account of the fracas, blaming the Irish. The material for this story was supplied by a correspondent from Perth, who was not present, but who had based his story on the many rumours which subsequently drifted about the countryside.

"The Irish emigrants who arrived in this settlement last season, under the auspices of Government and superintendence of the Hon. Peter Robinson, are carrying outrages to such extremes as almost to baffle the efforts of the civil authorities to keep them in check. On the 23rd of April, His Majesty's Birthday, a part of one of the militia regiments assembled for training at Morphy's Falls, in the Township of Ramsay, when such scenes of outrage took place as would require an abler pen than mine to describe. While a party, principally Scots, were drinking His Majesty's health in the house of Mr Morris, they were attacked by the Ballygibinets, as the Irish emigrants term themselves, the windows stove in and the floor and walls literally washed with blood. A gun was forcibly taken from one of the party in Morris's house and the person who carried it off was wounded by a shot fired at him when making his retreat with the prize. Since the 23rd, fresh outrages have been committed..."

It seems unlikely that the Irish would have attacked their neighbours without provocation. By and large, the settlement was a quiet one, without the violence which later characterised the Bytown Irish. However, we must remember that the Irish settlers had endured a great deal of trouble in Ireland from the landlords, from members of secret societies, and from those who had been driven through privation to crime; fighting in their own defence would have been natural under some circumstances.

It may be that the skirmish on the 23rd was little more than the result of tempers out of control as a result of strong drink. Had the matter rested there, all might have been well. However, the Irish got ready for reprisals. The next day a number of them marched back to Morphy's Falls, to have it out with one Thomas Glendinning. He was an Englishman, a veteran of the Napoleonic wars who was Captain of one of the militia companies, and he had been one of the most vociferous about the situation.

It is hard to know just what his grudge might have been. He had received a large land grant in return for his war service, and at Glen Isle, near Carleton Place, he already had a fine stone house which was one of the finest residences in Ramsay Township. (This house is still in use.)

It may have been at this point that the Irish dubbed themselves "the Ballyghiblins." Ballyghiblin was the parish in Ireland from which some of the people had come. When Robinson located the families on their lots in the fall of 1823 he had put some of the single men in a camp beside the Mississippi River, at a spot which is now in downtown Almonte. These fellows were hired to assist him with certain jobs. This became known as "the Ballyghiblin's camp." The idea of giving themselves a name may have stemmed from the then-prevalent custom of forming secret societies in Ireland which were formed to fight perceived wrongs.

Anyway, the group located Glendinning, and one of the settlers, Luke McGrath, felled him with a club. The group retreated, but two days later they were on the road again, with McGrath at their head, carrying a green flag. They headed for Glendinning's house at Glen Isle, but he saw them coming and hid in a secret recess in the fireplace, leaving his wife to face the mob. Frustrated, they eventually left.

By this time, other settlers were seriously alarmed, and they appealed to the local magistrates for help. Alexander Morris rushed to Perth with the story of the Glen Isle attack, with the result that an armed party came out from the village, accompanied by three magistrates.

The second of May was a Sunday. The Catholic settlers were in the habit of attending mass in private homes, there being no church as yet. On that day they were peaceably congregated at the home of blacksmith Cornelius Roche at Shepherd's Falls, which is now Almonte. Mass was to be celebrated at 11 o'clock. They were unaware that a large, armed party of men was approaching.

The raiders were divided into two groups; one went to "the depot of these emigrants" (the Ballyghiblin camp) while the other headed for the blacksmith's shop. Shots were exchanged, and one man inside the house was killed, and two people wounded, while one of the constables of the other party was also wounded. A signed affidavit made by the Perth group maintained that they were first fired upon by the people inside the house, but a later investigation proved that this was not true.

Now that violent death and wounding had entered the peaceful community, the authorities were seriously alarmed, and an official investigation was launched immediately. For his part, Peter Robinson was badly worried. He had been spreading the idea that the impoverished Irish, taken to a new country

and given the chance to make something of themselves, would do well here. If it could be proved that they were indeed "lawless banditti" as the older settlers charged, the experiment would be serioulsy affected, perhaps even discontinued. With plans afoot to ship out more people in 1825, he could not afford to have it said that his settlers were violent troublemakers. In his original memorandum he had said:

"If the experiment succeeds the system may be more considerably pursued in future years, dependent, however, upon the good conduct of those who may be anxious to avail themselves of the present offer, as well as on that of the future claimants for similar assistance , whom it is out of the power of Government to remove in the present year."

James Fitzgibbon, Assistant Adjutant-General, was sent to the area to conduct a thorough investigation. Sworn statements were taken from participants and witnesses on both sides, including the militia officers and the leading members of the Ballyghiblin faction. Fitzgibbon, a veteran of the 1812 war, was himself a native of the south of Ireland, and was therefore conversant with the concerns of the Robinson settlers.

Some of the local magistrates certified that they had accompanied the party which went to Ramsay on the Sunday in question. Setting out from Perth at daylight, they had spoken with a number of "old" settlers on the way, and were

"of the opinion that the people labour under such fear for the lives of themselves and their families , and the destruction of their property, that they will not mention many of the leaders in these riots. Several of the settlers have not slept in their houses for a week past, being in fear of their lives from threats held out against them."

William Loucks of Beckwith made a sworn statement before the magistrates:

"On Friday, the 23rd of April, I saw Bat Murphy, of the Township of Ramsay, strike the door of Mr Morris, at Morphy's Falls aforesaid, with a club (the door being shut) and throw stones at the window of the house, and that on opening the door from the inside I saw John French (generally residing at Morphy's Falls) strike a man at the door, likewise William Brown, who was battering the said house with a club. I saw a man knocked down of the name of John Munro, but cannot say by whom. Several others were present of Mr Robinson's settlers, who were acting notoriously, but I do not know their names."

"On the 24th I saw Luke, which I believe to be Luke McGrath, knock down Captain Glendinning in my house, in the upper apartment, with a club." He said that he had allowed only two men to go upstairs because a group of men had asked to speak to the Captain, and he was afraid of trouble.

William Murphy of Morphy's Falls testified that "*John Coklin (sic) one of Mr Robinson's settlers, on the day of the 23rd of April, broke Mr Morris's shop window with an axe handle; that John French struck the door of Mr Morris and also violently struck Mr Wilson of Ramsay with a club, and threw stones into the house whenever the door was opened. Bat Murphy I saw throw stones at the window of Mr Morris, and saw him strike on Benson with a stone on the head. William Brown I saw throwing stones at the house and having a club in his hand; he struck several but I do not know their names. They said and swore they would fight any Scotsman in the country. There were a number of Mr Robinson's settlers present with clubs. I saw a gun seized from John Fummerton by John Lackie and carried off by him... on the 24th I saw John French about Mr Loucks' all the noon of that day, saying that he would not leave the place till he had satisfaction of Mr Glendinning. He was armed with a gun. Twenty of Mr Robinson's settlers crossed the river that day and came to Mr Loucks' house, many of whom threatened Mr Glendinning's life.*"

"*On the 26th I saw a number of men which I believe were Mr Robinson's settlers pass through a field in which I was working, rank and file, with a green flag in front of them, carried by Luke McGrath. They were armed with guns and bludgeons, and going in the direction of Mr Loucks'. I heard several shots fired. Some told me they were at Mr Glendinning's, looking for him to fight a duel with one John Sullivan.*"

Following the tragedy at Shepherd's Falls, a number of the men involved were taken to jail at Perth, awaiting trial. Major Hillier, the Military Secretary to the Lieutenant Governor of Upper Canada, wrote that His Excellency was most eager to get to the bottom of the whole affair. He asked why " Fummerton, said to have fired on the 23rd of April" had not been apprehended; Fummerton was not a Peter Robinson settler and it was felt that if he had been promptly arrested the settlers might have been "satisfied and allowed the law to take its course."

"*It is easy to imagine,*" he wrote, " *that the settlers may have imbibed the idea that they were all to be held, without discrimination, the guilty party in every outrage, and that the laws were in force not for their protection but merely for their coercion.*"

He went on to say that this did not excuse the subsequent violence, and that the Lieutenant Governor wanted the settlers to know that no prejudice existed against anyone, " *except such as their acts as individuals may have excited.*"

Fitzgibbon arrived in the district on May 20, staying in the Almonte area for a week. He took sworn statements from Robinson settlers Patrick O'Keeffe, Cornelius Roche, Bridget Roche, Daniel Ryan and Bartholomew Murphy, as well as James Hawkins and Alexander Morris of the opposite faction. We should say here that the majority of settlers listed above had not taken part in the raids but were witnesses who had been in attendance at mass when the fatal shooting took place. Militia officers were also interrogated.

In June, Fitzgibbon released a report in which he summed up "what he thinks is an impartial review." In summary, the points he made are as follows:

That the old settlers were jealous of the new, with their government help, and that "religious and party distinctions greatly increased the agitation."

The person placed in charge of the new settlers was young, and without official authority in the district.

That the officers of the 4th Regiment, Carleton Militia, acted irresponsibly in giving alcohol to their men.

That there was a lack of communication between the sheriff and some of the Perth magistrates that made peacekeeping difficult.

That the sheriff, through illness, was not able to accompany the armed force to Shepherd's Falls where they were to arrest the troublemakers.

That his deputy, who organized the raiding party, was an Orangeman whose father was said to have been murdered by Catholics in Ireland.

That the magistrates did not use their authority over the party until firing began at the depot.

Fitzgibbon's interpretation of the events of May second was this. The deputy sheriff ordered some of his men to surround Roche's house, while he took the rest of the group to the depot, about a quarter of a mile away. This depot was a cluster of log huts which had been built to shelter some of the settlers, prior to their being moved to their lots in the spring. Those who had not attended mass, including, we suppose, some of the Protestants, ran for the river when they saw armed strangers approaching. They were fired upon, despite the protests of Colonel Marshall, who was with the Perth men.

Hearing the shots, the group surrounding Roche's house also fired, both through the walls and the window, as Mr and Mrs Roche and Con O'Keeffe later testified. Fitzgibbon was satisfied that the people inside, intent on their devotions, had no idea of their danger until they heard the shots. He was convinced that they had not started the shooting because only one pistol was found inside, and that had no flint in it.

He examined the walls of Roche's house, and found that the balls in the logs had been shot through the rear wall from outside. A flint was found to have been put into the pistol found in the house, and it was thought that the deputy sheriff's men may have inserted it later, so as to incriminate Roche.

One of the magistrates had put his finger into the muzzle of the pistol and, since his finger remained clean, he said that the gun had not been fired that day.

Other things, "too minute to detail" convinced the investigators that, on this day at least, the Irish were innocent of wrongdoing. It was thought that one man in the deputy's party, over-excited, might have discharged his gun by mistake, causing others in the party to follow suit.

"But," wrote Fitzgibbon, *"for the cruel conduct of the men who attacked Roche's house, in beating and wounding the people they found there, I can find no apology whatsoever."*

Indeed, the deputy sheriff and his men had returned the next morning, tearing the roof off Roche's house, and leaving only the four walls standing.

Next came the trial of those who were sitting in the jail, awaiting their fate. Ten magistrates officiated. Pat O'Keefe received no justice, for the two men accused of beating him were found not guilty. Luke McGrath and James Brown were found guilty of assault, and fined eight shillings and costs. William Roche was fined a similar amount for an assault on Daniel Shipman, a local mill owner, but Annever Cusack was found not guilty on a similar charge. A Fitzgerald was also found not guilty of an assault charge following the testimony of Luke and James McGrath and William Leahy.

Thomas Glendinning and John Fummerton were absolved of malicious shooting, and the later was found not guilty on a charge of beating John Leahy. Those who suffered the most were Bart Murphy, John French, Pat Sullivan and John Coughlin, who were convicted of riot, fined ten pounds sterling apiece, and given a two month jail sentence. This was a most severe penalty, when we consider that four pounds sterling had paid the cost of transporting a Robinson settler to Upper Canada and providing him with a year's rations.

Robinson was convinced that the riots were much exaggerated, and that his settlers were more sinned against than sinning. Certainly, the projected new emigration took place as planned in 1825, so officials in England must have been satisfied that the affair was an isolated case.

In time, all the settlers shook down together. Daniel Shipman, whose family had feared for their lives at the time of the riots, donated land to the Irish families on which to build the Catholic church on. John Sullivan, who had challenged Glendinning to a duel, settled down to become a school master in the district. Glendinning himself later moved to Chatham, Ontario. Blacksmith Cornelius Roche later moved to Montreal, where he practised his trade. Some of the other Ballyghiblins later moved to the United States.

The majority of the Peter Robinson settlers had not taken part in the riots at all, except as innocent bystanders. They stayed on in the district and made new lives for themselves. The memory of the riots went into the folklore of the district, never to be forgotten.

While the Irish continued to feel that they had been framed, there were others who continued to support the opposite viewpoint.

An article published in The Almonte Gazette in 1872, and later put into pamphlet form, entitled "Early Settlement of Ramsay Township" had some stern comments to make with regard to the events of half a century before. The author wrote that the settlers had been established in a camp which they dubbed "Ballyghiblin" on the site of what, in 1872, was McGuire's furniture store in Almonte.

"They received military rations and were fed upon the fat of the land. As the landlords in Ireland who had the selection naturally wished to rid themselves of the most improvident and unruly, it is no wonder that, with a few notable exceptions, they were disposed to follow their old system in Canada, leading idle and dissolute lives."

"For want of any other amusement they took to fighting among themselves, and as a variety , to beating and maltreating others. For any and no cause, unoffending men were beaten nearly to death. Some dared not sleep in their own houses, and to such a pitch had they got that on the morning of the first Sunday in May,1824, the militia of Perth and vicinity, under command of the authorities, made an attack upon the camp, killing one and wounding and capturing many of the most turbulent, which put an effectual stay to their outrageous proceedings."

"It is worthy to remark that of those who remained about the camp during the winter, very few ever came to any good, while those who settled at once on their land... are at the present time among the most respectable and wealthy people in the township. So much for seizing time and opportunity."

This is what, today, we call a "bad press." Very likely James Fitzgibbon's report was not made available to the general public at the time (we of course may now examine those official letters) and so the story would have been based on hand-me-down information. According to the late Dr.Dunn, writing the history of St.Michael's church, Corkery, the unfortunate man who was killed at Roche's house was not even a Robinson settler, but another Irishman who just happened to be in the wrong place at the wrong time.

On the humorous side, there is a story told by a priest of our own day, a native of the Ottawa Valley. Whenever his Mother would get cross, her husband would say "Oh you're a real Ballyghiblin!" Nobody knew just what a Ballyghiblin might be, but the expression had obviously been handed down from pioneer times.

The only tangible reminders of those long ago events are an historic sites plaque beside the Mississippi at Carleton Place, and Captain Glendinning's former home at Glen Isle.

A CHART, shewing the Interior Navigation of the DISTRICT of Newcastle, Upper Canada, and the proposed improvements on the Otanabee River &c.

Drawn by F.P.Rubidge, and engraved by T.Evans, for the Cobourg Star.

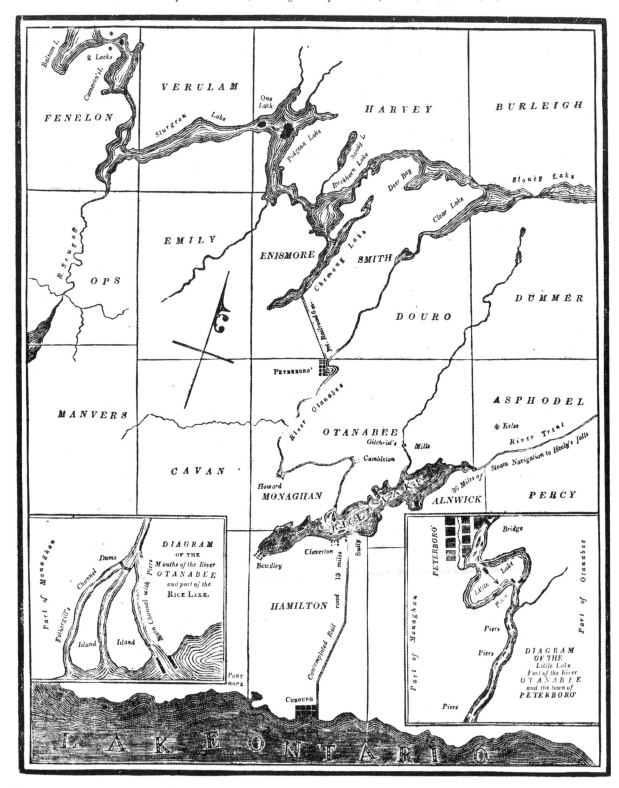

TABLE of DISTANCES.

COBOURG to RICE LAKE	18 Miles, Land carriage.	
RICE LAKE to PETERBORO'	27 By Steam-boat.	
PETERBORO' to CHEMONG LAKE	7 Miles Land carriage.	

CHEMONG thro' SMITH, ENNISMORE, HARVEY, VERULAM, OPS, CARTWRIGHT and FENELON, 81 Miles by Steam boat.
RICE LAKE to Heeley's falls in Seymour, 35 Miles, by Steam-boat.

The 1825 group

The second phase of Peter Robinson's emigration scheme was rather different from the first. There were many more emigrants in 1825 (2,024) and they embarked on nine sailing ships, the Albion, Amity, Brunswick, Elizabeth, Fortitude, John Barry, Regulus, Resolution and Star. The voyage time was half that of the 1823 sailing, with 31 days being the longest time at sea. Nevertheless, a number of people died during the ocean crossing, and others died soon after their arrival on dry land. These figures were probably in keeping with the mortality rate of that era, although tragic for those concerned.

Not all of the 1825 settlers were coming to an unknown future. At least thirty stopped off en route, joining family or friends in Quebec, Montreal or Kingston; it is not clear whether this defection was approved by the authorities. These friends may have included folk who came in 1823 but who did not remain on their lots.

Still others were related to the 1823 settlers. Some moved to the Ottawa Valley to be with them; in other cases they settled in the Peterborough District and were joined there by the earlier arrivals.

The ships docked at Quebec City at the end of June. The newcomers travelled by steamer to Montreal, then overland to Lachine where bateaux were waiting to transport them to Prescott. From there they proceeded to Kingston. They did not travel en masse, but formed smaller groups of a more manageable size.

At Kingston, the people stayed in a tent village, awaiting the arrival of Robinson, who had returned to Canada by another route. The weather was unusually hot, and many people fell ill, some fatally so. Tragic though this was, they were not the only people affected, for as Robinson was later to note: "the prevailing sickness, the ague and fever...at this time was as common among the old settlers as ourselves."

A chart of the Newcastle District showing the various townships, including those settled by the Peter Robinson families of 1825, including Emily, Ennismore, Douro, Smith, Asphodel and Otonabee. A small number went to Ops, Verulam and Marmora.
National Map Collection 3052.

Before joining the group, he had visited the Newcastle District to check out a travel route. This made better sense than marching two thousand people into unknown territory, although some modern critics believe that he should have gone straight to Kingston at that time.

He had hired a local guide to help him explore the terrain, and he was "highly gratified in discovering greater facilities of communication than I had expected." He felt that the land was excellent, and that supplies could be transported by water for more than half the distance involved. He chose a spot at the head of the Otonabee River which he felt was ideally situated for a supply depot.

His euphoria was somewhat diminished by the discovery that so many of his charges were sick, but he maintained that "everything possible has been done for their benefit by His Excellency, Sir Peregrine Maitland."

The Irish were quickly mustered, and prepared for the next leg of the journey.
"On the eleventh of August I embarked 500 on board a Steamboat and landed them the next day at Coburg on Lake Ontario,, a distance of one hundred miles; the remainder of the Settlers were brought up in the same manner, the boat making a trip each Week."

"Our route from Coburg to Smith, at the head of the Otonabee River, lay through a country as yet very thinly inhabited. The Road leading from Lake Ontario to the Rice Lake (twelve miles) hardly passable, and the Otonabee River, in many places very rapid, and the Water much lower than it had been for many Years."

Since the road was so poor, Robinson collected fifty pounds sterling from the local magistrates, and, pressing his healthier men into service, built up the track so that wagons could pass through. This work took ten days.

Meanwhile, the resourceful Robinson had "two scows" made, which were "transported on wheels. from Lake Ontario to the Rice Lake." These took ten days to build at a cost of twenty pounds each, and then he had to find experienced men to operate the boats. He hoped to hire "two crews of Canadians and a conductor" but had difficulty in finding the right men.
"I find the people of the country not only extravagant in their wages but also exceedingly awkward and troublesome," he complained in a letter to Hillier at York.

No doubt those approached felt daunted by the prospect of trundling two boats, which were fifty-six feet long, on wheels over twelve miles of makeshift road.

At that time, the Otonabee was navigable for twenty-four miles, but the water was extremely low that year. Members of the party were required to "deepen the channel" as Robinson put it, and even then the problem was not solved.

"To remedy the difficulty I had a boat constructed of such dimensions as I thought might best answer to ascend the rapids,and had her completed in eight days. So much depended on the success of the experiment that I felt a great anxiety until the trial was made, and I cannot express the happiness I felt at finding that nothing could more fully have answered or purpose,and that this boat, sixty feet in length, carrying an immense burden, could be more easily worked up the stream than one of half the size, carrying comparatively nothing."

An advance party tested the boat; Robinson took with him twenty "old settlers" who were skilled in axemanship, plus thirty of the healthier newcomers. He later reported that every one of the fifty had come down with ague and fever and that two of them had died; he felt that this proved that the rest, left behind in open country, were better off there than they would have been in the woods with the workers.

At last, everyone was moved up to Scott's Plains, which was later renamed Peterborough in Robinson's honour. The spot where they landed is now in down-town Peterborough, and the Red Oak Inn, complete with its Peter Robinson ballroom, now stands nearby.

While most of the settlers were soon to be sent out to their lots, Robinson proposed to erect a number of buildings near the river as his own headquarters. In September he wrote to Hillier to say that not all the people had in fact gone out to the country: "some are inclined to build on the town plot at the head of the Otonabee River, and it might be just as well..." By this time three-fifths of the people had ague and some were then incapable of beginning the work of land clearance.

Those who did go to their lots were dispersed in this way: those who had assisted in some way during the various phases of the trip were given first choice. The rest drew numbers out of a hat. Some leeway was allowed so that the settlers could trade among themselves, in order to locate near friends and relatives.

Peterborough.

Before moving on, let us catch a glimpse of the community beside the Otonabee. In 1818, a section of Monaghan Township was set aside as the site of a future town. By the time that the town plot was laid out in 1825 by surveyor Richard Birdsall, there was already a grist mill and a saw mill in operation. The grist mill, operated by Adam Scott, was described by Dr.T.W.Poole, writing in 1867, as "a poor apology for a mill, in the heart of the wilderness." He also noted that "an equally impotent distillery "was carried on in a small house in the vicinity.

Apart from Mr Scott's house,the first dwellings in that neighbourhood were erected under the direction of Peter Robinson. They were made of log,with gabled

windows and shingled roots. They faced Water Street. The largest house measured eighteen by twenty feet,and it was used for two purposes. It was to be a residence for Dr.Reade, whose services had been retained as a doctor for the immigrants, and it was also used as a temporary church, where later on, Father Crowley celebrated Mass.

The next two buildings were storehouses, where rations were kept. Some distance away there was a larger building, known as Government House, and it was here that Robinson and two other officials lived. Although it was also made of log it was larger than the private homes, being forty feet long by twenty feet wide. It had a door with a porch, and five windows. Inside, partitions separated the rooms, which included a reception room, kitchens, sleeping quarters and Robinson's bedroom-cum-study. A large, fenced-in garden ran down to the water's edge, where some outhouses were neatly arranged.

Who were the immigrants who settled down in the neighbourhood of Government House? One house sheltered the family of John Armstrong, who worked in the commissariat,dispensing rations. He later moved out to Douro Township. William Oakley opened a bakery, although it may have been Mrs Oakley who did the baking, as her husband was a shoemaker.

Immigrants named Boate and Sullivan opened taverns, which no doubt were used as a place of rest and refreshment for those who came into "town" to transact business with Robinson.

Others who remained were carpenter James Hurley; Timothy O'Connor who was too ill to work,and shoemaker Cottrell Lane. Another who practised his trade there was George Buck, a tailor. It made good sense for these tradesmen to begin work at the depot,where other settlers could find them,and patronise their shops.

During the winter of 1826,the community was visited by a number of dignitaries,including the Lieutenant Governor of Upper Canada, Sir Peregrine Maitland. With him were John Beverley Robinson and several other Canadians who had been instrumental in settling immigrants in the province. The party travelled from Cobourg by sleigh, crossing the frozen Rice Lake.

A banquet was held at Government House, during which a local address was given on behalf of the Irish settlers, praising the efforts of the government, Robinson and the King, and promising loyalty to the Crown. Referring to the recent war with the United States, the speaker noted that,in case of further hostilities, the Irish settlers would be willing to fight, "and if we have no better weapons in our hands, mow them down with our Irish shillelahs."

He concluded his remarks by requesting additional clergy "to administer to us the comforts of our Holy Religion" and "school masters to instruct our children."

A few days later the official party visited the outlying townships where more loyal addresses and letters of gratitude were received. In Ennismore they stayed at a shanty belonging to Eugene McCarthy, whose son Jeremiah later became Reeve of that township.

Life on the farm.

What was the experience of those who went out to their farms that first winter? To begin with, not all of the new immigrants made the perilous trip up the Otonabee. Instead,some faced a four day wagon trip to the Ottawa valley,there to join relatives whom they had not seen for two years. They were going to farms which were already partially cleared, where fresh produce had recently been harvested, and where well finished shanties were already standing.

Their shipmates in the Newcastle District had yet to clear the land,and they were greatly handicapped by the ague which struck many of them. Even those who succeeded in planting a crop often received a setback because of bad weather which ruined the harvest. This fact is graphically illiustrated by letters written to Peter Robinson by John Armstrong of Douro. Despite the fact that he had worked in the commissariat, he became entangled with government red tape.

Douro, May 18,1828.
Dear Sir:

To take the liberty of writing a few lines to you as I may not have an opportunity of speaking to you. My clerks have stopped six pounds ten shillings from me out of my own work. I would be satisfied if I thought that it was your order, but I know it was not. I have not received rations or pay for two months and a half of the time I was employed by you, which I am sure you know nothing about, nor I did not receive one pound of the year's rations that was coming to me when the business was over.

I had not one pound of victuals in my house at the time Mr Donnele came from York. He told me I was to get nothing more. He then told me I might take what flour and pork there was at Mr Burbridge's. I got one barrel of flour and 160 pounds of pigs heads and thirty pounds of pork when I was leaving Peterborough. I had not a pound of suet or flour for my family. When Mr Donnele saw me in such distress he gave me two barrels of flour which I thought extremely kind of him.

From the severe hurt I received I was prevented from getting a barn and root house, by which I lost 600 bushels of potatoes and 60 bushels of wheat this season. I was not able to work myself,nor was I able to hire hands to assist me.
I remain,Dear Sir, your very humble servant,
John Armstrong.

February 10,1829.
Dear Sir:

I suppose you will be very much surprised to see me in York at this time, but the great distress of my poor family has obliged me to come in hope of getting something to assist me in supporting them. I had a good prospect last summer until the hail storm destroyed all my fine crops. I had not left one week's provision in my house at the time I left it. What I did have was a little Indian corn Mr Keeler lent me while I could pay him.

Mrs Armstrong is keeping her bed these eight weeks,very ill, the doctor I believe has a very poor opinion of her and I was not able to get anything fit for her to take. If you would have the goodness to apply to the Freemasons for some little support for me, as I have the honour to be one myself.

Also my health is bad that I am not able to work for bread for my family. I would not let anyone see this letter but you, as I know, will do all in your power to help me. I hope my crops will be better this year. It is not for want of industry that made me in such want. I sincerely hope this letter will not offend you, for nothing but the greatest distress has made me write to you.
I remain, Sir, your much obliged and very humble servant,
John Armstrong.

This must have been a great blow to John Armstrong's pride. A former soldier,and member of a distinguished family,and married to a lady of noble birth, he had come to Canada because his brother, Robert Armstrong had come out in 1823 with the Robinson settlers. The men had married sisters.

John and Eliza Armstrong lost a baby son soon after their arrival in Upper Canada, and several other children were born to them here. One of these had arrived shortly before John's trip to York, an event which was probably the cause of Eliza's bedridden state. She did recover, giving birth to three more children in due course, and the family soon began to prosper. Some of their descendants live in Peterborough today.

There is no doubt that Robinson reacted to such letters with sympathy. Only a few years earlier, his own mother, left a widow with young children to support, had written a very similar missive to someone in authority, asking for help. In those days there was absolutely no social assistance or health care provision of any kind,and when people fell on hard times the outlook was often bleak.

Another anguished letter came from John Callaghan of Emily, asking for help for his son, who had got into some difficulty while working on the canal at Kingston. I find this letter fascinating for several reasons. It shows us that some of settlers ranged far afield before finally settling down to farm and it also shows that some of Robinson's people were recruited to work at Kingston, where labour was badly needed.

The letter also shows that some of the settlers, although impoverished, were of some consequence back in Ireland, where John Callaghan had obviously been looked upon as a spokesperson for others in his community. His skill at letter writing also testifies to a good education. Born circa 1781, when Catholics were still suffering under the Penal laws, he may have been educated at one of the hedge schools of that period.

Emily, February 13,1830.
Honoured Sir:

I have wrote to your Honour on October last, the same week after being with you, about my son's business at Niagara and my other son that went to the State of Pensel Vine and remained there until all the people were getting very sick,and he left it for fear of sickness. He came over to Niagara to his brother and gave him thirty dollers to send home to his father,and went from there to Kingtson Canal and stayed there for some time...he was at home when I came there from your Honour. He told me he had given Jerry thirty dollers to send it to me, which I did not get, and I was told he had given it to the Judge at Kingston the day of his trial."

Mr Callaghan did not say what his son had been up to (fighting, possibly?) but the boy was sentenced to a whipping. He pointed out that his family had never given any trouble in Ireland,and they had received excellent references when leaving.

I know very well that your Honour can do it...I am very sure that the Attorney-General will do it for you, and by so doing I am in duty bound to pray for you and friends during life. The Attorney- General was, of course, Peter's brother John.
His mother is these six months in a bad state of health,and if she knows that he is to be whipt she would lose her life, but we do not let her know anything about being whipt,and also,if he is whipt all my childer will go away from me through the mains of this thraxxin, and I have my dependence on your Honour.

I remain your obedient, humbel servant,
John Callaghan, Emily.

We can imagine the poor man reading over this letter to see if it might do,and then being struck by an afterthought, for he added an intriguing postscript. Some time before he left Ireland, he said,two young people had been tried before the magistrates of Cork for some infraction of the law, and had been sentenced to a month in jail,and a public whipping. The parents went to Callaghan, begging him to intercede with the

Recorder for them (we have some clue as to his beautiful Irish brogue, for he spelled it "entersaid") and *"according I did and he granted me the favour and set them at their liberty. I entrust and credit that you will entersaid with your Brother the Judge of the Surket...there is no time to spare."*
The said judge just happened to be another Robinson brother. Unfortunately we do not know whether young Jerry was spared his thrashing. Those were cruel times, when very severe punishment was given for very minor trespasses.

There is no doubt that some of Robinson's settlers did fall into mischief. The ship's surgeons named several as being fit for mischief or fighting; on the other hand, Robinson once wrote to his brother John to explain that other Irishmen, passing through, were idle rascals, "frequently exciting our people to mischief and leading them astray."

Early courts fined a number of men for being drunk and disorderly. One was fined for "fast driving." However, there is no hint that the Irish were any worse than other ethnic groups in this way, and there is every evidence that Robinson's settlers were hard working, devout people who soon built churches, worked hard at the land and set about getting an education for their children. These people were grateful for the opportunities given to them in Upper Canada.

Patrick Sarsfield, Earl of Lucan. A high ranking military commander in the army of King James II, he went to France after James' defeat by William of Orange. He was related to Mrs Garrett Nagle of the 1823 group, and also to Deborah Simcox Lehane of Emily.

Dispelling the Myths

When I first began to investigate the families of the Peter Robinson settlers it was because I wanted to know what the people were like as individuals. I knew that there had to be more to them than their usual profile of shadowy figures who were part of a government sponsored emigration scheme. While Peter Robinson deserves his place in history for successfully promoting assisted emigration from Ireland to Upper Canada in the 1820s, I felt that not enough has been said about the families themselves, who had to cope with what was often a hostile new environment.

At school, I often drove my history teacher mad by asking "but what happened to the people?" when taught that there were 4,000 casualties in a certain battle, or that some treaty had changed the course of history. After all, I reasoned, if each of us doesn't count for something in this world, then why are we put on earth at all?

I found that some historians and researchers have concluded that the Robinson settlement scheme was a failure. Some of the reasons given were that they didn't stay on the land; they were shiftless people who didn't make the most of their opportunities here; they were not the right type to become farmers. (This despite the fact that many of the Robinson settlers had been farmers in Ireland!) I believe that such conclusions are nonsense.

The question might be asked, then, how have I come up with a different viewpoint when others, presumably, have had access to the same primary sources as myself? The answer is that I have attempted to study as many of the individual families as possible, to see if any fit into the mould suggested above.

Another factor is that some writers appear to have simply repeated the myths which have been handed down for years, while a look at the original problems out of which these accusations grew reveal a paper tiger. Let us look at some of these myths now.

Few of the people stayed on their land.

A superficial glance at the land records of the townships involved shows that many families did not stay on their lots. This does not mean that they were too lazy to farm. Some drew poor land, and had to move to find something better. Robinson's agents were well aware of this and every effort was made to help the families relocate. Sometimes this meant moving across the line to the next township. It was never intended that these people should stay together as a tightly knit group, although

originally Robinson tried to locate them together for their mutual support and convenience.

Sad to say, others disappeared from their lots because they died. Some did not even get as far as their farms, having died en route. The mortality rate was appallingly high, especially among the 1825 group. Widows and widowers quickly remarried, especially when there were young children to care for. When widows and single women married they changed their names and so are hidden from the view of the casual researcher. This doesn't mean that they were not still in the district. Another mistaken idea is to discount women and children in a consideration of the Robinson settlers. Men may have been given land, but other members of their families also made their contribution to the development of the community.

It was not until I began to study the families as a group that I realised the extent of early death through illness or accident. In some cases people suffered from malnutrition because of their low standard of living in Ireland; they were unable to withstand the rigours of the Canadian climate or to withstand the various diseases which were rampant in an era before the value of sanitation was fully understood.

More than 2500 men, women and children came to Canada with Peter Robinson in the 1823 and 1825 groups, all told. By 1828 there had been 182 deaths among the group; 34 among the 1823 arrivals and 148 in the 1825 group, whose numbers on arrival outnumbered the former by more than four to one. These deaths included a number of infants born after their mothers left Ireland.

Between 1823 and 1826 a total of 96 infants and children died, the majority in the Newcastle District. Sixty-seven men died in that period, including 21 in the Bathurst District and 46 in Newcastle. Surprisingly enough, the women fared best; only 19 died in that five year period, despite the fact that childbirth was dangerous in that era. If we were to extend the period of study, however, the figures would change considerably; many of the surviving men actually had two or three wives in all, death in childbirth or as a result of consumption having claimed their mates.

A happier reason for disappearance from the farm was that life in Upper Canada offered the settlers a chance for self improvement. It has been said that Robinson chose only a small number of tradesmen to come to Canada, just enough to smooth the path of the other immigrants. Here again, the picture is slightly distorted; I have found that at least 89 men were in fact tradesmen or professional workers.

Robinson actually employed some of them in the communities where he set up government depots, while others were employed for a time in the embryo villages, returning to their land at a later date. Some did stay in the towns which evolved, but who is to say that they were failures if they earned an honest living at the trade for which they had been trained?

The following came out to Upper Canada.

Bakers, 2	Nailors, 1
Blacksmiths, 8	Plasterers, 1
Butchers, 4	Saddlers, 1
Carpenters, 12	Sawyers, 3
Clerks, 4	Schoolmasters, 3
Coopers, 4	Shoemakers, 16
Engineers, 2	Tailors, 3
Fishermen, 4	Tradesmen, 2 *
Masons, 9	Turners, 2
Millers, 1	Weavers, 5
Millwrights,1	Wheelwrights, 2

* unspecified.

While some of these people might have picked up comparatively unskilled jobs, we cannot suppose that the majority, many of them middle aged, somehow managed to learn such trades in Canada. These jobs often called for a seven year apprenticeship, starting in boyhood, with an additional period as a journeyman before a man could set up in business for himself.   The main exception was the schoolmaster, who might be a man with a good education who decided to fill in a gap locally when there was nobody to teach the young.

What might be true is that possibly some of these men failed to mention their skills when applying to come to Canada, feeling that they would have a better chance of being selected if they had no visible means of support. Many of those who were accepted were labourers, or else "reduced farmers", small land owners who were hard hit by the economy.

Some of the surviving references show that other men were employed as gamekeepers, gardeners or land agents on large estates. These men were hardly destitute but in some cases they had several unemployed sons, who would qualify as needy persons.

An examination of family records shows that, while a large number of people ultimately went to the United States, this seldom happened in the first generation. The popular time for moving south seems to have been the 1850s. What usually happened was that the original land owner died, one son inherited the farm, and the others had to look about for some other means of support. They repeated the pattern set down by their fathers and grandfathers; they migrated in order to take up free or low-cost homesteads.

Families from the Newcastle District moved to such states as Iowa, Minnesota, North and South Dakota. Curiously enough, the Bathurst District families moved south in fewer numbers, choosing to go north to Renfrew County where new townships were being surveyed.

It should be pointed out that, in moving to new locations in the mid-nineteenth century, the Robinson settlers were not unique. This was part of a general movement by Canadians in that era. Between 1850 and 1880, almost every Ottawa Valley family had at least one family member in the USA, and this trend was only halted by the opening up of the Canadian West, when native -born Canadians joined the stream of incoming settlers from Europe in the rush to obtain homesteads in Manitoba, Saskatchewan and Alberta.

Now to the question of the Irish being lazy, shiftless people! I am tired of this stereotype being applied to our Irish pioneers. In an earlier book, Valley Irish, I concentrated on a quite different aspect of the Irish settlers of the Bathurst District, people who worked hard to build up their communities, who were devout in the practice of their religion, whether Catholic or Protestant, and who believed in the value of a good family life.

One reviewer was critical because I had chosen not to repeat the tired old stories of the drunken, rollicking lumbermen, or to catalogue the exploits of troublemaking groups. His review was a list of all these facets of history which I had "missed."

The point here is that not all the Irish were rogues, and not all the rogues were Irish! There is no doubt that the Robinson settlers included a few difficult characters, given glowing recommendations by magistrates who hoped to see the back of them. The ships' surgeons quickly discovered the livelier spirits in their midst, and recorded for posterity the deficiencies in their character. The vast majority, however, were simply poor people who only needed a new environment in order to better their lives. Poverty is not a crime!

Incidentally, I have investigated the family trees of a few of these "fighting Irish" and have found that, in later generations, there have been just as many good citizens and high achievers among them as the other families can boast. It may well be that this aggressiveness has been translated into the drive and determination which is necessary to success. It is true that descendants are not likely to have told me about any bad hats in the family, unless it is far enough back in time for their exploits to be viewed through a romantic haze, but I have read many old newspapers, whose editors were quick to report any minor scandal, and these Irish families seldom made news. In fact, it seems that they were so eager to avoid the perceived disgrace of being written about in the papers that in the early days they failed to submit obituaries which is a blow for the modern researcher.

As a group, the Peter Robinson settlers did occasionally have a "bad press", as we term it today. The chapter on the Ballyghiblin riots tells the story of a clash between some of the 1823 group and their Scottish neighbours. A thorough investigation of this altercation completely exonerated the Irish , proving that they were provoked by jealous men who had not received any like assistance from the government, as the Robinson group had.

Even so, newspaper articles right up to the turn of the century continued to paint a black picture of the Irish, saying that they would not stay on the land, that they were lazy, that they had been given an unfair advantage. Not surprisingly, the authors usually had a Scottish background. Old grudges die hard.

A similar jealousy was felt in the Newcastle District, where again Robinson's people were given aid which the earlier comers had not had. This fact is recorded in Dr.Poole's history of Peterborough County, published in 1867.

"The immigrants were, not unnaturally, regarded at first with coldness and distrust by the previous settlers, and it has been said of them that, while their rations lasted, they contented themselves in idleness and sloth, and only put forth the exertions necessary to persons commencing life in a new country, when compelled to do so by cutting off their supplies."

An inspection made by Robinson's appointees, following the first year of settlement, shows what was achieved by the Newcastle group. A total of 1264 acres of land had been cleared. These people had acquired a total of 33 oxen, 65 head of cattle and 143 hogs. They had produced a large amount of foodstuff, including close to 64,000 bushels of potatoes and over 9000 pounds of maple sugar. So much for the lazy Irish.

In that same year, an attack on these people was printed in The Colonial Advocate,which was published by the Scottish William Lyon Mackenzie. It said,in part:" *Mr Robinson's Irish settlers: we have information which may be depended upon, stating that these people have an ardent desire to go to the United States, and that they frequently desert. No less than thirty of them decamped recently in one night."*

This was immediately challenged by a number of prominent men, including Thomas Stewart, a magistrate from Douro Township.

He said that the story was *"entirely false and without foundation. I am living here in the midst of them...I have always found them satisfied and happy. Some of them have told me with tears in their eyes that they never knew what happiness was until now. In general they are making great exertions in clearing the land,and the exertions have astonished many of the old settlers. I conceive that this is in general owing to the great care Mr Robinson has shown in regard to their complaints, and in studying their wants."*

Mr Stewart went on to say that, before Robinson's people arrived, he and the other established settlers did not like the idea of their coming,and that many rumours and fears did circulate among them. " All turned out to be equally false with those of The Colonial Advocate."

If this was the case,why did Mackenzie print the story? To understand this we have to know something of the man himself. He was very much against the establishment and the fact that Upper Canada was run by a group of Anglicans who had a great deal of power under the Crown. He objected to the fact that tithes must be paid to the established church by members of other faiths, and that members of some faiths had to have their marriages performed by Anglican priests. He felt that too little was being done for the average farmer in Upper Canada, and that the government should take steps to improve roads, markets and so on, for this struggling class.

One would suppose that Mackenzie would have some sympathy for the Irish, who had suffered under a similar regime in Ireland, but ironically, Robinson's settlers came under the wing of the Family Compact, and this, coupled with the fact that they had received preferential treatment, probably coloured his thinking.

In 1837, Mackenzie led an unsuccessful rebellion in Upper Canada, aimed at getting some redress for these grievances. Among the militiamen who set out to quell this uprising were a number of the Robinson settlers from both the 1823 and 1825 groups. They had sworn their loyalty to the Crown, out of gratitude for the help they had received, saying that they would always be ready to fight on the side of law and order. It was a homespun army that they faced in 1837; many of the rebels were armed only with hoes and mattocks. The rebellion collapsed like a damp squib. Even so,the chance to fight back must have given some satisfaction to Robinson's people, who had been so rudely libelled a few years earlier.

Robinson himself has come in for some criticism from historians, despite the fact that he seems to have taken his duties seriously. Many letters have survived which bear this out; he was constantly reporting his moves to other officials, including his brother John.

Two main charges have been levelled against him. One is that he was largely to blame for the illness and death of some of the settlers while they were encamped at Kingston, awaiting his arrival from England. The other is that he did not give all applicants an equal chance of being selected for passage to Canada.

Robinson did not sail from Ireland with the second group of settlers in 1825. Having seen his people safely on board at Cobh he left for London, where he had business. On June the ninth he sailed from Liverpool, bound for New York. It was July 28 before he reached Niagara,and from there he went to Cobourg, arriving on the third of August.

The voyage of the nine emigrant ships took only a month, which may have surprised Robinson, considering the fact that the 1823 trip took double that time. Thus the new arrivals had some time to wait before Robinson could arrive, a delay that was prolonged because he went to take a look at the Newcastle District before moving the group there. This was prudent, for when in 1823 he had expected to settle all his families in Ramsay Township, he found the district half settled already.

The situation at Kingston was not good.. The people were housed in tents, sanitary facilities were non-existent, and Kingston was experiencing a heatwave, " *the thermometer having stood at 100 degrees Fahrenheit for the last ten days."*
More than 300 of the new arrivals fell ill, and thirty-three died. The situation can be equated with refugee camps in some third world countries today. The people of Kingston, including members of some religious orders, did what they could to assist the Irish visitors, but all in all it was not a propitious beginning to life in the New World.

These facts cannot be disputed, yet at the same time we must not attempt to rewrite history, judging matters by today's standards. What if Robinson had arrived earlier than he did? These people would have been living in similar conditions near Peterborough while they waited to be taken out to the land allotted to them. They would still have been exposed to climatic conditions which were different from Irish weather, (1825 was a hot,dry year for this part of Upper Canada) they would still have had poor sanitation, because that was par for the course in 1825, and there would still have been mosquitoes and swamps, and waterborne diseases such as cholera and typhus.

If we choose to argue that Robinson could somehow have planned things better, let us consider this. The settlers were not left to their own devices by any means. In Robinson's absence his place was taken by his brother, John Beverley Robinson, who accompanied the families to Kingston and remained with them. In addition to this, two of the ships' surgeons, doctors Connin and Reade, were not only with the camp at Kingston, but they also settled in the Peterborough area, so that continuing care was available to the people. Few settlers of the 1820s had a similar privilege.

On July 6, John wrote that he had housed *"the settlers in tents at Point Frederick... where they are much more comfortable than in barracks, each family, nearly, having a tent."* At that point 713 persons, more than a third of the group, had arrived at Kingston.

Not all of the new arrivals were properly grateful for this regimented life, for another officer wrote of the outrageous conduct: of one particular man, "towards the Persons who had been appointed by Mr Robinson to take care of them." Apparently the local inhabitants were fascinated by the mushrooming camp, and John Beverley Robinson noted that he found *"the soldiers rather troublesome as they kept going down
to the camp. I applied to the Commanding Officer for an order to prevent them going near the camp, which was enforced immediately."*

The settlers continued to straggle into Kingston; at one point John wrote to Hillier to ask " *Pray have you heard of my Brother's having sailed out?"* noting in passing that 470 more Irish were *"hourly expected at Prescott."* A few days later he *"found Dr Reade with about one thousand settlers, generally in perfect health, behaving in a very quiet and orderly manner".*

At that time, Peter Robinson was probably still on the Atlantic, nearing the east coast of America. The immigrants would have to wait another month before he joined them. Why could he not have left Ireland earlier, so as to arrive at the same time as the settlers? The fact of the matter is that he stayed in Ireland until the last minute, to supervise some necessary repairs to the ships. In May, he had written to John, telling him that he had just overseen the loading of the ships and the embarkation of the passengers, whom he described as "the working poor." He concluded by telling his brother to "write to me at New York." It appears that he left no stone unturned in order to ensure the comfort and safety of his charges.

When he reached Canada, he received a shock when he discovered that so many people were sick. He later noted that three-fifths of them had the ague. Illness quickly claimed him, also, and he noted in a report on the first of September that *"I was
suffering much from a violent fever when I wrote to you last, brought on in great measure by the excessive heat; it left me for a day or two and the ague succeeded, this I hope I have got rid of also."*

Despite his own illness, Robinson was on his feet very quickly, supervising the building of scows which were to be used on a later leg of the journey. I have found nothing to support the theory that Robinson was in any way careless of his responsibilities, or negligent in carrying them out.

Let us now examine the idea that Robinson was unfair in his selection of the fortunate few who would be taken to Canada from Ireland. Peterborough historian Howard Pammett, writing his Master's Thesis over fifty years ago, said that there was "every evidence that the selection of emigrants was both impartial and unfair, and was for the most part restricted to a small district 20 miles by 40 miles..." He suggested that the colonial Robinson was dazzled by the aristocrats who wined and dined him, and that he may have been duped by landlords who were eager to rid themselves of potential troublemakers in their districts. I find it hard to believe that a member of parliament, and a member of a most prominent family in Upper Canada, would be overawed by a body of Irish magistrates.

It may well be that Robinson found it easier to process people in the districts where he had set up a communications network in 1823, than to go into unknown areas where he would have to make new contacts. As he noted at the time, *some would not go in 1823, suspecting deception, but have since changed their minds.* It seems reasonable that such people would be considered first, if their applications had already been cleared by the officials. It is evident by the number of unsuccessful applications and character references which are still extant that many more would have come than were actually taken in 1823, why should they not have been given first consideration the second time around?

A great many people from County Cork did come to Canada under the leadership of Peter Robinson, as Mr Pammett noted, However, we cannot say that Robinson confined himself strictly to that county when selecting applicants. Recruiting centres were set up at a number of places, mainly in County Cork, and the people had to go to the nearest one. Sometimes this meant walking some distance from Kerry, Tipperary, Waterford or Limerick, counties which border on Cork. When the passenger's place of origin was shown on the ship's list, this was often the place at which he had registered to come to Canada, which was *not necessarily* the same as his birthplace or current residence. Actual birthplaces given in different documents, or research conducted by descendants of the emigrants often substantiate this point.

In any case, I do not think that it much matters whether Robinson deliberately confined his choice to residents of a small area or not. He may have been overwhelmed by the number of applications and have decided that one poor Irishman is much like another. Then, too, he may have believed that future schemes would encompass other applicants.

There is some truth to another charge, that he promised to take out some families who could be considered special cases. I believe that this was not an arbitrary decision but that it was based on a desire to link up separated families, who had relatives in Upper Canada as a result of the 1823 settlement.

Robinson encouraged the 1823 settlers to write to their people in Ireland, inviting them to come here in 1825. You will find several examples of such letters elsewhere in this book. He followed through on his promise to link up families whose menfolk had come in 1823; we have evidence to show that parents were brought out to join children, that wives and babies came to join husbands, that brothers and sisters came to join siblings. both 1823 and 1825.

There is evidence, through stories handed down in families, that some of the second group were chosen in return for some special service, or for compassionate reasons; Robinson pointed out that he chose some older farmers and tradespeople, who did not conform to the guidelines set down by Parliament, because he believed that they could add something to the pioneer communities by virtue of their life experience.

A study of the family names and places of origin of the two groups of settlers indicates that there were many relationships between the two; it is possible that there were even more than are immediately verifiable. Some genealogists have found that some families were connected by marriage even before the group left Ireland, although there is no mention in the ships' lists of such a bond.

In order for us to get a totally clear picture of the reasons behind Robinson's choice of settlers, we would need to undertake a far more comprehensive study of the inter-relationships between the various families who came to Canada. Obviously that it outside the scope of this book. I hope, however, that I have at least opened the door to some thought as to the character of Peter Robinson, and the reasons behind his actions.

We must remember that he had to work under very different conditions in the 1820s than we know today. Imagine that you are a travel agent, given the responsibility of shepherding a group of 2000 people to another country. You may not use the telephone, computer, air mail service or modern maps. You may not travel by air, or use cars and buses. You must charter sailing ships and stock them with a month's supply of food, without refrigeration.

In order to solicit your travellers, you must travel rough roads on horseback, and when they want to pick up their tickets, they must walk several miles.

If the tourists become ill while in your care, you can turn them over to the accompanying doctor, bearing in mind that there is no hospital, no wonder drugs, no x-ray machines or other diagnostic tools.

When you arrive in that foreign country, you must cut down trees to build accomodation for your flock, for no hotel is available. There are few roads for you to traverse the interior, so you may have to travel by water- first building your own boats. Could you do it? Peter Robinson did.

PR PR PR PR PR PR PR PR PR PR PR

Peter Robinson's Settlers

More than 2500 people came from the South of Ireland to Upper Canada under the leadership of the Hon. Peter Robinson in the 1820s. One of these families alone, the Boyles of Pakenham, has been found to have more than 1,000 descendants. Even allowing for the fact that some people did not have children (many joined religious orders, while others died unmarried) it is still possible that two million or more people may have come from these founding families! This means that today there are thousands of descendants of these "Peter Robinson families" across Canada and the United States.

Are you one of them? Your surname may not be on the list of Peter Robinson's pioneers, and perhaps you think of yourself as a Canadian or American associated with a different ethnic group, yet you may still find ancestors in this book. Don't forget that married women took their husband's surnames, and not all the settlers married into other Irish families, although a surprising number of the Robinson settlers did intermarry.

When I began the research for this book, many of my acquaintances had never heard of the Peter Robinson settlements, including some who are keen amateur historians. In due course I discovered that many of my neighbours are actually descendants of these settlers, but they were unaware of the fact because their surnames suggest other ethnic origins.

A word of caution!

Please do not go flying off to Ireland to research your family history, based on the information in this book, without doing some preliminary checking. While all the information given here is published in good faith, some of it may at times be misleading.

Throughout the Peter Robinson records, information given seems to vary from one list to another. There is often a good reason for these discrepancies, but it does make it hard on the genealogist. Accordingly, I shall attempt to explain a number of points for the sake of those who will be using this book as a research tool.

Questions & Answers.

My ancestor is listed as having come from Doneraile, County Cork. Are you absolutely sure that this is correct?

No. In some cases the place given in documents was the actual place of birth; in others it referred to the current place of residence, which was not always the same thing. Another possibility was that the place named was the centre where your ancestor registered to come to Canada, which may not have been his home parish.

This is particularly true when people came from Counties Tipperary, Limerick, Kerry and Waterford and most of the recruiting centres were in nearby County Cork.

Your best bet is to check through the Peter Robinson papers, which can be found at the Public Archives, Ottawa; the Ontario Archives, Toronto; or in Peterborough. You may be able to compare more than one document there, including ships' lists; location tickets; character references.

I have already checked these papers and I find that one brother came from one place and the other from somewhere different. How could this be?

Even in the eighteenth and nineteenth centuries, people did move from one place to another in search of work. However, do remember that an emigrant might cite his town or village, or even his parish, and in Ireland they have both civil and ecclesiastical parishes!

Just imagine your Canadian ancestors saying that they came from Ramsay Township or Lanark County, or "near Almonte" or "St.Mary's parish." All could be correct, yet a researcher in a different country would wonder at the discrepancy. In researching your Irish genealogy, try to have old and new maps, plus a checklist of parish registers on hand.

You haven't spelled our surname correctly. Why?

In most cases, I have used the spelling as it appears in documents of the 1820s. Mistakes made by clerks, illiteracy on the part of some immigrants, or a conscious decision to change the spelling, made by the family at a later date, may all contribute to the difference.

Phonetic spelling of a Gaelic Irish surname also led to changes. Mealey was written as Maley, Meade as Maid, Dennis as Dinnis, Keane as Kane, and so on.

In the Irish language, "mac" means "son" and "og" can mean younger (as in junior) or grandson. Thus many Irish names begin with Mc,Mac or O. These prefixes were often dropped at some point, perhaps to be taken up again later. Please note that in listing such names in the following chapters I have followed the Irish habit of placing O'Brien under B, O'Grady under G, and so on.

What about the ages you have given for my ancestors? Are these definitely correct?

Take these with a large pinch of salt! In many cases there are discrepancies between the ages given on the ships' lists, location tickets, in census records, on tombstones. Men often added or subtracted a few years so that they would be eligible to draw land, which was supposed to be limited to a certain age group.

Women often subtracted a few years as time went by. Why tell all to the census taker, perhaps a neighbour known to have a nosey wife?

Even the dates on tombstones have occasionally been found to be wrong. Don't forget that these were erected by survivors, who might not have access to exact information.

Do remember that in the nineteenth century, ages given in official documents were often those to be reached on the following birthday. Depending on the time of year when the information was gathered, this could throw out your calculations by a year or two.

According to the ages on the ship's list, my female ancestor was too young to have been the natural mother of some of the children. What are the implications of this ?

She could have been their stepmother. Many women died in childbirth and their husbands had to remarry quite soon if there were young children to care for. This fact is hard to spot because there was often a gap of perhaps only two years between the first and second families.

Was her husband old enough to be the father of those children? A good number of the younger Robinson settlers were actually brothers and sisters of the married couple. There are even cases where nephews or cousins accompanied the family. In some cases these young people temporarily took on the surname of the family head. When over 50,000 people applied to come to Canada with Robinson, it is not surprising that many people altered the facts to their advantage.

Could some teenagers actually have been servants?

There were a few cases where apprentices may have travelled with their masters. It is doubtful whether there were any servants as such, as only persons in great need were supposed to take part in this emigration scheme.

My ancestor used an alias. What could this mean?

Today, the use of an alias may hide some doubtful activity. This was not the case among the Peter Robinson settlers. Some ticket holders had cold feet at the last moment and sold their tickets to friends. The new people, afraid that they would be turned down, travelled under the assumed names of the original family. So many people applied to come that, for the sake of fairness, tickets were not legally transferable.

There were other reasons for the use of an alias, which I have discovered in talking to descendants of people who used them. In some cases, people used the name of a stepfather but later reverted to their birth name. When families wished to include a cousin or a fiancee in their group, those people would temporarily "adopt" that family name.

A little mystery reared its head when I was checking the reports made by government officials, following later inspections of the townships where the Robinson groups settled. Why were there a number of young men who had been given land as Peter Robinson settlers, but who did not appear in any of the ships' lists? Some cross-checking proved that the lads had indeed come out on the ships hired by Robinson, but were listed under a different name. If you are puzzled as to what became of a lad in your family - perhaps he doesn't appear in settlement lists, land books or census records, do check out some of the young bachelors of the day. Who knows what you might find?

Family tradition says that my ancestor came out with the Peter Robinson settlers, but you haven't mentioned him. Why not?

I have only listed those who appear in the ships' lists or other records. This is not to say that you are wrong. Here are some possibilities:

He may have travelled under an alias. He may have come at a later date to join his family who did come out with Peter Robinson. He may have come out under his own auspices but obtained land through Peter Robinson, who was Commissioner for Crown Lands for some time after the 1823 and 1825 migrations. I am currently investigating a story which indicates that a third group came out under Robinson's leadership in 1826, settling in the neighbourhood of the Rideau Canal. Should this be true, perhaps your ancestor might have come with them.

My name is Robinson. Could I be descended from Peter Robinson?

Peter Robinson was a bachelor. He did have married brothers and sisters, however. I shall include a few words on the subject of this family, since I have received letters from researchers, asking this question.

Can the genealogist learn anything from the surnames of the Peter Robinson settlers?

It is easy to spot many of the Gaelic Irish surnames, such as O'Sullivan, O'Twomey and McCarthy. Other names, such as Boland, Boyle, Dowling, Foley, Healey, Hennessy, Ring and Ward are anglicized forms of old Irish names.

Some of the Peter Robinson settlers with Norman Irish names were Barrett, Barry, Bryan, Burke, Costello, Cusack, Dillon, Fitzgerald, Nagle, Power, Purcell, Roche, St.Leger, Wall and Walsh. Many of these families went to Ireland in the twelfth century.

The Dulmages, Millers, Switzers and Teskeys are undoubtedly descendants of the Palatine settlers , Protestants who fled to Ireland in 1709. A later chapter will be devoted to this story.

The Robinson family

The Hon. Peter Robinson, 1785-1838.

Peter Robinson was born in New Brunswick in 1785, the eldest child of Loyalist Christopher Robinson, an officer in the Queen's Rangers, and his wife, Esther Sayre. Their children were:

Peter   1785-1838 (unmarried)
Mary   1787-1863 (Mrs Stephen Heward)
Sarah   1789- 1863 (Mrs James Boulton)
John B.   1791-1863 (m. Emma Walker)
William B. 1797-1873 (m. Eliza Ann Jarvis.)
One other.

The family moved to Upper Canada in 1792, spending six years at Kingston before moving to York. Christopher Robinson died in 1798, and Esther immediately applied to the Lieutenant Governor for assistance, describing herself as a "distressed widow"

with "six fatherless children to participate in her distress."

Her idea was that her late husband's post, that of Deputy Surveyor-General for Upper Canada, should now be given to her eldest son, Peter. Since he was only 13 years of age he had to wait a while for such an appointment; he was given it some thirty years later! However, in due course an administrator was appointed to look after Christopher Robinson's estate and in 1805 Esther Robinson married him.

Esther's sons and grandsons did well in politics and the law. Her son John, later Sir John Beverley Robinson, became Attorney-General of Upper Canada in 1813, even before he was called to the Bar.

Peter Robinson fought for the Crown, commanding a rifle company in the War of 1812-1814. He was mentioned in dispatches after the capture of Detroit, and he took part in the defence of Michillimackinac.

After the war he turned to politics. In 1817 he was elected to the Legislative Assembly for Upper Canada, representing the east Riding of York. He served two terms, from 1817-1820 and from 1821-1824. Later he served on both the Executive and Legislative Councils.   He served in Upper Canada in several posts; he was Commissioner of Crown Lands, Clergy Reserve Commissioner and Surveyor-General of Woods.

When the British government decided to try out an experimental emigration scheme, sending poor Irish families to Upper Canada, Sir Peregrine Maitland approached Sir John Beverley Robinson, asking him to recommend someone to oversee the scheme. His elder brother was an obvious choice.

With the War of 1812 fresh in their minds, the government needed settlers, local to the Crown, who could provide man power for the new militia. Veteran Robinson knew as well as anyone else just how necessary this was; during that war the British army had had one thousand miles of frontier to defend and too few troops with which to do it.

As an ex-officer he had experience in organization and getting people and equipment from place to place; this skill was vital to the success of the proposed operation. As a member of parliament he had the stature and the background to inspire confidence in the people he was to lead into Upper Canada.

There is no doubt that Peter Robinson was able to earn that confidence. Despite the fact that many of the Irish people feared encounters with hostile Indians or wild animals, more than fifty thousand of them were ultimately willing to go.

Some of the settlers died soon after their arrival in Upper Canada, a prey to infectious diseases because of malnutrition. Robinson himself, although born into better circumstances, did not survive them by many years. He died, unmarried, in 1838.

Researchers may like to know about two other men who settled in the Peterborough area in 1825 as a result of the Robinson emigration. They were two ship's surgeons, Reade and Connin, who accompanied the settlers to the depot and then applied to stay. They cannot be considered as part of the settlement scheme, as they received more land than did the ordinary emigrants.

Francis Connin was supposed to receive 800 acres, and a letter written by him from Cobourg in 1825 suggested that he would like some of it in Otonabee Township because of its nearness to "Cobourg and Lake Ontario, whereby supplies might be obtained with greater ability than townships more remote."

Dr Reade apparently returned to Ireland and brought out more settlers in the 1830s. These were not government-sponsored like the Robinson settlers, although it is possible that some of them might have been related to the 1825 group. (I say this because some of the family names which appear in later censuses are similar to those in the Robinson group.) Apparently a clean cargo was wanted for the return voyage of timber ships which went to Britain, and people filled the bill, thus making the voyages more economical. Such ships, then, were made available for emigrants, with rough bunks being installed for the return journey.

The Hon. Sir John Beverley Robinson, died 1863. PAC 7467.

The Families

Abbot, Jeremiah, 25
Ship	Stakesby, 1823
Origin	Rathcormac, County Cork
Location	lot 9, con 12, Lanark Twp

Ahern, Jeremiah, 40, labourer.
Ship	Star, 1825
Origin:	Newmarket, Cork
Location	N lot 13, con 9, Emily
Family	
Johanna	22
Margaret	1

Jeremiah Ahern died in Emily on October 23, 1825. His daughter, Margaret, born at the depot, died on October 13, 1826.

Ahern, John, 28
Ship	Stakesby, 1823
Origin:	Castletownroche, Cork
Location	E lot 20, con 7, Pakenham
Family	Bridget, 27 (d. Aug.6, 1823)
Thomas	3
Jane	3 months. (d.July 29, 1823)

John Ahern first located on October 6,1823. He later moved to lot 22, con 4, Pakenham Township, a lot earlier allocated to Patrick Sullivan. Francis Jessop, who was appointed to inspect the progress of the settlers, observed in 1834 that "this unfortunate man occupied lot 20 until 1826 when he threw it up and commenced his migrations, occupying in succession each rejected lot as the other settlers fled the township. The last was best."

John Ahern's wife and baby died during the voyage to Canada. The birth must have taken place shortly before they left Ireland, and probably neither one was in a suitable condition to travel.

Allen, Edmond, 39
Ship;	Resolution, 1825
Origin	Deniskea, Tipperary
Location	E lot 3, con 7, Douro
Family	Bridget, 38 (nee Fleming)
John	19
William	17
Mary	14
Edmond	7
Robert	5
Bridget	3
Johanna	

John Fleming, 66, father in law; Bridget Johnson, 11, granddaughter.

Two Allen sisters: Mary (Mrs Leahy) and Julia, (Mrs Tangney.) The baby is a child of Mary Leahy, and is said to have died soon after the picture was taken.

Ship's notes state that one man died and one child was born.

Edmond Allen died in 1860. His tombstone indicates that he was a native of Galbally, Limerick, which is at variance with the ship's list. His children married as follows: John (Catherine Ryan); William (Bridget Sullivan); Mary (Michael Sullivan); Edmond (Ellen Clancy); Robert (Johannah Green); Bridget (Patrick Sullivan). A daughter Catherine was born to the Allens after their arrival in Canada

Allen, James, R.C.

Ship	Hebe 1823
Origin	Clogheen, Tipperary
Location	W lot 18, con 11, Ramsay
Family	Mary, wife
Margaret	7
Catherine	4
Nora	wife's sister.

By 1826 there were six people in this family group.

Two births and two deaths had taken place in the interim.

The Allens soon moved to E lot 19, concession 10, Huntley Township. James obtained his land patent in 1838. One record gives James Allen's birthplace as "Hospital,Cork."

Andrews, Richard, 42. Shoemaker.

Ship:	Resolution, 1825
Origin:	Brigown, County Cork
Location:	N lot 8, con 5, Smith Township.
Family:	Susanna,38;
Jeremiah	16
Ellen,	12
Eliza	10
William	7
France	3

In 1827, Richard was listed as a shoemaker, "working at his trade in Peterborough." A report of this era said that "one man had died" but it is not known whether Richard was that man.

Armstrong, John, 32. Protestant.

Ship:	Resolution, 1825
Origin:	Kilfinane, Limerick.
Location:	all of lot 10, con 8, Douro Twp.
Family:	Eliza, 30 (nee Massey)
Mary	15
Samuel	16
Francis	9
Thomas	8
Wheeler	7
Robert	3
Charles	1
Born in Canada:	
Eliza Frances, b. 1826	
William Henry, b. 1829	
Charlotte, b.1832	
Jane Amelia, b. 1835	
Mary Letitia, born 1836.	

John Armstrong

When this family came out in 1825, John Armstrong worked in the commissariat, doling out rations to his fellow settlers. Although he was in a favoured occupation, doing clerical work in a Peterborough office, his adjustment to the new land was no easier than that of his shipmates.

Five additional children were born in Upper Canada, but several of this family died young, and Mrs Armstrong suffered ill health for a time because of childbirth complications. When he began farming, John was injured, and on top of that, two successive crops failed

In due course, the family prospered. They had three homes in all. The first, a traditional log house, was in Peterborough. Next came "Maple Forest" at lot

Captain John Armstrong, who travelled on the ship Resolution in 1825.

Eliza Massey, Mrs John Armstrong.

10, concession 8, Douro. Finally they built their permanent home, "Beechwood", in a setting which later became a gold club. John died in 1853 at the age of 65.

Francis Armstrong married Jane Martin, a Kingston girl, and after her death, Elizabeth Armstrong, a third cousin from Richmond. This indicates that other members of this family must have come to Canada at another date. Thomas married Mary Ann Carew, Robert married Elizabeth Tamblyn, Wheeler did not marry, and Mary Letitia became Mrs F. Lee. William H. Armstrong drowned in the Otonabee River in 1848.

Genealogists may wonder what became of Samuel and Mary, the teenagers who travelled to Canada with the Armstrongs. Descendants who have done considerable research say that they were not part of the family. Not only are they missing from family birth records but also they were too old to have been the children of John and Eliza. The theory is that they were servants, or possibly relatives of some kind.

It is interesting to note that a young man named Samuel Adams, a Peter Robinson settler not appearing in the ships' lists, took up land next to the Armstrongs in Douro. In the early days, he, too, worked as a clerk in the government office at Peterborough. While I have no proof whatsoever, it is

my theory that this may have been the Samuel who accompanied the Armstrongs to Canada.

Armstrong, Robert, Protestant

Ship:	Hebe, 1823
Origin:	Kilfinane, Limerick
Location,	W lot 7, con 12, Ramsay Twp.
Family:	Margaret, wife (nee Massey)
Jane,	born 1813
Frances,	b. 1814
Thomas,	b. 1815
Sophia, b.	1817
Rebecca, b.	1820
Elizabeth,	1821.

<u>Born in Canada:</u>
Mary, b. 1824
Francis Massey, b. 1828.

Robert Armstrong, an 1823 settler, was a brother of an 1825 settler, John Armstrong.
Their wives, Margaret and Eliza Massey, were sisters. Robert and John were the great grandsons of Lord Decies. The Massey girls were the granddaughters of Hugh, Lord Massey, their father being the Hon. Francis Massey. The girls grew up at Suir Castle in Golden, Tipperary.

Thomas Armstrong was a small boy when he travelled to Canada on the ship Resolution in 1825. He was a son of John Armstrong and Eliza Massey.

It was not long after this that the family moved to Gloucester Township, near Ottawa. In 1841 the Bytown Gazette printed the death notice of Margaret, who died in June at the age of 59, noting that she was the daughter of the Hon. Francis Massey, of Suir Castle. The same paper recorded the marriage of her son Thomas, to Maria Hardy in 1844.

Among several prominent descendants of this family is **Earl Armstrong**, Reeve of Gloucester from 1952-1968. He also served as Warden of the County of Carleton.

Two men served the Methodist Church: **Robert Armstrong**, son of Thomas and Maria, was a lay preacher, and his son, another **Robert**, was a Methodist minister. The latter, Rev Robert Armstrong, BA., Ph.D, 1876-1930, was a missionary to Japan for a quarter of a century and he was also the author of a number of books. His daughter Nellie married Rev. R. G.Newman, and their son , **Rev. Paul Newman** is a minister in Japan.

Other branches of this family were Anglican. **Canon Clement McFadden** was a great grandson of the first Robert Armstrong, for the baby Mary who was born soon after the family arrived in Canada, grew up to marry Samuel McFadden of Ashton. Samuel's father and uncle were military settlers of the 1816-1818 period.

Birth records of John Armstrong's children show that the family had not always lived at Kilfinane; in fact, they had moved about considerably. This may have been because he was a captain in the King's County militia, a fact which weighed in his favour when Peter Robinson was selecting families to come to Upper Canada.

Just why the Armstrongs came to Canada, we do not know. However, Robert and Margaret ventured out in 1823, bringing with them five daughters and one son. Two more children were born to them in Ramsay Township, where they settled first. Their farm was not far from Ashton, where some of their children eventually settled. (Ashton is on the border between the townships of Beckwith and Goulbourn, which are contiguous with Ramsay and Huntley.)

By 1834, Thomas had his own farm at lot 3, con 11, Ramsay,, but he was still living with his parents in the twelfth concession. Robert, then in his fifties, was described in an inspection report as "an aged man with a helpless family of young females." Perhaps having six daughters had worn him down!

Barragy, Patrick, 35

Ship	John Barry, 1825
Origin	Deniskea, Tipperary
Location	E lot 5, con 9, Emily
Family	Margaret, 29
Patrick	4

Patrick was given these references before leaving Ireland:
"I certify that I am acquainted with the bearer, Patrick Barragy, these many years back, and I certify that I always considered him honest and industrious, that I never heard him charged with anything deleterious or disloyal."
Ballinatemple, June 30, 1823.

"The bearer, Patrick Barragy, has been employed in my garden, and about my pleasure grounds and park, for seven years. I believe him a well-conducted man and one who can make himself useful in a garden."

Patrick also made himself useful to the officials aboard ship, who noted that he "assisted in cutting up and distributing rations on the voyage."

In a report of 1826 it was noted that he was "living with an old settler." He died on August 12, 1846 and was said to be 66 at that time, so very likely he was one of those who deducted a few years off his age when applying to come to Canada.

Barrett, William, 35

Ship:	Resolution,1825
Origin:	Kilworth, County Cork
Location:	S lot 15, con 9, Emily Twp
Family:	Johanna, 35
John,	13
Mary,	11
William,	9
Norah	7
Johanna	4
Edmond,	1

In 1826, William Barrett was one of those unlucky settlers who was stricken with the ague.

In 1825 the parish priest of Tullow had given him this reference:

"I have known William Barrett for many years. He not long since lived respectably and comfortably in Ballygally, and always supported his Character as an honest man."

Barry,David

Ship:	Stakesby, 1823
Origin:	Mallow, Cork

Settled: Unknown. He could have been one of the young single men who was employed at the Ramsay depot by Robinson and located later.

Barry, Edmond, 26.

Ship:	Stakesby, 1823
Origin:	Castletownroche, Cork
Location:	NE lot 20, con 4, Goulbourn

Barry, Edmond, 41, RC

Ship:	Stakesby, 1823
Origin:	Mallow, Cork
Location:	W lot one,, con 3, Darling Twp.

Other members of this family may have followed him to Canada at a later date. In 1835 a Pat Barry on an adjoining lot was listed as paying his annual dues to the parish priest.

One of these Edmonds was temporarily absent in 1826, listed in a government report as working as a baker in Kingston,Ontario.

Barry, James.

Ship:	Hebe,1823
Origin:	Castlelyons, Cork

Alias **Patrick Mealey.** See separate entry.

Barry, James, 38

Ship:	Albion, 1825
Origin:	Doneraile, Cork
Location:	E lot 11,con 10, Asphodel Twp.
Family:	Bridget, 37
Margaret,	16
Bridget,	14
Catherine	7

John	5
Ellen	2

The ship's surgeon reported that this was "a decent family."

Margaret Barry died at age 17, September 24, 1826. A government report which was compiled after that said that there were then seven in the family.

In 1855, James Barry disclosed his present age as 55 years.

Barry, John, 32, RC

Ship:	Stakesby, 1823
Origin:	Mallow, Cork
Location:	E lot 11, con 4, Ramsay Twp
Family:	Fanny, 19, wife.

Note that in a different document, John's place of origin is given as Churchtown, Cork.

Barry, John, RC

Ship:	Hebe 1823
Origin:	Buttevant, Cork
Location:	W 6, Con 6, Goulbourn Twp
Family:	Margaret, wife
Thomas	24
Margaret	16
John	14
Ellen	7

John Barry soon moved to another part of this township, where he claimed land as a military settler. His son Thomas took up land on the East half of lot 6, con 6.

Barry, John, 32, butcher

Ship	Fortitude, 1825
Origin:	unknown
Location:	W lot 9, con 5, Douro Twp
Family	Eliza, 29
Patrick	8
Thomas	2

One child was born in Canada. Eliza is said to have died at the depot on October 13,1825. However, I have found a different source which indicates that it was John who died. Researchers may wish to check this out.

Barry, William

Ship	Hebe, 1823
Origin	Churchtown, Cork
Location:	W lot 15, con 11, Ramsay
Family	
Richard	23
James	21
William	15
Mary	18
Ellen	18, twins

William senior was a widower when he came to Canada. His son Richard farmed the west half of lot 16, con 11, Ramsay; James the east half of lot 15, con 11.

A fine old barn in Emily Township. Moses Begley's blacksmith shop formerly stood to the right of the picture.

D.W.McCuaig photo.

Begly, Moses, 45, blacksmith
Ship	Amity, 1825
Origin:	Knockatemple, Cork
Location:	S lot 16, con 10, Emily
Family	Norah, 44

Begley did not go out to Emily at once, but remained in Peterborough for a time, working as a blacksmith. Other members of his family came to Canada at the same time; a daughter was Mrs Michael Buckley.

Benson, John, 32, Protestant
Ship	Stakesby, 1823
Origin:	Charleville, Cork
Location	E lot 7, con 10, Ramsay
Family	Mary, 28, wife
William	7
Francis	5
Robert	3
John	1

John Benson senior was born at Tralee, County Kerry. By 1826 he had cleared seven acres of land on his lot, and a new birth had boosted his family to seven people.

By the time of a later inspection, eight years later, he had managed to clear forty acres, but this was apparently judged to be "all that is fit for cultivation."

Blackwell, John, 41, Protestant
Ship	John Barry, 1825
Origin:	Killeedy, Limerick
Location	S lot 17, con 1, Emily
Family	Prudence,39
John	22
Margaret	19
Catherine	17
James	15
Mary	13
Abigail	11
William	8
Anne	6
Edward	3

Ship's notes: "A very excellent family, Protestants, of good and industrious daughters. Blackwell was instrumental in saving the ship." (This referred to a difficulty which took place in the Gulf of St.Lawrence when crew and passengers were obliged to man the pumps.)
"He brought out a lad from Cork, engaged to serve him three years, who has, to his great loss, left him on some frivolous excuse. The family deserves every encouragement. Blackwell has behaved wholly to my satisfaction."

Boate/Boot, James, 40
Ship	Brunswick, 1825
Origin	St. Michael's, Limerick

Location	N lot 22, con 5, Emily
Family	Catherine, 40
William	15
Ann	13
Eliza	11
Fanny	9
Catherine	5
James	1

There was one death in this family in 1826. William Boate later owned his father's farm plus the south half of this lot, and also the south half of the adjoining lot in the sixth concession.

He appears in the 1851 census with wife "M.A."; sons William and James and daughters "M" and Isabella.

A plaque at St.James' Anglican church, Emily Township, says that land for the cemetery was deeded to the church by William Boate and his wife, Mary Ann, in 1855.

Boland, Jeremiah, 34, mason.

Ship	John Barry, 1825
Origin	Cashel, Tipperary
Location	E lot 4, con 6, Emily
Family	Mary, 32
Edward	12
Mary	7
Joseph	5
Ann	4
Thomas	2

The ship's surgeon described Jeremiah Boland as "a well conducted, proper man."

This was a reflection of the assessment made in a reference given to him in Ireland, of which the following is an extract:

"We, the undersigned magistrates know the bearer, Jeremiah Boland, a native inhabitant of the City of Cashel for a long period of years. He has a wife and four children, their ages being 18, 14, 7 and 5 years. The said Jeremiah Boland being inclined to go out to that part of His Majesty's Dominion called Canada in North America, and having applied to us for a testimonial of character, we have no hesitation recommending him for an honest, well conducted and local man".

You will note a discrepancy in the ages of the children. There may be an error here, but I have left this reference in for the benefit of genealogists who may find it useful.

Bolster, John, 40, carpenter

Ship	Brunswick, 1825
Origin	Mallow, Cork
Location	S lot 8, con 4, Smith
Family	Grace, 38
Thomas	17
Catherine	15
William	13

Eliza	1
John	9
Nathaniel	six months

Bolster, Joseph, 45, weaver

Ship	Brunswick, 1825
Origin	Kilshaney, Cork
Location	S lot 1, con 5, Ennismore
Family	Margaret, 25
John	22
Joseph	20
Thomas	19
William	17
Richard	13
Elizabeth	11
Nathaniel	8

There was one death in this family by 1826.

John Bolster received the north half lot 3, con 5, and his brother Joseph was given the south half of lot 1, con 6. He can be found there in the 1851 census.

Bourke, Edmond, 34

Ship	Fortitude, 1825
Origin	Kilbolane, Cork
Location	W lot 10, con 6, Marmora
Family	Mary, 26
Michael	18
Mary	9
Bridget	5

Another child was born in 1826. Edmond was a farmer, who managed to clear eight acres in his first year on the land.

Kilbolane is in the neighbourhood of Kanturk, Cork. An interesting fact in the Peter Robinson papers is a reference given as follows: " we the undersigned do hereby certify that we know the bearer, Edmond Bourke of Gowran in the County of Kilkenny to be a man of honest and industrious habits and that he is the father of three children, one male, two female."

I have no way of knowing whether this is the Edmond listed above, or a namesake who did not come to Canada. If it should prove to be the right man, then this may be one of the cases where the place of origin given refers to a centre where the family obtained tickets.

Bourke, Patrick, 34

Ship	Elizabeth, 1825
Origin	Kilbolane, Cork
Location	E lot 43, con 14, Smith
Family	Catherine, 22
Denis	20
Thomas	17
William	born June 6, 1826

According to a report issued in 1827, Patrick Bourke was sick all during the summer of 1826. Denis was Patrick's brother and in the early days he resided with him. Thomas Bourke and wife Elizabeth are shown in the 1851 census with two children at home.

Bourke, Simon, 38

Ship	Elizabeth, 1825
Origin	Kilbolane, Cork
Location	S lot 1, con 4, Emily
Family	Catherine, 37
Edmond	15
Nancy	14
Jeremiah	12
Mary	10
James	7
Margaret	5
Michael	3
John	one week

Simon Bourke was "very ill all summer" in 1826.

Boyle, Henry, 20, Anglican

Ship	Stakesby, 1823
Origin	Bandon, County Cork
Location	E lot 18, con 6, Pakenham Twp

Henry Boyle was single when he came to Canada but in 1835 he married Martha McAdam Reade, a young widow. This marriage was short-lived as Martha died at an early age; Henry subsequently married an Irish girl, Catherine Sealey.

Henry's land was poor and he tried several farms in turn, each one proving to be unsuitable. He lived in Huntley and Ramsay Townships before finally settling in Wilberforce Township. There are a great number of Henry Boyle's descendants in Renfrew County today.

Clyde Lendrum, a descendant of Henry Boyle, has spent some years researching family history. Some of his findings have appeared in the Boyle Bulletin, published by **Garvin Boyle.** Mr Lendrum says that there were many teachers and engineers in his branch of the family. Others have helped to develop Canada. *"My uncle, William Boyle, was water boy for the construction crew of the Canadian Pacific Railway when it came into North Bay. My grandfather, Robert Boyle, drove a team and the family worked west from North Bay along the CPR, working in the early mines of Sudbury. Two of Uncle Bill's brothers were diamond drillers and they drilled all over North America, and parts of South America. Hugh Boyle left Peru during a revolution and caught a boat from Lima to San Francisco arriving there the day after the great San Francisco earthquake. He worked on the relief crews."*

William Robert Boyle, a grandson of settler Henry, was a pioneer of Neudorf, Saskatchewan. He built the village hotel there, and later headed the village council. For many years he was manager of a local

R. D. BOYLE.

A thoroughly reliable and representative house engaged in the manufacture of harness and saddlery and the handling of turf goods and stable supplies is that of R. D. Boyle located on Main street. The business is an

old established one and has been carried on by its present proprietor for thirty years. The harness produced by Mr. Boyle enjoys an enviable reputation among the horse owners of Cobden and vicinity. Road, track and driving harness, both single and double, bridles, and all strap work constitute the general production of the house, and being all hand made, and of the best material, are unexcelled for strength, durability and finish. Only skilled hands are employed and all kinds of repairing is promptly attended to. Mr. Boyle is a long resident of Cobden and one of the representative business men.

This advertisement appeared in an industrial advertising paper which included the Cobden area. R.D.Boyle was the father of Edward G.Boyle of Hollywood.

lumber yard, and he build many flights of stairs in neighbourhood houses, being paid one dollar per step. Mr Boyle celebrated his 100th birthday in 1972 at Lethbridge, Alberta, where he lived in a nursing home. Telegrams were received from the Queen, Prime Minister Trudeau and the Premiers of Alberta and Saskatchewan.

Edgar Boyle and the one that didn't get away. Mr Boyle's ancestors travelled on the Stakesby in 1823.

In 1983, ten years after his death, "Boyle Place" was dedicated to his memory at his adopted town of Neudorf. Boyle Place consists of six senior citizen housing units, erected at a cost of $210,000 as a combined project of the federal, provincial and municipal governments.

Later in the book you can read the story of another of Henry's descendants, **Teenie Mayhew.**

Boyle, Thomas, 32, Anglican.

Ship	Stakesby, 1823
Origin	Ballymoden, Cork
Location	W lot 18, con 7, Pakenham
Family	Mary, 32
William	8
Mary	5
Charles	4
Esther	1

Thomas was a brother of Henry Boyle. The Peter Robinson papers give their place of origin as Clonmeen, Cork, but this must have been where they signed on to emigrate, as the family says that Thomas was in fact born in Bandon. Ballymodan, given as Henry's place of origin, is a Church of Ireland parish at Bandon.

Thomas Boyle was married to Mary Checkly. There was another child, born as they were passing through Ramsay on their way to Pakenham, but this baby apparently did not survive. However, it may also have been Esther because ages given often meant those to be attained on the following birthday.

The Boyles drew poor land on Pakenham mountain so they tried several farms in turn. When Thomas was laying claim to a Huntley property in 1834, a land agent recommended him by saying that "Thomas Boyle has ever borne the highest character for industry and good conduct."

Mary Checkly Boyle died in 1836, and six months later the widower married Mary McAdam.

The Boyle children married as follows William: 1. Elizabeth Curtis; 2. Sarah Jane Whitehead. Mary: Charles Curtis. Charles: Ann Dickson. Esther has not been traced.

Charles and Ann Boyle had an interesting grandson. His name was Edward Boyle, and he was the son of as Cobden couple, Robert Dickson Boyle and his wife, Mary Murphy. His ancestor, Thomas, would have been quite intrigued had he lived into the era of the motion picture industry, but he would have been even more dumbfounded to learn that his great grandson would go to Hollywood and win an Oscar! Edward's story is told later in the book.

William Boyle and three of his daughters: Nell (Lankin); Josephine (Hunt) and Janet (McNab.)

Bresnahan/Bristnahan, Daniel, RC

Ship	Hebe, 1823
Origin	Liscarrol, Cork
Location	lot 20, con 10, Huntley
Family	Honorah
Bridget	25
Julia	20
Joanna	18
Mary	14
Thomas	14
John	12
Catherine	10

Note that Daniel was the brother of all these children. Honorah Bresnahan was their widowed mother. Daniel went to the United States in 1826. His mother continued to farm this property with the aid of her younger son, Thomas.

Bresnahan, Maurice, 24, RC

Ship	Stakesby, 1825
Origin	Buttevant, Cork
Location	E lot 11, con 11, Ramsay

Maurice was a single man when he came to Canada. By 1826 he had cleared three and a half acres of his land, but was also working at Brockville as a tenant farmer.

Brick, Patrick

Ship:	Regulus
Origin:	Listowel, Kerry
Location:	N lot 11, con 6, Ennismore Twp

Patrick Brick is listed with the Patrick Shanahan family on the Regulus. It is known that he lived with them when he first came to Canada so perhaps he was related to them.

It is interesting to note that the surname Brick in Ireland originates almost exclusively from Kerry.

In due course, Patrick married Ellen Driscoll, a girl who had come out on the ship Brunswick with her parents, Michael and Nora Driscoll. According to census records, the Bricks had at least eleven children. They were Maurice; Catherine; Hanorah (Mrs Fitzpatrick); Mary (Mrs Hogan); Ellen (Mrs Peter McAuliffe); Patrick (m. Miss Hartney); Johanna (Mrs Nathaniel Travis); Michael; Margaret (Mrs Simon Perdue); John (m. Miss Moloney) and William.

Maurice Brick's first children were twins, Patrick and Thomas. Twins ran in the Driscoll family.

O'Brien, Denis, 35, cooper

Ship:	Resolution, 1825
Origin:	Mitchelstown, Cork
Location:	W lot 3, con 5, Douro Twp
Family:	Bridget, 26
James,	5
Johanna,	4

1826 report" "self and wife sick during summer."

O'Brien, John, 34, RC

Ship:	Stakesby, 1823
Origin:	Kanturk, Cork
Location:	lot 1, con 2, Ramsay Twp

1826 report: "tradesman, at work in Montreal."

O'Brien/Brien, John, 40

Ship:	Albion, 1825
Origin:	Litter, Cork (Fermoy district)
Location:	Asphodel Twp; later Emily
Family:	Margaret, 40
Thomas,	15
Ellen,	12
Johanna,	1

Ship's notes: "well behaved."

O'Brien, John, 38

Ship:	Brunswick
Origin:	Adare, Limerick
Location:	Asphodel Twp
Family:	Margaret, 28
John,	16
Denis,	14
Mary,	10
Patrick,	8
Johanna,	6
Ellen,	infant.

A most unfortunate family. The father died in Asphodel on September 24, 1826. Margaret died in December. Baby Ellen had died Sept 30. The family had suffered with the ague for most of the summer.

O'Brien, Martin, 44

Ship:	John Barry, 1825
Origin:	Kilfidane, Clare
Location:	E lot 31, con 6, Otonabee
Family:	Honora, 34
John,	17
Patrick,	15
Mary,	13
Bridget:	a baby who died en route.

1826 report: "absent without leave." This sometimes indicated a temporary absence when a man was employed in a nearby community.

O'Brien/Bryan Maurice, 37

Ship:	Resolution, 1825
Origin:	Mitchelstown, Cork
Location:	E lot 4, con 5, Douro Twp
Family:	Mary 33
Morgan,	17
Honora,	13
John,	11
Thomas,	7

William,   4,
Margaret,   1

In 1826, Morgan O'Brien was listed as 'living with his brother-in-law." Morgan had E lot 6, con 5, Douro. St Joseph's church was later built on land belonging to him.

Thomas O'Brien died August 13,1826.

Maurice and Mary appear to have had some additional children born to them in Canada, for in the 1851 census we find Maurice, 22; Michael, 18 and Catherine,16 living with them. In that year, the family lost a child from "scarlet faver" (sic).

O'Brian/Bryan, Michael, 33
Ship	Resolution, 1825
Origin	Brigown, Cork
Location	E lot 3, con 5, Douro
Family	Julia, 28
Mary	12
John	8
Eliza	6 (d.Aug 11,1826)
Michael	4
Ship:	Resolution, 1825

Ship's notes: "one child born; one child died."
It may have been Mary who died, for Michael and Julia had another daughter named Mary , born circa 1834.

O'Brien, Thomas, RC
Ship	Stakesby, 1823
Origin	Mallow, Cork
Location	lot 10, con 11, Ramsay

1826 report: "at work with a farmer in the country."

O'Brien, Timothy, 32, RC
Ship	Stakesby, 1823
Origin	Liscarrol, Cork
Location	E lot 8, con 7, Ramsay
Family	Katherine (nee O'Leary)
Patrick	9
Joanna	8
Jeremiah	5
Julia	2

Born in Canada:
Ellen (died age 21; John; twins, George and Thomas (the latter died at 15), Mary.

1826 report: seven in family, including one birth. Ten acres of land cleared.

This home was a "station" in which Mass was celebrated by a travelling priest in the 1820s and 1830s. Mrs O'Brien wrote an excellent letter to her brother in Ireland, urging him to come out in 1825 with the second wave of Peter Robinson settlers. In it she mentions a

The Foley plot at St Patrick's, Ferguson Falls. The marker in the foreground is that of Johanna O'Brien, Mrs John Foley.

Thomas, who had obtained work. This may be the Thomas O'Brien of the previous entry, though it could refer to a man of a different surname. Her husband,Timothy, was actually born in Kanturk, so the difference in places of origin for the two O'Brien men may not be significant. Mallow might be simply the place where Thomas applied to come to Canada.

Some of the O'Brien children married as follows: Patrick: Hanorah; Joanna: John Foley,PR; Jeremiah: Catherine Foley; Julia: John Madden,PR.

Ramsay Township, February 20,1824.
Dear Brother:

I embrace the opportunity of writing you these few lines to let you know that I and my family is well, thank God for His kind mercies, and I hope that this will find you the same.

I am happy to inform you that we have had a most

39

The wedding picture of two descendants of 1823 settlers, Frank O'Brien and Ellen Madden.

I expect that you will have more time to prepare than we had, and I therefore press upon you the necessity of bringing with you plenty of clothes, both for bed and body, for that is our greatest want here. You cannot bring too many with you for they will all be needed. I also entreat you to bring with you all the pots and pans, earthenware and other cooking utensils that you have.

I do not wish to encourage my brother John to come to this country if he would not resolve to work better than he did at home. If he would think of coming, if no misfortune has happened since we left home, I think he could bring out some money with him. He could get land cleared for ten or twelve dollars fit for cropping.

If he would keep from the drink he might do well, but the rum is very cheap - four shillings and sixpence per gallon - and some of our settlers likes it too well, which may prove their ruin, for a drunkard will not do well here, any more than at home.

Tell David Bonnell that I think he would do well in this country. Give my love to my sister. I will add no more now, but remain your loving and affectionate Sister,
Catharine O'Brien.

The four O'Brien children who had accompanied their parents to Canada all survived. One of Patrick's sons was **Dr. David O'Brien**, who practised medicine in Renfrew in the 1880s. While at McGill, David became a friend of William Osler, the well known surgeon. David married Theresa Foran and several children were born to the couple, although, sadly, three died at the time of a diphtheria epidemic. A surviving boy, John Robert, graduated in medicine from McGill in 1899 and practised for many years in Ottawa.

agreeable passage, and was all along, and still is, amazingly well treated. I cannot describe to you how kind and attentive Mr Robinson has been to administer to our comfort and convenience, and we are now most agreeably situated on a good lot of land with good neighbours all around us, in a flourishing settlement. Thomas has got, and has the prospect to get, plenty of employment at one dollar per day of wages and found in board and lodging, but he is inclined to work on his land, and notwithstanding working out considerable he has got about four acres chopped down, and hopes to have an acre or two again by spring. We have every prospect of doing well and having plenty.

This is a most delightful country, I believe none in the world more healthy. No sickness of any kind affects us, nor any of the settlers here; no want of bread for all have plenty to spare, and no man living, willing to work but may live happy.

The wages for labouring men is ten to twelve dollars per month and found, or by the day from half a crown to three shillings.

Now, brother, I have given you a short sketch of the country, and I am now going to invite you to come. Peter Robinson is going home for more settlers and carrying this letter along with him, and I beg of you, brother Robert, that you will come and embrace the opportunity, for you may never have the like again.

A fine house near Appleton, built by Frank O'Brien in 1903. The wing to the right was added in 1980.

Lieutenant Kathleen O'Brien, a graduate of the Royal Military College, Kingston.

A granddaughter of this doctor, **Lieutenant Kathleen O'Brien,** graduated from the Royal Military College, Kingston, 1986,with a degree in mechanical engineering. Not only is she one of the first female graduates of RMC, a distinction in itself, she has also travelled far from the lifestyle of her ancestor Katherine O'Brien by becoming an officer in the armed forces!

Mary Anne O'Brien, a daughter of pioneer Patrick, married Patrick Manion of Huntley. Their son, Robert Manion, is featured later in the book.

Johanna O'Brien married John Foley, PR. She became the mother of some railroad millionaires. Their story can be found in the Foley section of the book.

Newspaper clippings.
Almonte Gazette, Jan.1868.
Married in Huntley on the 12th instant by the Rev.E.Vaughan, Mr Peter Doyle of the Township of Drummond to Miss Catherine O'Brien, eldest daughter of Patrick O'Brien Esq., councillor of the Township of Ramsay.

(We were complimented with a piece of wedding cake, for which we wish them the compliments of the season, a happy and prosperous future, and hope the nuptial-tie will prove (Deo juvante) a blessing to both.)

Nov.11,1874.
At her son's hotel, Carleton Place, on the 19th inst., Hanorah, wife of Patrick O'Brien Esq., of Ramsay. Deceased had been suffering from asthma for the last four or five years, which debilitated her very much, but no serious apprehensions were entertained until the Monday previous to her death, when a severe attack of bronchitis set in. She was attended by Dr McEwen of Carleton Place and also her son, Dr David O'Brien of Renfrew,, but was unable to endure the necessary remedies for her complaint.

Her remains were conveyed on Saturday, followed by a very large concourse of friends and acquaintances, to the Roman Catholic church at Almonte (where a Solemn Requiem Mass was sung for her happy repose) and thence to the new Catholic burying ground for interment. R.I.P.

Carleton Place Canadian, 1883.
Two years ago, Miss O'Brien of Ramsay went to visit her sister, Mrs Eccles of Dakota. Though only 19 she took up 160 acres and has since been fulfilling the legal requirements of settlement, A few days ago she was offered $3000 but respectfully declined. Her friends are glad of this great good fortune- a swifter way of getting wealth than remaining in Ramsay and raising poultry, even for so good a market as that of Carleton Place.

The O'Brien connection at the Eccles farm near Grand Forks, North Dakota. Julia (Mrs William O'Brien) and Frank Foley in the car; - ?, Myra Eccles, Kate Eccles, Henry Eccles, John Foley. Elmer Foley in front.

This girl was a daughter of John O'Brien and Johannah Lahey, John being one of the children born in Upper Canada to settlers Timothy and Catherine. The Mrs Eccles was her sister, Catherine O'Brien Jr.

April, 1873
Gone to Pembroke

Dr. O'Brien, who has recently taken his degree in McGill College, Montreal, has taken up residence in Pembroke for the practice of his profession. As a student he was noted for close application and rapid progress made in his studies, and we have no doubt that as a doctor he will be equally successful. We wish him all prosperity.

O'Brien, Timothy, RC

Ship	Stakesby, 1823
Origin	Newmarket, Cork
Location	Darling Twp
Family	Mary, 34
Margaret	12
Bridget	9
Denis	3

Timothy O'Brien died in 1828, leaving his widow with several young children. Since his son Denis was listed as being 13 years old at that time, it is difficult to know his correct birthdate. Mary O'Brien apparently worked on, erecting a house on lot 21, con 10, Darling (they had originally drawn lot 4, con 2) and the family managed to clear five acres of land by 1834. Women were not then eligible for land grants but widows were usually permitted to hold farms in trust for their eldest son.

Brislane, John, 41

Ship	Star, 1825
Origin	Shandrum, Cork
Location	E lot 9, con 10, Emily
Family	Margaret, 39
Margaret	22
Edmond	19
Honora	17
Elizabeth	15
Jane	12
Janny	9
Nancy	7

Edmond Brislane drew the west half of the lot on which his father settled. During their first full year on the land the family produced 200 bushels of potatoes, 100 bushels of turnips, 60 bushels of Indian corn, and 100 lbs maple sugar.

Brown, James, 19, RC

Ship	Stakesby, 1823
Origin	Lismore, Waterford
Location	E lot 19, con 5, Ramsay

James went to the USA before very long.

Brown, William, 16, RC.

Ship	Stakesby, 1823
Origin	Lismore, Waterford
Location	W lot 19, con 5, Ramsay

This was a brother of James Brown. William worked as a boatman on the St. Lawrence in 1826.

Bryan, David, 32.

Ship	Fortitude, 1825
Origin	Templetenny, Tipperary
Location	unknown
Family	Anne, 34
Kennedy	12
John	8
Kitty	5

Bryan/Brien, Patrick, 30

Ship	Resolution, 1825
Origin	Deniskea, Tipperary
Location	W lot 23, con 5, Otonabee
Family	Honora, 30
William	8
Anne	6
John	4
David	1

Elizabeth Carroll, 17 (sister-in-law)

Buck, George, 45, tailor

Ship:	Elizabeth, 1825
Origin	Knockatemple, Cork
Location	lot 19, con 10, Otonabee
Family Mary,	40
Thomas	18
William	16
George	13
Ellen	8
John	6
Patrick	2

This family at first remained in Peterborough, where George set up a tailor's shop. Meanwhile, his son Thomas went out to the country and made a start at clearing the land; in 1826 he was said to be "chopping on his father's lot." Thomas himself was given the west half of this lot.

The 1851 census shows George and Mary with their sons George and Patrick, still in Otonabee Township, accompanied by a Canadian-born Patrick, age 19.   Thomas is shown in the township as a widower with ten children, ages four to 18.

Researchers should be careful when working on this family, as there was a prominent family in the same district who had quite similar first names. They were of English background and apparently came to Canada circa 1834.

Buckley, Cornelius,

Ship:	Hebe,1823
Origin:	Liscarrol, Cork
Location	W.lot 17, con 10, Huntley Twp
Family	Catherine
Cornelius	15
James	1 year

In 1826, Cornelius was described thus" "has been absent, but is now returned to his land."

Buckley, Daniel, RC

Ship	Hebe, 1823
Origin	Churchtown, Cork
Location	E lot 3, con 12, Goulbourn Twp
Family:	Mary (Daniel's mother)
James	(brother)
Ellen	(sister.)

1834 report: "left this country in 1826."

Buckley, Edmond, 45

Ship:	Stakesby, 1823
Origin:	Kanturk, Cork
Location:	E 3, con 10, Goulbourn Twp
Family:	Katherine, 20
Ellen	22
Mary	14

Edmond Buckley died in Goulbourn before 1826.

Buckley, James, shoemaker

Ship	Hebe, 1823
Origin	Churchtown, Cork
Location:	W lot 1, con 12, Goulbourn Twp
Family:	Wife, Ellen.

A baby was born to this couple before 1826. 1834 report: "resides in Huntley, works at his trade."

The 1851 census does show a James Buckley, shoemaker, with a large family, but his wife's name is given as Mary. If this is the same James Buckley, it is possible that Ellen died, for Mary's children were born from about 1831 on.

Although James Buckley's place of origin is given as Churchtown, other documents say that his birthplace was Mallow, Cork.

Buckley, John

Ship:	Hebe, 1823
Origin:	Croom, Limerick
Location	unknown.

Note in 1826 records: "gone".

Buckley, John, 41

Ship:	Brunswick, 1825
Origin:	Colemanswell, Limerick
Location	W lot 7, con 8, Emily Twp

Family:	Johanna, 32
Timothy	13
Catherine	10
John	9
Mary	6
Ellen	1

Note: John Buckley, alias Maurice Fitzgerald. See entry for the latter.

Buckley, Maurice, 35

Ship:	Stakesby, 1823
Origin:	Fermoy, Cork
Location:	Ramsay Twp.

Buckley, Michael, 31

Ship	Amity,1825
Origin:	Knockatemple, Cork
Location	N lot 16, con 10, Emily
Family:	Bridget, 27, nee Begley
Honora	15
Ellen	12
Michael	10
Manus	3
Benjamin	1

Bridget was a daughter of Moses Begley (see separate entry.)

Ship's notes" Has a very honest, well conducted family."

Michael Buckley senior was sick all through the summer of 1826. One member of the family died in that year.

Reference, given in Ireland:
Cork, May 7, 1825
"This is to certify that Michael Buckley is a man in reduced circumstances and unable to pay his passage to America. That during the late disturbances he gave valuable information to the magistrates which placed his life in danger, and that he is still obnoxious to his neighbours on that account. Moses Begly, his father-in-law, is also a reduced farmer and blacksmith, without means of support"

Buckley, Patrick, RC

Ship:	Hebe,1824
Origin:	Churchtown, Cork
Location	lot 23, con 3, Ramsay
Family	Bridget, wife
James	7
Daniel	4
John	3
Timothy	2
Elizabeth	born in Ramsay

Patrick worked off the farm in the early days, for a note written by an inspector in 1826 says "absent without leave, but in Canada."

Buckley, Timothy, RC
Ship: Hebe, 1823
Origin   Churchtown, Cork
Location   E lot 12, con 6, Ramsay
Family: Mary, wife
Margaret   3

This family later moved to E lot 23, con 3.

1834 report: "residing on his land and doing well." He was obviously making a success of things, for in 1831 the parish priest's diary recorded that the family gave him ten shillings as their annual dues.

Buckley, Timothy, 34
Ship   Elizabeth, 1825
Origin   Churchtown, Cork
Location: lot 2, con 10, Goulbourn
Family: Julia, 20
Timothy   14
Catherine   9
Margaret   6
Margaret   17 (a sister).

This is obviously an extended family. Timothy was too young to have been Julia's father; if she was his wife, then he must have married twice, for she could not have been the mother of the children.

Although Timothy travelled with the 1825 group, he settled in the Bathurst District, which usually did not happen unless people had relatives there. He may therefore have been connected with some of the Buckley families of 1823.

A butcher by trade, Timothy did not farm his land but worked at his trade in the district. In 1834 he was reported to be "doing well."

A Wealthy Man.

Eleven families of Buckleys travelled to Upper Canada with Peter Robinson, and most of them came from County Cork. The most enterprising of them all was one Daniel Buckley, a descendant of one of these families, who grew up to become a wealthy man. He lived in Huntley Township.

In the early days, life was hard. Although the original settlers had been equipped with tools and rations, they still had to clear the land, and there was little money to spare. Crops could rarely be sold because all produce was needed for survival, and the only cash crop at first was potash. (Ashes left over from burning stumps during land clearance were placed in a container and water was allowed to leach through them. The result was lye, an essential ingredient in soap making.)

This was all too much for Daniel Buckley. He decided to help the family along by making his own money. A local blacksmith was brought into the act, and sworn to secrecy. In those days the blacksmith turned his hand to making many different articles, everything from tools to household fixtures. Horses were few and far between in the early days, and the smith needed to diversify. On this occasion, a blacksmith made a mould for manufacturing American half dollars.

This needs some clarification. Before Confederation, many different types of coin were legal currency here. Spanish pieces of eight, English guineas, French sous and Mexican gold were all acceptable in Upper Canada. Dan figured that a few home-made half dollars could get by undetected. He went into operation, making pewter coins, with a coating of silver. Just how he got hold of the silver is unclear. Perhaps he had to begin by melting down some real money.

For a while, Dan enjoyed great success. We know that the average daily wage of a labourer was less than a dollar. Dan could afford to make a few coins each month and then take life easy for a time. Just two of those coins would have purchased a gallon of rum then, if Dan was inclined to give a party. Perhaps, though, he was prudent enough to hide his new-found wealth from the neighbours.

Unfortunately for Dan, his sister was less cautious. On one occasion she went to Bytown on a shopping spree, taking some of the family money with her. This must have been without Dan's knowledge, for she filled her purse with unmilled coins, which were instantly recognized as counterfeit by the merchants in town.

The constables arrived at the run, and Dan was soon apprehended and hauled before the magistrates. He was given a stiff jail sentence, and told to stay out of Huntley after his release. Later, an official report noted that Daniel Buckley had left the district. We know why.

Burgess, Daniel, 44, cooper.
Ship: Albion, 1825
Origin   Kilbride, Cork
Location: lot one, con 4, Smith Twp
Family: Avice, 44,
William   23
Emanuel   22
Sabina   21
Elizabeth   20
Mary Anne   19
Henry   18
Daniel   15
Avice   10

Ships' notes: Daniel senior: "a plausible and I suspect a designing character." William: "a good young man, a cooper by trade."

This family was dogged by bad fortune. Daniel senior died in Smith Township September 11, 1826, Mary Anne on Sept 21, and her mother on September 23.

Sabina went to Kingston and Elizabeth to Prescott. In 1826, Emmanuel was shown to be living with his father, although at that time their residence was given as Emily Twp, not Smith as recorded earlier. In any event, the 1851 census for Emily shows the family of a Daniel Burgess who appears to have been Daniel junior.

Byrnes/Burns, George, 25
Ship	Resolution, 1825
Origin:	Brigown, Cork
Location	W lot 5, con 4, Douro Twp
Family:	Kitty, 24
Patrick	4
Mary	born April 9, 1826

Cahill, Thomas, 38
Ship:	Elizabeth, 1825
Origin:	Listowel, Kerry
Location	S lot 7, con 7, Ennismore
Family	Johanna, 36
John	17
Michael	15
Mary	14
Johanna	9
Thomas	4
John	1

Ship's notes: "a good and honest family." There was a birth and a death in this family in 1826.

Cahill, Bartholomew, 25
Ship:	Stakesby, 1823
Origin:	Fermoy, Cork
Location:	unknown

Callaghan, Daniel, RC
Ship and origin unknown, but this man is listed in the location papers and was given land on lot 27, con 1, Beckwith Twp. He was accompanied by a wife, Bridget.

Callaghan/Clahane, Denis, RC, 22
Ship	Hebe, 1823
Origin	Kilnagowan, Cork
Location	E lot 19, Ramsay Twp
Family	Jude, wife
Mary	1 year

This family is also listed as having occupied lot 3, con 7. Denis was a brother of Timothy Callaghan. Denis died in 1828. His mother then lived on his lot, and in 1834 she petitioned to be allowed to leave the land to her daughter's children. At that time she was being assisted by her son-in-law, Hugh McDonald, the father of two sons.

"I mention this," the government inspector wrote, "as Timothy Clahan has gone to the United States and the two elder sons are dead, to show that there are heirs for the lots...the widow prays to be allowed to keep them for her grandchildren."

Callaghan, Edmond.
See Lynes.

Callaghan, Eugene,
Ship:	Regulus, 1825
Origin	Ballyclough, Cork
Location	W lot 23, con 6, Smith

1826 report: "has been working with H. Gardiner; now chopping on his own land."

Callaghan, Jeremiah, 35
Ship:	Regulus, 1825
Origin:	Mallow, Cork
Location:	E lot 13, con 10, Emily Twp
Family:	Kitty, 34
John,	14
James,	12
Michael,	7
Mary,	3
Ellen,	2
Baby,	born 1826

Callaghan, John, 34
Ship:	Star, 1825
Origin:	Freemount, Cork
Location:	E lot 5, con 1, Ramsay Twp.
Family:	Patrick, 15

This John Callaghan was a brother to Denis and Timothy Callaghan, who joined them in 1825. He never did live on his lot but took possession of his brother Timothy's farm when it was vacated by him. John and Patrick cleared six acres of land in their first season. Unfortunately, John died in 1828.

Callaghan, John, 44
Ship:	John Barry, 1825
Origin:	Clonmeen, Cork
Location:	N lot 5, con 5, Emily Twp
Family:	Norah, 38
David,	23
Cornelius,	22
Jeremiah,	20
Ellen,	18
Owen,	16
Dennis,	14
John,	12

Jeremiah took up land on the northern half of lot 6, con 6, Emily.

Callaghan, Patrick
See Lynes.

Callaghan, Thomas, 42.

Ship:	Amity, 1825
Origin:	Brigown, Cork
Location,	N lot one, con 2, Marmora
Family:	Judith, 36
Thomas,	19
John,	17
Mary,	15
Patrick,	13
Jeremiah,	10
Margaret,	8
Catherine,	6
Johanna,	2

In the ship's notes, poor Thomas was described as "quiet, well-behaved and slothful!" Two members of this family died after arriving in Canada, and the whole family suffered with the ague throughout the summer of 1826.
Thomas Callaghan junior was allocated the west half of lot 3, con 3, Marmora, and his brother John drew the east half lot 2, con 2,

Callaghan, Timothy, 22

Ship:	Hebe, 1823
Origin:	Kilnagowan, Cork
Location:	lot 5, con 1, Ramsay.
Family:	Margaret (widowed mother)
Joanna,	18 (sister)
Catherine,	15 (sister)

This family also lived at one time on lot 5, con 7, Pakenham Twp.
Timothy was a widower when he came to Canada. Kilnagowan is near Churchtown.

Callaghan, Timothy, 34

Ship:	John Barry, 1825
Origin:	Drishane, Cork
Location,	W lot 11, con 12, Asphodel Twp
Family:	Nancy, 29
Ellen,	14
Jeremiah,	11
John	8
Timothy	3
Mary	1

Ship's notes: " a quiet family. A child born on the John Barry." This could have been Mary, as ages usually referred to those which would be attained on the next birthday.

Reference, 1825

We the undersigned Clergy and Gentry do know the bearer, Timothy Callahan to be a perfectly honest, sober, diligent and reliable man and likewise an intelligent labourer- as such we recommend him."

Application by Timothy:
I have four children in Distress and a wife for the work."

In 1826, Timothy was erroneously listed as being absent without leave, but he had actually died. He had left his family in Peterborough while he went out to his farm to build them a shelter, but he died before he could rejoin them.

Callaghan, William, RC

Ship:	Hebe, 1823
Origin:	Kanturk, Cork
Location	lot 20, con 10, Huntley
Family	Bridget, wife

"Absent without leave" in 1826.

Callaghan.
Several examples have been discovered of passengers on the emigrant ships who impersonated ticket holders in order to get aboard, but none is more heart-rending than a story told to Peter Robinson in a letter, which reached him at a Cork hotel in May of 1825.

"The bearer, David Callaghan of Mallow, a mason by trade, leaves town today in quest of his son Jeremiah, being apprenticed by him and wants two years of his apprenticeship served. Young Callaghan eloped last night from his father's service with the intention of going to Canada, and his intention is to slip in if possible with some family who are about to emigrate. You will do this poor man a favour by not granting passage to his undutiful and disobedient son. His sudden disappearance has plunged a poor industrious family into extreme distress and agony of mind.
I learn that the son of the bearer has purchased a ticket of some other Callaghan for one pound, and will impersonate his wavering namesake.
I am, Sir, yours sincerely,
W. Jones, Parish Priest, Mallow."

Whether the youth actually came to Canada, we cannot say. Certainly there were a number of Callaghans who came out at that time, with boys of the right age to have exchanged places with the flitting Jeremiah.

There is no Jeremiah of suitable age among the emigrants but he may have adopted an alias for the trip, as many did.

Here is a letter written on behalf of another Callaghan who apparently was turned down. Whether they came here at a later date is not known, but it is included here for the sake of genealogists.
To Mr Robinson Esq.,
Ballyghiblin, Cork.
The humble address of Pat Callaghan of Liscarrol.
Humbly sheweth that he and his family will never

recover their present distress if you be not so kind as to take him and family to Kanada. You promised here in Doneraile to carry him, and he still hopes you will not leave him...if you take him he will daily and hourly as in duty bound forever pray.
Michael Callaghan of Mount Corbett in the Parish of Churchtown, Cork.

Cannon, William, 44

Ship	Elizabeth, 1825
Origin:	Coole? Cork
Location:	unknown
Family:	Mary, 40
Denis,	21
George,	19
Catherine	18
Frank	15
Mary	13

Carew, Michael, 34

Ship:	Fortitude, 1825
Origin:	Deniskea, Tipperary
Location:	N lot 5, con 5, Ennismore Twp
Family:	Anne, 30 (nee Hogan)
Bridget	14
Patrick,	8
Michael,	6
John	4
William,	2

Illness and death marred this family at first. Anne gave birth to a little son during the voyage to Canada, naming the child Lewis Fortitude Carew after the captain and the ship. Unfortunately the baby did not survive, and he was buried at sea.
During their first summer in Ennismore Michael senior suffered from the ague. However, he recovered and the couple went on to have more children, including a son, James and a daughter, Ann.
Their children married as follows: Bridget: Michael Crough; Patrick: Ellen Sullivan; Michael: Elizabeth Donnelly; John: Margaret; then Ann Sloan; James: Mary Ann Doran; Ann: Dennis Conroy, PR. William did not marry.
In 1852, Michael Carew, then age 68, moved to Mukwa Township, Waupacca County, Wisconsin, with his wife and their children John and Ann and their families. These people were among the earliest settlers of that county, which had been opened to settlement by a treaty made with the Menominee Indians in 1849. At a later date, descendants of the Dorans of Emily Township also settled in this district. The family lived at Bear Lake, so John Carew was nicknamed "Lake John" to distinguish him from other John Carews in the area.
Ann Carew, with his husband Dennis Conroy,
 a descendant of the Conroys of Douro) also settled at Bear Lake, and their farm is still in family hands.

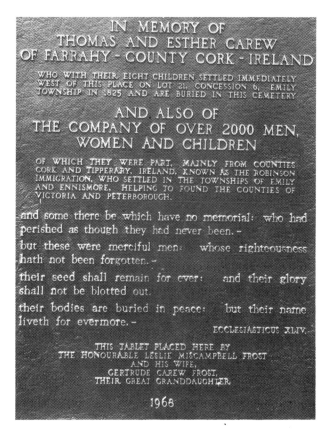

A plaque beside St. James Anglican church, East Emily pays tribute to the memory of Thomas and Esther Carew, and to others who travelled with the 1825 settlers. The plaque was placed there by The Hon. Leslie Frost, Premier of Ontario, whose wife Gertrude was a descendant of the Carews.

James Carew married Mary Ann Doran in Coburg in 1852 and soon after this they joined the rest of the family in Wisconsin. James was a veteran of the American Civil War.

Carew/ Casey, Thomas, 43.

Ship:	Resolution, 1825
Origin:	Farraghy Cork
Location:	S lot 21, con 6, Emily Twp
Family:	Esther, 41
Anne	21
Samuel	19
Sarah	15
Richard	13
Thomas	11
Esther	9
John	7
Robert	2

Samuel Carew drew land on the south of lot 19, con 6. In 1826, his father suffered badly with the ague, but even so, in that season the family managed to produce 500 bushels of potatoes, 100 bushels of turnips, 30 bushels of Indian corn and 50 lbs maple sugar.

Among the distinguished citizens who have their roots in Emily Township, the Carews have been well to the fore. One of the more prominent members of this family was **John Carew**, who served as Conservative MPP for South Victoria at the time of the First World War. He was a descendant of Thomas and Esther Carew who came on the Resolution. John, their great grandson, was born in Emily Township in 1862, a son of John Carew Jr and his wife, the former Jane Wilson.

John Carew III went into the lumber business, establishing himself in Lindsay. His territories extended throughout the Haliburton region. Listed in the Parliamentary Guide of 1918 as "a lumber manufacturer", he operated a mill in town, was president of the John Carew Lumber Company, and vice president of two brick-making companies. His lumber company was one of the larger employers of labour in the area at the turn of the century.

At the age of 23 he married Margaret Ann Kelly of Verulam, and they had seven children. Their eldest son, **Francis John Carew** was in his middle twenties when the First World War broke out. He served as a Liutenant-Colonel in France, appropriately enough as an officer in the Canadian Forestry Corps. In civilian life he was president of the Haliburton Lumber Company.

While his son was away at the war, John Carew served his country on the home front. He was elected to the Ontario legislature in 1914, serving until 1919 under the Hearst regime.

Soon after the war, two young lawyers, war veterans, moved to Lindsay to practice their profession. Their names were Cecil and **Leslie Frost**, both discharged with the rank of captain. Leslie had been severely wounded and had spent months in hospital before returning to civilian life. The brothers fell in love with two of John Carew's daughters, and marriage followed.

Gertrude Carew was Leslie's choice. When he later decided on a political career, she was well equipped to support him in his ambition, as the daughter of a former MPP.

Leslie Frost was elected to the legislature in 1937 as the Member for Victoria, and he continued to serve the province until 1961. He became Premier of Ontario in May, 1949.

While "Gert", as she was known to her friends, did not attempt to share the limelight with her husband, it was an accepted fact that she had a strong influence on the Premier. Her moral convictions and her sense of what was fitting were regarded as being a significant factor in the shaping of Ontario policy.

A story that is told about Gertrude Frost shows the sort of person that she was. Once, she and her husband were travelling from Toronto to Lindsay when their chauffeur-driven car was stopped by an officer of the O.P.P. The young man turned white when he realised that he had flagged down the Premier of Ontario! Gert Frost took charge of the situation at once. "Go ahead and give him a speeding ticket, he deserves it!" she said.

Later, the young policeman was given a commendation for his record in recognition of his courteous handling of an awkward moment.

This advertisement appeared on an old map of the Peterborough area.

Carey, Florence, 25, RC
Ship: Stakesby, 1823
Origin: Ballyhooly, Cork
Location: W lot 11, con 3, Ramsay Twp

Note that Florence was a man. This was a fairly common name for a boy in nineteenth century Ireland, being an awkward English translation of a Gaelic saint's name. The name Florence for a girl was popularized only after Nurse Florence Nightingale achieved fame; she in turn had been named for Florence, Italy. Florence Carey was drowned in August, 1825.

Carey, John
Ship: Hebe, 1823
Further details unknown. John Carey "left the group at Morphy's Falls." This community is now Carleton Place.

Carey, John, 38
Ship   Fortitude
Origin: Kilworth, Cork
Location   E lot 18, con 7, Emily Twp
Family: Mary, 36
Patrick   16
Catherine   11
Mary   3
Johanna   2
Elizabeth, 33 (Mary's sister) One death took place in this family in 1826.

Casey, James, 50
Ship: Fortitude, 1825
Origin: Kilbenny, Limerick
Location: E lot 7, con 4, Douro Twp
Family: Mary, 46
Maurice,   26 (alias Maurice Clancy)
Michael,   23
Mary   20
Judith   18
Kitty   14
James   12
Johanna   8
John   4

Michael Casey drew the west half of the lot occupied by this family. However, his father died in 1826 and Michael then moved in with his mother and the others.

Casey, Margaret, 18
Ship: Stakesby, 1823
Origin: Mitchelstown, Cork.
No further information is available on Margaret Casey, but on the ship's list her name appears below that of the Mansells, who came from the same place in Ireland.
She may be the Peggy Casey mentioned in a letter written by Michael Cronin. (See Cronin.)

Casey, Thomas, 35
Ship: John Barry, 1825
Origin   Kilbrien, Cork
Location: E lot 19, con 9, Otonabee Twp
Family: Johanna, 30
James   11
Mary   9
Timothy   7
John   5
Johanna   1

Ship's notes: " a very good family. Behaved well on passage."
1826 report: Thomas "has never been well since his arrival in Canada.

Clancy, John, 30, shoemaker.
Ship: Albion, 1825
Origin: Rock Mile Creek, Cork
Location: NW lot 19, con 11, Otonabee
                      NE lot 19, con 12.
Family: Eliza, 30
Ellen   16
William   14
John   5
Johanna   3

Ship's notes: "a well behaved man."
In their first full year on the land, this family raised 300 bushels of potatoes, 50 bushels of turnips and 30 bushels of corn. They were also the proud possessors of one cow.

Clancy, Maurice, 26, blacksmith.
Ship: Fortitude, 1825
Origin   Kilbenny, Limerick.
Location: E lot 5, con 4, Douro Twp
Notes: "alias Maurice Casey." See entry for the James Casey family. 1827 report "working at his trade."
Maurice was married to Margaret Lenihan. A later census reports that a daughter, Mary, was born in Ireland circa 1825, while children born in Douro included Michael, Ellen, Johanna and Margaret.
If the census taker was correct in his report of Mary's birth, then it is possible that Maurice's wife remained in Ireland - possibly because she was pregnant - joining her husband at a later date. Neither she nor Mary appear on any ship's list.

Clancy, Patrick, 40
Ship   Resolution, 1825
Origin   Kilworth, Cork.
Location: N lot 15, con 9, Emily Twp
Family   Mary, 33
Thomas   12
Denis   10
Maurice   8
Daniel   4

Patrick   2
Martin   May 1, 1825 - Sept 20

In 1826, a John Clancy, who had received part of lot 22, con 6 Emily, was living with this family. He was Patrick's brother who had come out to Canada at an earlier date, moving to join the rest of the group in 1825.

The 1851 census for this township shows Patrick Clancy, 65,
Mary,   60
Patrick, 28
Ellen,   14

Cleary, William, 45

Ship	Resolution, 1825
Origin:	Doneraile, Cork
Location:	W lot 23, con 10, Otonabee Twp
Family;	Mary, 40
Timothy,	20
John	17
Mary	15
Johanna	12
William	10
Catherine	3
Baby	1826

Catherine Cleary died and was buried at sea.
Wiiliam Cleary senior was "sick during the summer' of 1826.

Coghlan/Coughlin, Jeremiah, 22

Ship:	Stakesby, 1823
Origin:	Mallow, Cork
Location:	not given

Coghlan/Coughlin, John

Ship	Stakesby, 1823
Origin	Bandon,Cork
Location:	lot 13, con 3, Ramsay Twp
Family:	Mary, wife.

One child was born to this couple soon after their arrival in the township. John worked for a while at Kingston, and never returned.
1834 report: "not heard of since 1826. Wife kept possession of the lot until her death, by will leaving the lot to her son, a child of ten years of age, in charge of John Cadogan."

John Coghlan had taken part in the Ballyghiblin riots, as a result of which he had been given a jail sentence and a fine. We know that he worked at Kingston following his release, and it is likely that he was employed at the canal, as a number of the Robinson settlers were.

Coghlan/Coghlin, Timothy

Ship	Hebe, 1823
Origin:	Doneraile, Cork
Location:	unknown
Mary	wife

Colbert, John

Ship:	Hebe, 1823
Origin:	Clogheen, Tipperary

Note: "left at Morphy's Falls." (Now Carleton Place.)
Alias **John Mara.** See Mara.

Collins, Cornelius, 43, RC

Ship:	Stakesby, 1823
Origin:	Glanmile, Cork
Location:	E lot 2, con 12, Goulbourn Twp
Family	Katherine, 40, wife
Anne	22
Richard	20
Margaret	17
David	14
Daniel	11
Katherine	7
Johanna	5

One birth occurred in Goulbourn and was reported at the time of the 1826 inspection. Richard Collins, although he initially lived with his parents, was given the next farm to theirs, the west half of the same lot. He left his land in 1829 and his father petitioned to get it, planning to turn his own farm over to his son Daniel.

Collins, John, 40

Ship:	Albion, 1825
Origin:	Askeaton, Limerick
Location:	W lot 19, con 11, Emily Twp
Family:	Johanna, 40
Michael	20
Timothy	18
John	16
Catherine	14
Edmund	12
James	8
Bridget	3
Maurice	1

The ship's surgeon remarked that John had "an unhappy temper."
Michael and Timothy Collins each received half of lot 6 in con 11.
A report of 1827 noted that John was "recovering from ague" and that Timothy had in the previous year "worked all summer at the Welland Canal."
The 1851 census for this township shows Michael with wife Johanna and children Mary Ann; Elizabeth; Timothy; Catherine; John; Johanna; Bridget and Maurice; also John with wife Mary and children Timothy, Mary, Johanna, Catherine, Bridget, Thomas, Cecilia and Amelia.

Collins, John, 48

Ship	Regulus, 1825
Origin	Listowel,Kerry
Location:	S lot 1, con 3, Ennismore Twp
Family	Joanna, 44
Denis	23
Mary	16
John	14
Thomas	12

Michael	9
Morgan	4
Joanna	1

There were two deaths in this family in 1826. They received a land patent in 1834.
John junior eventually received the south half of lot 3, con 2, and Michael the north half. Thomas had the south half of lot 2, con 2.

Collins, Patrick, 34
Ship:	Brunswick, 1825
Origin:	Mallow, Cork
Location:	S lot 11, con 6, Ennismore Twp
Family:	Julia, 33 (nee Bourke)
Mary	16
Michael	14
John	9
Eliza	4
Catherine	2

There was one birth in 1826, at a time when the family was "sick all summer."

Collins, Richard, RC
Ship:	Hebe,1823
Origin:	Kanturk, Cork
Location:	W lot 1, con 11, Goulbourn Twp
Family:	
Thomas	21
Daniel	20
Mary	16
Cornelius	14

Thomas drew the east half of his father's lot, and Daniel the east half of lot one, con 12. In 1826, Richard senior was listed as having five in his family; Thomas by this time had married and was living elsewhere. Richard junior later moved to Huntley Township but left that farm also in 1829.
Researchers may wish to investigate the possibility that Richard senior could have been a brother of Cornelius ("Con") Collins who also came out in 1823. The pair had adjoining lots in Goulbourn Township and some of the names in the two families are similar. For instance, Con had a son Richard, and Richard had a son Con..

Condon, David, 50
Ship:	Brunswick, 1825
Origin:	Brigown, Cork
Location	E lot 10, con 2, Douro Twp
Family:	Mary, 45 (died 1854)
Michael	24
Bridget	22
Margaret	20
Ellen	16
Johanna	12
John	9
Patrick	7

David Condon died at sea during the voyage to Upper Canada. The lot on which this family lived was allocated to his eldest son, Michael. Another record gives the family's place of origin as Carrigwell, Cork.

The Michael Condon home was one the stations where Mass was celebrated in the early days, prior to the building of the church. Michael's son Patrick became a priest.

Condon, James, 43, weaver
Ship	John Barry, 1825
Origin	Templetenny, Tipperary
Location	W lot 29, con 2, Otonabee
Family	Margaret, 38
Richard	24
Judith	18
Mary	16
William	12
Honora	6

Ship's notes: "a very good, quiet, industrious and willing family."
Richard Condon was given a lot adjoining that of his father, E lot 28, con 2. In 1827, however, he was still residing with his father

Condon, John, 44
Ship	Brunswick, 1825
Origin	Kilworth, Cork
Location:	S lot 10,con 5,Ennismore
Family	Johanna, 44
William	20
Richard	17
John	11
David	5
Michael	2

Johanna Condon is listed as a widow, so evidently her husband died en route to their new home. Their son William took up this farm but he eventually moved to the USA.

Nobody in the Condon family starved as in their first year on the land they were able to raise 300 bushels of potatoes.

Condon, John, 30, tailor
Ship	Resolution, 1825
Origin	Mitchelstown, Cork
Location:	lot 25, con 12, Otonabee
Family:	Sarah, 24
Martin	7
Henry	6
James	1

Condon, Richard, 32, butcher
Ship	Stakesby, 1823
Origin	Mallow, Cork
Location	stopped at Montreal, with Peter Robinson's consent.
Family	Mary, 19
Sarah	8 months.

Condon, Thomas, 42
Ship	Resolution, 1825
Origin	Kilworth, Cork
Location	E lot 25, Otonabee Twp
Family:	Margaret, 40
James	21
Bartholomew	16
Patrick	14
Ellen	10
John	8
Mary	5
Thomas	1

Reference.
I have never heard of anything to show prejudice of the character of bearer Thomas Condon.
Edward Barry, Fermoy, 1824.

James Condon was given the west half of the lot on which his father settled.
The ship's notes state that "two men settled at Quebec; one child died."
Researchers may wish to consider the fact that there may possibly have been some connection between this family and that of Richard Condon, an 1823 Peter Robinson settler who located in Montreal, Quebec.

Connell, Callaghan, 40
Ship	Brunswick, 1825
Origin	Mallow, Cork
Location:	S lot 18, con 11, Emily
Family:	Judith, 30
Denis	14
Mary	6
Margaret	9 months

Reference, Mallow,Cork.
The bearer, Callaghan Connell, lived with me this fifteen years back as plowman and general labourer, during which time he conducted himself sober, quietly, and as to honesty I had to entrust him frequently with large sums of money from here to Fermoy, which trust he fulfilled to the satisfaction of Mr Walker and myself."

This family is no longer represented in Emily Township.

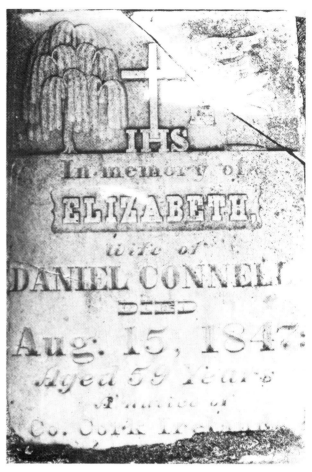

Elizabeth and Daniel Connell travelled from Freemount, Cork, to Upper Canada in 1825.

Connell, Daniel, 35
Ship	Elizabeth, 1825
Origin	Ballyclough, Cork
Location:	S lot 4, con 4, Smith
Family:	Mary,30
Norah	14
Catherine	12
Denis	6
John	5
Philip	2

A report printed in 1827 showed that Daniel was working at Port Hope at that time.

Connell, Daniel, 40
Ship	Elizabeth, 1825
Origin	Freemount, Cork
Location:	lot 4, con 10, Emily
Family	Elizabeth, 36
George	20
James	17
Elizabeth	14
Mary	11
Daniel	8
John	5
Timothy	2

George Connell received the east half of lot 3, con. 9, Emily. The 1851 census shows a George Connell, wife Hanora and children Elizabeth, 4 and Mary,3.

Mr Simon J. Connell of Emily Township, who also features in our cover photo.

Connell, John, 34

Ship	Regulus, 1825
Origin	Mallow, Cork
Location	N lot 18, con 11, Emily
Family	Mary, 30 (nee Sweeney)
Denis	14
Callaghan	10
Catherine	8
John	4

In the 1851 census we see John Connell, age 60, his wife Mary, 60, and sons Denis, 30 and Callaghan, 28. Denis Connell married a Harrington girl from Tipperary.

Our cover photo shows Mr Simon J. Connell, who is a direct descendant of John Connell and Mary Sweeney. The name Simon is a legacy of the Harrington family and there have been six Simon Connells to date.

Mr Connell, a retired assessor, is an expert on the history of Emily Township and was chairman of the committee which sponsored the book "Lilies and Shamrocks." He recently edited a booklet entitled "Some Facts From St. Luke's Past."

St. Mary's Church,
MALLOW.

Certificate of Baptism

Name of Person Baptised... *John Connell*

Name of Parents... *John Connell*
Mary Sweeney

Date of Birth...

Date of Baptism... *29th March 1821*

Sponsors... *Mary Bryan*
C Bryan

Celebrant... *f. X.*

I certify this to be a correct Extract from the Registry of Baptisms of above Church.

Signed... *Daniel Hallissey.*
Dated at Mallow... *20th May 1972.*

An extract from the register of baptisms at St. Mary's church, Mallow, refers to John Connell Jr. who travelled to Canada on the Regulus with his parents when he was a small boy, settling in Emily Township.

Connell/O'Connell, William, tailor.

Ship	Elizabeth, 1825
Origin:	Liscarrol, Cork
Location:	W lot 1, con 10, Goulbourn
Family:	Margaret, 30
Michael	18
Margaret	16
Mary	13
Norah	10
Judith	7
William	5
Ellen	3

This is an interesting family because although they came out with Peter Robinson in 1825 they did not settle in the Peterborough area but went to the Bathurst District where the 1823 group settled. This usually means that there was a relationship between the 1825 family and somebody in the first group.

The tombstone of William O'Connell Sr. and his wife, Margaret Flynn, at Corkery. The couple came out with Peter Robinson in 1825.

However, researchers among their descendants have not yet found such a connection.

Michael Connell was drowned at some time before 1827. If the ages given are correct, then obviously neither he nor Margaret could have been the children of Mrs Connell. They may have been siblings

William senior farmed his land until the 1830s, when he went to Merrickville to follow his trade as a shoemaker. This fact is noted in a government inspection report of 1834.

Some members of the family either remained in the locality or returned here at a later date, as descendants can still be found, living in Huntley Township. They use the older spelling, O'Connell.

Reference, signed by the parish priest of Liscarrol:
I certify to know the bearer, William Connell, since my residence in this parish. I know him to be an honest, industrious man.

Connor, Daniel, 33

Ship	Albion, 1825
Origin	Kanturk,Cork
Location:	lot 13, con 10, Ramsay
Family	Bridget 26
Judith	16
Margaret	14
James	12
Ellen	8
Bridget	5

Mrs William O'Connell (nee Esther Meehan) was a daughter of 1823 settler, Michael Meehan, whose wife was Esther Manion.

William O'Connell junior, who travelled to Canada on the ship Elizabeth, in 1825.

Ship's notes: "a decent family."
Although these people came out with Robinson in 1825, they settled in the Bathurst District, which points to the fact that they probably had family already in that area. No County Cork Connors came with the 1823 group, but perhaps the connection was through Mrs Connor's side of the house.

I suggest that researchers look for possible marriage records for their children, where their mother's maiden name will probably be given. Exercise some caution, though, as it is unlikely that the three elder children belonged to Daniel and Bridget. They may have been siblings.

The Connors raised 400 bushels of potatoes, 300 bushels of turnips and 50 bushels of corn in their first full year on the farm. They must have had some resources, as at that time they owned a cow and two hogs.

One source lists their place of origin as Glanmile, Kanturk.

Connor, Hugh

Ship	Hebe, 1823
Origin	Croom, Limerick
Location:	"left the group at Prescott."

Connor, Jeremiah, 35

Ship:	Albion, 1825
Origin	Killeigh, Cork
Location	unknown
Family:	Mary, 30
Margaret	9
Jeremiah	7
Johanna	3
Daniel,	born June 3, 1825

Connor, Timothy, 38, blacksmith

Ship	Star, 1825
Origin	Newmarket, Cork
Location:	lot 11, con 11, Ramsay
Family:	Margaret, 32
Benjamin	12
William	11
Timothy	10
Margaret	4
Patrick	1

Another 1825 family who settled in the Bathurst District. This man settled only two farms away from Daniel Connor, already mentioned. Timothy Connor worked as a blacksmith in Ramsay Township. He died in 1826 and the land was claimed by his son William when he came of age.

This fine stone house in Huntley Township was built by William O'Connell Jr. following the Great Fire of 1870. It is now the home of his descendant, Peter O'Connell and his family.

D.W. McCuaig photo.

Connery, Michael, 18
Ship: Stakesby, 1823
Origin: Doneraile, Cork
Location   not given.

He may have been one of the young bachelors who was kept by Robinson at the depot by the Mississippi , hired to perform various duties. Some of these young men received farms later.

Conroy, David, 34
Ship   Amity, 1825
Origin: Ballyclough, Cork
Location,   E lot 1, con 9, Douro.
Family: Catherine,30 (nee Sullivan)
Edmond   11
Patrick   9
David   5
Catherine   3
Born in Canada
John, 1834.

Ship's notes: one child died. The head of the family was "generally well behaved, but I consider him a stubborn character."

Edmond Conroy grew up to marry Mary O'Brien; John married Elizabeth McGrath, daughter of Patrick McGrath and Abby Ahern.

The Conroys settled in Douro. Their eldest son, Edmond, became the father of eleven children, and one of these, another David, remained in the district and lived to be 100. In 1934 The Peterborough Examiner sent a reporter to interview the old man, who was then 93 years of age.

"The so-called economic depression is a joke to David Conroy, oldest resident of Peterborough city and county..." the article began. Mr Conroy described "the almost insurmountable trials and hardships endured by the original settlers of his native Douro Township, alongside of which present-day problems appear to assume lesser proportions."

Predictably, he noted that the present generation (of 1934) didn't know what hardship was, compared to the pioneer experience. In the 1860s he had worked in the shanty for seven dollars a month; before that, his parents and grandparents had had even tougher experiences as they struggled to establish themselves in Douro.

When his people arrived there was not even a wagon trail between Peterborough and Douro, and the land on which they built their first cabin was hilly and stony, quite unsuitable for farming.

"Each of the settlers received a government grant of twenty dollars, and a cow and cowbell was given to each family," he said "and a team of oxen was also provided for the use of the community."

Born in 1840, David Conroy worked as a shantyman, farmer, drover, lumberman and contractor. In the shanty, the daily diet consisted of potatoes,

David Conroy and his wife, Catherine Allen. The picture was taken in front of their home, now demolished, which stood at 33 Hunter Street in Peterborough.

pork and bread. The weekday fare was boiled pork; the Sunday treat was fried pork. The noon meal for each man consisted of a loaf of bread and a large slab of salt pork. There was no tea or coffee, so they had to melt snow if they wanted water to drink with the meal. The shanty foreman, Dick O'Rourk, would not allow the men to light fires in the bush at meal time, and if they did get one going when he wasn't around, he would soon appear and kick snow on it.

The diet seldom varied during the four months of winter spent in the bush. Mr Conroy said that, during his

whole time in the bush,"I never saw the shanty by daylight except on Sunday. We had to be out to work before sun-up and would not return to camp until sundown."

***   ***   ***   ***

Three examples of projects undertaken by David Conroy (1839-1939) and Sons. Top, the Buckhorn dam. Centre, the Smith Street bridge at Peterborough, looking north up the Otonabee. Below, at Rosedale on the Trent Canal, just above Fenelon Falls.

Ninety year old Mary (O'Brien) Conroy with her grandson, Ed, circa 1907. Mr Conroy claimed that this was the first Ford car in Peterborough. One of the headlights was kicked off by a cow.

The David Conroy family: Back: Johanna (Josephine); Frank; David; Bob; Ed; Mary; Herb. Front: Lucy; Catherine Allen Conroy; Eleanor; David Conroy, 1840-1940; Daisy; Fred. Of this family, the youngest, Eleanor, is still living at the time of writing. She resides in Edmonton.

He worked at lumbering on the river for ten years but that came to a halt when he *"got the disease the doctor couldn't cure."* That is, he fell in love with Catherine Allen, a girl fifteen years his junior, whose people had also come out with Peter Robinson. Three generations had come out at that time, including her father, grandparents and great-grandfather.

Married in 1873, the couple farmed on the old Conroy homestead, but their savings were soon exhausted to the point where their only assets were *"two children and a cow."* David began buying up lambs for an Otonabee dealer, earning a ten per cent commission, but since the top price for a lamb was $2.50, he didn't do too well. On top of that, he had to walk from farm to farm because he could not afford a horse.

On borrowed money he went into business for himself as a cattle drover, and, having become successful at this, he again borrowed money to go into the contracting business. Among other things he constructed the Smith Street bridge, as well as dams or bridges at Keene, Buckhorn, Indian River, Balsam Lake, Beaverton and Toronto.

He also put in a tender for Peterborough's Hunter Street bridge but was turned down. He was later grateful that he had lost the contract as the final cost of the completed structure was far higher than his tender

Although Mr Conroy became successful in the business world he was unable to read, or to write anything other than his own name. As a boy he had lived under conditions which deprived him of any formal schooling. He was proud of the fact that he could dictate a good business letter, though.

His eleven children were all well educated. Among them were two doctors, a pharmacist, a nurse, two teachers, a contractor and a ranch manager. Other successful professional people are numbered among their descendants.

Corbet, Katharine, 20

Ship:	Stakesby, 1823
Origin	Mallow, Cork

No further information. In the ship's papers, Katharine was listed after the Shea family, also from Mallow.

Corkery, Michael, 39, RC

Ship	Stakesby, 1823
Origin	Carrigrohan, Cork
Location	E lot 10, con 3, Ramsay
Family	Mary, 39, wife
Ellen	20
Elizabeth	18
Patrick	16
Bridget	10
Mary	8
Michael	3
Denis	Born Ramsay Township

This cupboard was used in the 1820s and 1830s as a "mass table" by Father John MacDonald of Perth when he made his periodic visits to Ramsay Township. Once the property of 1823 settlers Michael and Mary Corkery, it is still treasured by one branch of this family.

Carrigroghan is about three miles from the city of Cork.

Patrick Corkery was given the other half of this same lot. He married Mary Donohue. Elizabeth married Michael Foley, who was not apparently connected with the Peter Robinson Foleys, having come to Canada earlier on. Mary married Michael Tierney, and Denis's wife was called Margaret. Ellen Corkery did not marry.

After the arrival of the 1825 settlers, Michael Corkery wrote to Peter Robinson at York, as follows:

Honourable Peter Robinson, Superintendent of Irish Emigrants.

We congratulate you on your safe arrival here with all those under your patronage. We are doing very well, thank God, and enjoy good health. My daughter is married to an old settler in Lanark but we have got a young son as an increase which makes up the number.

We had a good crop last year out of which we sold Mr Bain six barrels of flour but my eldest daughter's illness together with buying clothes and necessities for winter prevented me buying a yoke of oxen which are indisputably necessary on a farm. We have a good crop

This composite photo of the Corkery connection was made up by the late Basil Mossey. The people in the photos are described from left to right, beginning in the top row.

Canon Patrick Corkery,1844 - 1916 was pastor of several Ottawa Valley parishes. Corkery was named in his honour.

Father Frank Corkery, 1884- 1956. He was a nephew of Canon Corkery.

Canon John Burke, 1896-1961 was another nephew.

Father David Corkery, a nephew of Father Frank, is currently the pastor at the Church of the Resurrection in Ottawa.

Sister St Dunstan and Sister Francis Xavier, nursing sisters of the Grey Nuns of the Immaculate Conception. (Two sisters of Father Frank.)

Sister St.Roch, of the Sisters of St. Joseph. Canon Burke's sister.

Father Leo Curtin, 1898-1966, SFM. Served in China, Dominican Republic, West Indies and Canada. A cousin to Father Frank.

Sister Mary Margaret of the Sisters of Mercy, with her niece, Sister Mary Isabel.

Sister Isabel Oatway, a teaching sister of the Sisters of Providence. A niece of Father Frank.

Sister Hope Corkery, twin sister of Father David Corkery and a nursing sister of the Sisters of St. Joseph.

Sister Geraldine Boyle, another niece of Father Frank, who is a teacher of the Sisters of the Missions.

Sister Eleanor O'Brien of the Sisters of the Missions.

All these people were connected with pioneers Michael and Mary Corkery of Ramsay Township.

this year also, out of which I expect I can sell about 24 barrels of flour and 100 bushels of potatoes; but as I have no market convenient, nor oxen to convey it where there is a market, I don't know how to manage.

Now as there are some of your later settlers convenient to me who will, no doubt, be supplied with rations, if you would be so good as to cause the above-mentioned flour and potatoes to be bought for them of me, it would favour me to the extreme and enable me to buy a yoke of oxen and other necessaries.

My son-in-law, Michael Foley, who you may recollect gave you some trifling money for his father and mother which he expected would come out under your banner - you will recollect on the day you were going away, at Colonel Powell's, Perth - he has got no account from them this year and as they did not come out with you, he is uneasy to know whether they presented themselves, or perhaps you might have a letter from them. If convenient, write a few lines in answer to me. You may direct to Rev.John MacDonald (for Michael Corkery) or to Mr Ben Delisle.

Your obedient servant,

Michael Corkery.

Michael Foley and his wife Elizabeth later moved to Ramsay Township to be near her family. While I don't know whether the senior Foleys arrived later, an elderly couple does appear in a later census, and they do not seem to be connected with other district Foleys.

By 1826 the Corkery family had cleared 30 acres of land, including a beaver meadow. In the first two growing seasons they raised, among other things, 1200 bushels of potatoes. An 1834 report noted that they had an excellent dwelling house, and that they were "trying for additional land." An inspector wrote: " a large family and are remarkable for their industry and good conduct."

In the early days of settlement, Mass was celebrated in private homes, and one of the "stations" used was the Corkery home. Several publications have noted that this was the house of Patrick Corkery but this is only technically correct, as for a number of years he lived at his parents' home.

Father John MacDonald, a missionary priest who operated out of Perth between 1823 and 1837 noted in his diary in his last year of tenure "eleven Masses said. That is to say I had Mass at different stations in Ramsay, Pakenham, Lanark and Beckwith eleven times from January first to August 23rd 1837, besides sick calls, at different homes."

This meant that several Masses were said at eleven different places. Stop two covered "January 2,3,4,5,6,7 at Michael Corkery" and stop ten meant "June 3,4,5 at Michael Corkery. One branch of the family still treasures a cupboard or "mass table" which was used by Father MacDonald at the Corkery home.

Notes and comments from the priest's diary have recently been translated from the Gaelic and put into book form by Mr Duncan MacDonald of Brockville, who has given permission for quotations to be used here. In 1837, Mass was also said at the home of Timothy O'Brien, another Peter Robinson settler.

From the priest's diary, June 22, 1834 "went twenty miles to Corkery's to marry Patt Corkery" (sic.)

Mr Norman Paul of Ramsay attended a country school when a large part of his class was composed of Corkery children and their cousins. One day, the school was visited by **Father Frank Corkery,** a descendant of the pioneers named above, and a nephew of **Canon Patrick Corkery.** Mr Paul remembers him as "a big, stout man."

The priest was on his way to call on his brother, and he asked the teacher if the Corkery children might accompany him. Six delighted youngsters scrambled into the buggy and made for home.

Before long, they were all back at the school. Their parents were away from home. Undaunted, the priest decided to visit some Foley cousins, so he asked to have all the little Foleys released from lessons. Another six children replaced the Corkerys in the buggy.

Costello, Michael, 43

Ship:	Amity, 1825
Origin:	Listowel,Kerry
Location:	S lot 9, con 6, Ennismore Twp
Family:	Honora,40
James	24
Daniel	23
Michael	21
Patrick	19
Mary	16
John	11
Maurice	8

Michael senior died in Ennismore on October 26, 1826. Daniel drew the north half of lot 8, con 6, Michael junior the north half of lot 9 and Patrick the north half of lot 7. Patrick later went to the USA.

A large group of Costellos can be seen in the 1851 census. The family head was a "D.Costello."

Cotter, James, 45

Ship:	Fortitude, 1825
Origin:	Brigown,Cork
Location:	E lot 10, con 6 Douro Twp
Family:	Ellen, 38
Edmond	23
Maurice	21
Patrick	21
Mary	14
Johanna	12

This is the former Michael Costello house on lot 9, concession 10, Emily Township. His parents, Michael and Honora Costello, were Ennismore settlers of 1825. He married the widow O'Neill, whose farm this was.

D.W. McCuaig photo.

Catherine	8
Margaret	7
James	3

One member of this family died in 1826.
Edmond Cotter settled on the west half of his father's lot. Maurice and Patrick were twins, who were living with their father in 1826.

Cotter, Thomas, 25

Ship:	Stakesby, 1823
Origin:	Fermoy, Cork
Location:	unknown.

Cotter, William, 38

Ship:	Regulus, 1825
Origin:	Fermoy, Cork
Location:	S lot 22, con 7, Emily Twp
Family:	Jane, 32
John	15
Edmond	13
William	11
Mary	9
Thomas	7

Jane	5
Ellen	newborn

Couche, Henry, 41, shoemaker

Ship:	Resolution, 1825
Origin:	Mitchelstown, Cork
Location:	E lot 2, con 10, Douro
Family:	Susanna, 32
Susanna	19
Christopher	17
Henry	15
Mary	12
Anne	9
Elizabeth	7
Jane	3
Thomas	infant

This was a most unfortunate family. Henry senior died at the Peterborough depot August 10, 1825, followed by Susanna on the 16th. One child also died. Christopher Couche took over his father's lot.

Cronin, Jeremiah, 27

Ship:	Brunswick, 1825
Origin:	Charleville, Cork

Location: unknown
Family: Catherine, 22
Ellen   4
Eliza   2

This Jeremiah was a tailor by trade.

Cronin, Jeremiah, RC

Ship: Hebe, 1823
Origin: Buttevant, Cork
Location: lot 15, con 5, Beckwith Twp

Jeremiah was a shoemaker, and in 1826 he was found to be working at his trade at Perth. An 1834 report says that "Cronin never occupied this lot. Believes it not worth cultivating, Follows his trade in this neighbourhood or on the Rideau."
A further reference is made to him in a letter written by Michael Cronin; apparently Jeremiah was actually a Ryan but he used Cronin as an alias.

Cronin, Michael, RC

Ship   Hebe, 1823
Origin   Mitchelstwon, Cork
Location   W lot 18, con 10, Huntley
Family   Mary, wife

By 1826 these people had two children. Michael Cronin went to work at Brockville for a time and became ill there. However, he recovered and returned to his farm, receiving his Crown patent in 1836.
In an 1834 inspection report he was living on that farm and was listed as "doing well"

Huntley, October 26, 1823.

My dear Mother:
I take the opportunity of writing you these few lines, hoping to find you and the rest of the family in as good health as I am at present, thanks be to God. We sailed from the Cove of Cork on the 8th of July and arrived in Quebec on the first of September. we had as favourable a voyage and as pleasant as ever was performed, to this country, and as good useage as any person could expect.
Then from Quebec to Montreal we came in the steam boat, that is I am informed 180 miles and from Montreal we came in waggons to a barrack called La Chine, only nine miles from Montreal, and from thence to Prescott in boats which is 130 miles, and from Prescott to the place which we are all encamped there this month back.
(Beside the Mississippi River, where Almonte is now.)
The whole crew of settlers which came in both ships were sent out from this place in squads, in numbers from six to thirty to look for their lands, with a pilot to show them their respective lots and it was on Thursday last I made out my own farm, which was the 23rd of October, and as to my own judgement I take it to

be as good a farm as any in the country.
Mr Robinson our superintendent is uncommonly humane and good to us all. He at first served us our bedding and blankets and all kinds of carpenters' tools and farming utensils, and sending people which are in the habit of building log houses with the whole of us, and each man's house is built in the course of two days. And Mr Robinson promises us a cow to the head of each family next September.
Since we came on shore each man is served out in the day with one pound of bread or flour and one pound of beef or pork, and each woman,boy and girl the same. I do recommend you my dear Mother and to Denis and Mary and Jude to get yourselves ready early next spring to come here. Mr Robinson tells me he is to go back to Ireland early next spring to bring a good many more settlers...
*   ... and not to forget to bring William, and to tell he is 14 years of age, and to bring as many pots as you can with you here, and clothing, and have Denis go to my uncle's son Michael Cronan and sister and to show them the letter and perhaps it might encourage them to come here.*
This is as good and free a country as any in the world and each man is paid 12 dollars a month throughout all America and each woman six dollars each. A dollar is five shillings here. Jeremiah Ryan *which came here*

in place of my brother Denis is hired in Prescott at 24 pounds a year, and Peggy Casey is hired in the same place at six dollars a month, and sends her Mother an account that she has a very good place.
Signed, Michael Cronin.

The Peggy mentioned above is probably the Margaret Casey mentioned earlier.

Cronin,Timothy.

Ship: Regulus, 1825
Not on the ship's list, but found among the Peter Robinson settlers in 1826, on N lot 23, con 4, Emily Twp. There were seven people in this family, including one birth.
In 1826 Timothy Cronin was keeping a school in his neighbourhood.

Courtney, Timothy, RC

Ship: Hebe, 1823
Origin: Buttevant, Cork
Location: W 22, con 10, Huntley

Timothy was found to be absent from his land during the 1826 census.

Cranly ,John, 30
Ship: Resolution, 1825
Origin: Deniskea, Tipperary
Location: W lot 12, con 5, Douro Twp

Family: Margaret, 25
John   1
Mary

Baby Mary was born during the voyage from Ireland but died in Douro November 13, 1825.
This family manufactured fifty pounds of maple sugar during their first spring on the land.

Crotty, Michael, 21

Ship	Hebe, 1823
origin	Lismore, Waterford
Location	W lot 2, con 10, Goulbourn

1826 report: "labourer, at work in the country."

Crowley, Charles, 34

Ship	Star, 1825
Origin	Ballyhooley, Cork
Location	W lot 10, con 3, Douro Twp
Family	Nancy, 32
John	14
Murphy	12
Mary	8
Norah	6
Nancy	3

This family had the ague in the summer of 1826, and one person died. Fifty years later this lot was occupied by John Crowley.

Crowley, Cornelius, 34

Ship	Elizabeth, 1825
Origin	Timoleague, Cork
Location	S lot 25, con 12, Smith
Family	Hannah, 34
Florence	15
Cornelius	4
Timothy	2

Another child was born to this family soon after their arrival, possibly in 1826. Note that Florence is a boy's name. In the nineteenth century it was often bestowed in honour of St Finghin, an Irish saint whose name was for some unknown reason anglicized as Florence, although pronounced Fineen in Gaelic. The short form Flurry was often used.

Crowley, Patrick, 45

Ship:	Amity, 1825
Origin	Templetenny, Tipperary
Location	E lot 16, con 15, Ennismore
Family	Elizabeth, 40
James	19
Honora	16
David	14
Michael	12
Catherine	10
Patrick	8
Julia	4

Ship's notes: "a quiet, well disposed man."
James was ill with the ague all through the summer of 1826. Somebody in this family died at that time, possibly James, for very soon after, Patrick Crowley was said to be "living on his son James' lot" which was E lot 20, con 13.
Members of this family can be found in the 1851 census for this township, but researchers will have to be careful as there were a great many other Crowleys in this district, some of whom came at a different time from the Peter Robinson settlers, although similar first names are repeated.

Cunningham, James, 33

Ship	Fortitude, 1825
Origin	Kilbenny, Limerick
Location	E lot 18, con 6, Emily
Family	Mary, 35
Mary	6
John	4

This family was "sick during the summer" of 1826.

Cunningham, James, 47

Ship	Regulus, 1825
Origin	Adare, Limerick
Location	E lot 4, con 11, Ops
Family	Anne, 42
Robert	24
Martha	23
John	21
William	19
Thomas	17
James	16
Joseph	13
Barbara	11
Mary	9
Eliza	7
Jane	6
Josiah	4
Hannah	2

John Cunningham was given the East half of lot 3, con 11. Three members of this family died by 1827.

Cunningham, Roger, 38, RC

Ship	Hebe, 1823
Origin	Fermoy, Cork
Location	lot 5, con 11, Goulbourn
Family	Margaret, wife
Mary	14
Catherine	7
Anne	2

This family located on October 25 and received a Crown patent in 1836. By 1826 there were seven in the family, including a recent birth.
1834 report: "This man is an excellent settler. Has a large young family, also a brother with three sons who

These are the nine children of William Curtin who came to Canada as a boy on the ship Star, with his parents. Timothy and Catherine Curtin.

came out last year."
Roger Cunningham was born at Grange, County Cork.

Curran, John
Ship	Stakesby, 1823
Origin	Lismore, Waterford
Location	W lot 13, con 11, Ramsay
Family	Sarah, wife
Margaret	(sister)
Joanna	12
James	9
Mary	
Thomas	4

The 1826 report lists a birth and a death. The death was Mary, on July 22, 1823. In 1827, John Curran also died. His widow later married William Riordan. (See entry for Riordan, William.)

Curtin, John, 32
Ship	Star, 1825
Origin	St.Anne Shandon, Cork

Location	S lot 12, con 7, Ennismore
Family	Margaret, 30 (nee Devine)
Joseph	6
John	4
Mary	2

Also with this family was Margaret's brother, **William Devine,** 20

Curtin, Timothy, 34, mason.
Ship	Star, 1825
Origin	St.Anne Shandon, Cork
Location	lot 6, con 2, Ennismore
Family	Catherine, 29
Mary Ann	17
Thomas	15
William	7
Cornelius	4
David	1

Thomas later took up land in Smith Township.
Obviously Catherine Curtin could not have been the

mother of Mary Ann and Thomas, and it is unlikely that Timothy was their father, unless he deducted a few years from his age, as some settlers did. Perhaps they were siblings of the couple. Two members of this family died in 1826.

Cusack, Anniver, 29, shoemaker
Ship: Stakesby, 1823
Origin: Charleville, Cork
Location: E lot 1, con 5, Pakenham Twp.

Anniver Cusack remained a bachelor. At the time of the 1826 inspection he was "at work in the country" but he later returned to his farm, obtaining a Crown patent in 1836. At the time of the 1834 inspection, however, it appeared that farming was a part-time occupation as he was "mostly engaged in his trade of shoemaking at Pakenham Mills."

In later life he received some injury which rendered him a semi-invalid and he turned over his farm to some neighbours in return for board and lodging at their home. He remained there until the time of his death.

One New Year's Eve he went to Pakenham to see the new year in, but he did not return to his lodgings in the country. He was found on the road the next day, frozen to death. The subsequent inquest led to a verdict of accidental death, but the temperance men of the district used the tragedy as an example, writing to the newspapers about the evils of drink. The coroner, however, pointed out that the victim had not taken a drink for two years.

Dahill/ Dunhill, Michael, 28
Ship: John Barry, 1825
Origin: Colemanswell, Limerick
Location: unknown
Family: Ellen, 30
John,   14
Thomas,   12
Catherine,   10
Mary   8

This family must have been connected with others who were already in this country, for two women met them at the boat and travelled with them here.
This was a Protestant family.

Dahill, Patrick
Ship: Hebe, 1823
Origin: Newmarket, Cork
Location: W lot 26, con 7, Ramsay Twp
Patrick's   birthplace was Mallow, Cork.

1826 report: "at work with a farmer in the country." In 1834 it was noted that the land had been sold, that Dahill had always remained in the neighbourhood, was cheated out of land, and wished to get it back. Patrick appears to have moved to Pakenham

Township, where he is recorded in 1835 with a wife and four daughters.

Daley, Denis.
Not found on the ship's list, but is in the location book at E lot 21, con 3, Pakenham Twp.
1826 report: "working as a mason at Perth."

Daley, James, 30
Ship: Albion, 1825
Origin: Buttevant, Cork
Location: W lot 11, con 10, Asphodel Twp
Family: Ellen, 26
Mary   3
Patrick   21

Patrick, who used the name Daley, was listed as a brother-in-law. He obtained E lot 19, con 7, Asphodel. Ship's notes on James: "an excellent man, worthy of encouragement." Sad to say, the excellent man died soon after his arrival in Asphodel.

James Daley also used the name James Healey. There was possibly a relationship between his family and the Patrick Healey family who also came on the Albion. The latter group obtained an adjoining lot in Asphodel.

Daley, John, 46, cooper
Ship: John Barry, 1825
Origin: St.Mary Shandon, Cork
Location: E lot 34, con 13, Smith Twp
Family: Mary, 40
John   21
Bridget   20
Henry   19
James   12
Michael   10
Eugene   9
William   5
George   1

Ship's notes: a good, industrious, obliging and willing family. Himself by trade a cooper."
Henry Daley was given the west half of his father's lot. John Daley senior died in Smith February 17, 1826, and his son William on April 9. By 1827, two more children had died. This was indeed a sad introduction to her new life for poor Mary Daley.

Daley, Owen, 43
Ship: Star, 1825
Origin: Kilmeen, Cork
Location: E lot 20, con 7, Smith Twp
Family: Johanna, 36
Honora   21
Andrew   19
Catherine   14
John   11

Johanna   8
Eugene   2

Andrew Daley received the west half of his father's lot. His brother John was one of the unfortunates who died while the Peter Robinson settlers were encamped at Kingston. A report tabled in 1827 showed that Andrew was then living with the rest of the family, and that Owen had suffered with the ague in the summer of 1826.

Dawson, Mary, 40
Ship:	Fortitude, 1825
Origin:	Callan, Kilkenny
Location:	N lot 19, con 8, Emily Twp
Family:	Patrick 18
Norah	15
Richard	10

Mary Dawson, widow, died in Emily Township October 29, 1826.

Deane, Cornelius
Location: N lot 7, con 5, Smith Twp
There is no trace of this man in the ships' lists (perhaps he travelled under an alias or is included with a family of a different name) but he was given land with the Peter Robinson settlers. He worked as a clerk at the Peterborough depot.

Deleury/Delohary, John, 24 RC
Ship:	Stakesby, 1823
Origin:	Mallow, Cork
Location:	lot 21, con 5, Pakenham Twp
Family:	Bridget (Biddy) 20, wife

One report says that John drowned at Kingston in October, 1825. However, an 1834 report seems to indicate that he was still alive, having sold his lot to a William Harris and moved to lot 27, con 6, which had formerly belonged to Henry Mahoney.
Furthermore, a note in the parish priest's diary in that same year indicated that John and Biddy were living in Pakenham Township with three children.

Dillon, Edmond, 45
Ship:	Star, 1825
Origin:	Kilfinane, Limerick
Location:	E lot 22, con 10, Otonabee Twp
Family:	Elinor, 45
Michael	22
Deborah	18
Patrick	14
Mary	13
Margaret	5

Michael Dillon was allocated the west half of this lot. He was drowned in the Otonabee rapids, May 21, 1826. Edmond had the ague during the summer of 1826.

The family remained in the township, and in the 1851 census Patrick and his wife can be found with their children, Edmond, Barney, Michael, Elinor, Hugh and Ann. The family had two log houses on the farm, and in the second one sheltered Widow Dillon, 71; Margaret, married woman, also Eliza, William and Frances.

Dimond, William, 46
Ship:	Star, 1825
Origin:	Kilfinane, Limerick
Location:	S lot 1, con 1, Marmora Twp
Family:	Margaret, 40
Edmond	24
Patrick	22
John	18
William	16
Henry	14
Thomas	10
Michael	8

Edmond Dillon, a carpenter by trade, was allocated the north half of this lot. A report printed in 1827 said "this family have suffered a good deal from sickness since arriving in this country."

Divine/Devine, William, 20
Ship:	Star, 1825
Origin:	St.Anne Shandon, Cork
Location:	Ennismore Twp

A brother of Margaret, Mrs John Curtin, who also travelled on the Star.

O' Dogherty, John, 37
Ship:	Resolution: 1825
Origin:	Brigown, Cork
Family:	Ellen, 26
Anne	15
Kitty	12
Judith	5
John	2
Mary	26

No record of location. John senior "died at the Monaghan depot. Anne, 15, now in Kingston."

Dohorthy/ Dougherty, Joanna
Ship:	Hebe, 1823
Origin:	Newcastle, Limerick
Location:	unknown

Dohorthy/ Dougherty, John
Ship:	Hebe, 1823
Origin:	Churchtown, Cork
Location:	E lot 23, con 7, Pakenham Twp.
Family:	Judith (wife)
Patrick	10
Edward	6

| Daniel | 3 |
| Michael | (born in Ramsay). |

A hanging offence.

November first, 1825, was the date set for the hanging of John Dougherty at Perth. His family had come to Upper Canada with the Peter Robinson settlers two years before, settling in Pakenham Township. Two years later, Judith Dougherty, the mother of several young sons, was in dire distress. Her husband was in the Perth jail, sentencing to death for "maiming a cow."

Unpleasant though the crime was - he had cut out the animal's tongue - it is hard to conceive of this as a hanging offence, yet in those days, such was the case. At that time, several men had already been hanged in what is now Eastern Ontario, for such crimes as horse stealing or cattle rustling. Back in Ireland the death penalty was still given for poaching and theft.

This offence against a neighbour's cow was particularly serious because cattle had only recently been introduced in to the neighbourhood, usually one to a family, as part of the privileges given to Robinson's settlers. John's act was a strike against government property, as well as a blow to a neighbour.

Judith Dougherty was distraught, as well she might have been. She was stranded in the bush in a strange land with five children under twelve to provide for; her position was desperate. She decided to send a petition to Sir Peregrine Maitland, who was Lieutenant Governor of Upper Canada and "Major General Commanding His Majesty's Forces in North America."

Perhaps friends advised her to do this; she was illiterate and had to get someone else to write out her letter. Perhaps more than one person was in on the act, for the language is that of an educated person of the day. We can imagine them anxiously bending over the sheet in the light of a tallow candle in that small shanty in the wilds of Pakenham Township.

The Petition of Judith Dougherty:
Most humbly sheweth:

That your Petitioner is at present one of the most wretched women on earth, with five children in a Strange Land, in the poorest of circumstances, and to complete my misery my husband John Dougherty is at present confined in the Gaol at Perth under sentence of DEATH, thus situated, having no other earthly hope, your Petitioner trusts that the miseries of a wretched family will be permitted thus to appeal to Your Excellency.

Your Petitioner prays Your Excellency in the most supplicating manner that you will be graciously pleased to permit her husband to return to, and live again in the world to be the help and support of his unfortunate family. Your Petitioner begs and entreats

Your Excellency in the name of Him who wills not the death of a sinner; Your Excellency's general character for humanity inspires Your Petitioner with hope that, when you view me and my poor wretched children, standing on the very brink of destruction, Your Excellency will be induced to prevent the impending CATASTROPHE and restore to my arms the husband of my most tender affections and to his children a fond and loving father.

And Petitioner with her little children shall incessantly pray to the Father of all Mercies that when the Messenger of Death shall approach Your Excellency to summon you to appear before the Tribunal of the King of KIngs, the reward of a great and merciful Act may cancel the charges of human frailties and verify that Beatitude, Blessed are the Merciful, for they shall obtain Mercy.

With impatient anxiety and trembling hope, your Petitioner remains Your Excellency's unhappy Petitioner,

Judith Dougherty   X her mark.
Pakenham Township, September 22, 1825.

Meanwhile, Sir Peregrine had already decided to investigate the case, and even before Judith's petition reached him he had directed Major Hillier to write to Sheriff Powell at Perth, in connection with this and several other cases which had recently been tried there.

Powell explained that in some of those cases the death sentence had not been imposed, although burglary and horse theft were among the crimes committed, but he felt that it was justified in Dougherty's case because his act was "alarming to the neighbourhood" and that "the conviction was on the fullest and most satisfactory evidence." We must remember that this was only a few months after the Ballyghiblin riots, and that Sheriff Powell was responsible for keeping order in the district.

While the case was being debated, Dougherty took matters into his own hands. Before the sentence could be carried out, the sheriff was obliged to write "escaped" alongside the culprit's name in his record book.

Winter must have come early that year. Inadequately dressed for the weather, Dougherty got his feet frozen as he fled into the countryside. In due course he won a reprieve and was allowed to rejoin his family, but he paid a dreadful penalty for his crime. He lost several toes as a result of his flight from jail.

Donaghue, Patrick, 44
Ship:	Stakesby, 1823
Origin:	Mallow, Cork
Location:	lot 11, con 4, Ramsay Twp
Family:	Anne 40

Katherine	7
Margaret	4
Mary	2

This Patrick Donaghue died in Ramsay in 1823. A son, who may have been a posthumous child, was born to the couple in Ramsay. When a government inspector visited the farm in 1834 he noted that it was held by "the widow Donaghue" and the land let on shares. A nine year old son was "placed in the care of David Kemp, Ramsay." In that same year, the parish priest noted "widow of Patt, absent."

Donahue, Patrick.
Ship:	Hebe, 1823
Origin:	Newcastle, Limerick
Location:	E lot 18, con 2, Ramsay Twp.

Patrick, a single man, had cleared four acres of land by 1826, at which time it was noted that "he has been at work on the Canal, and is now sick."

Donoghue, Arthur, 45
Ship:	Brunswick, 1825
Origin:	Kilbehenny, Cork
Location:	S lot 4, con 8, Ennismore Twp
Family:	Abby 40
Daniel	23
Timothy	19
John	17
Thomas	15
Francis	12
Catherine	9
Elizabeth	6
Arthur	1

Daniel Donoghue took up the south half of lot 13, concession 8, while Timothy had the south half of lot 8, concession 8.

In 1826 Arthur senior was listed as "recovering from ague" but he died in 1832. He was a brother of Daniel Donoghue. (see next entry.)

Donoghue, Daniel, 48
Ship:	Elizabeth, 1825
Origin:	Newtown, Cork
Location:	N lot 13, con 8, Ennismore Twp
Family:	Elizabeth, 40
Denis	23
Maurice	21
Daniel	19
William	17
Michael	15
Johanna	12
Mary	10

Denis Donoghue had the south half of lot one, con 10, Emily Twp; Maurice south lot 2, con 10, Emily: Daniel Jr. north lot 7, con 9, Emily.

The whole family was sick during the summer of 1826.

Donoghue/ O'Donoghue, Jeffrey, RC
Ship:	Hebe, 1823
Origin:	Liscarrol/ Ballyghiblin, Cork
Location:	lot 15, con 10, Huntley Twp
Family:	Mary, wife
Katherine	3
Joseph	2

Margaret Lacey, sister.

At the time of the 1826 inspection, Jeffrey was at work in Perth. His family had increased by two persons.

He received his Crown patent in 1836, but is said to "have sold his lot for little or nothing" and moved to lot 16, con 10, originally given to Richard Barry, who never did occupy it. Inspector Jessop wrote in 1834 that "Donoghue has never left the country but has been very unfortunate through continued sickness." In another record, this family can be found on lot 17, con 11, Ramsay.

Donovan, Cornelius, RC
Ship:	Hebe,1823
Origin:	Fermoy, Cork
Location:	W lot 5, con 11, Goulbourn Twp

In 1826, Cornelius Donovan was working at Perth as a sawyer. In 1834 he was found to be absent from the land, and another Robinson settler, Roger Cunningham, petitioned to buy it, as it lay beside his own farm

Donovan/ Donogan, Michael, RC
Ship:	Hebe, 1823
Origin:	Buttevant, Cork
Location,	E lot 18, con 4, Ramsay Twp
Family:	Bridget Donovan.

In 1826, Michael was found to be "absent without leave" and it is not known whether he returned to the farm. Bridget Donovan, who may have been a sister, is said to have "stopped at Lachine."

O'Donnell, Patrick, 40, mason
Ship:	Resolution, 1825
Origin:	Brigown, Cork
Location:	S lot 1, con 2, Ennismore Twp
Family:	Martha, 35 (nee McMahon)
Edmond	25
Catherine	20
Ellen	15
Patrick	14
Jane	11
Mary	8

Edmond O'Donnell, also a mason, took up land on the south half of lot 21, concession 6, Ennismore. His wife was Catherine Doran.

Patrick junior was married twice, first to Sarah Scanlon, and after her death to Margaret Wren. Jane became the wife of James Hickey.

Ship's notes: "one child born."

Patrick O'Donnell senior died in 1827.

Patrick O'Donnell Jr., who was a lad of 14 when he travelled on the Resolution with his family in 1825.

On the left, Michael O'Donnell, son of Patrick O'Donnell and Sarah Scanlon.

Doody, John,	32, butcher.
Ship:	Fortitude, 1825
Origin:	Ballyhooley, Cork
Location:	went to Montreal after landing.
Family:	Eliza 29
Patrick	8
Peggy	6
Thomas	2

Reference written at Prescott by the ship's surgeon:
John Doody, a butcher, conducted himself with propriety on the passage and is, I understand, a good tradesman, and much conversant with the cutting part of his trade.

Doogan/Dorgan, Timothy, 40	
Ship:	Fortitude, 1825
Origin:	Mallow, Cork
Location:	N lot 14, con 11, Emily Twp
Family:	Julia, 34
Daniel	19
Michael	12
John	6
Patrick	4
Ellen	1

Daniel Dorgan, alias **Daniel Mahoney**, was a first cousin of Timothy Dorgan. See entry for Mahoney for further details.

Dooling/Dowling, David	
Ship:	Hebe, 1823
Origin:	Charleville, Cork
Location:	lot 23 con 12, Beckwith Twp
Family:	Mary
Catherine	
Nelly	
Edmond	
John	
Joanna	
Norah	
Anne.	

No ages are to be found for this family but only Norah and Anne were under the age of 14 on arrival in Upper Canada.

Although Edmond Dowling is found in most of the original records with this name, it seems that he was actually known as Edward. This is found in censuses and on his tombstone. We shall therefore use the latter name. Single when he came to Canada, he obtained part lot 24 in con 12, Beckwith, and his brother John received part lot 27.

In 1834 the government agent noted that David Dowling had settled on his lot in 1824 but that George Burke, superintendent of the military settlement at Richmond, maintained that an earlier settler named

King already had the deed to this land. Dowling moved onto his son Edward's lot, while still hoping to gain title to the farm which had been allocated to him. By this time they had cleared 36 acres of Edward's land and had put up "an excellent barn."

The Edward Dowling farm was one of the stations used by Father John MacDonald, the travelling priest from Perth, for Mass in this township. Beckwith Township had very few Catholics, being settled mostly by Anglicans and Scots Presbyterians, but the Dowling farm was close to Catholic settlers in Ramsay, being on the "town line."

Edward Dowling is mentioned in the Belden Atlas of 1880, which says that he was a native of County Cork, born in 1807, whose family came in 1823. This cannot be quite right, as he accepted a farm in 1823 and would have been at least 19 then. His tombstone says that he was 87 when he died in March, 1891. He served as a Justice of the Peace for thirty years.

He married Mary Leahy, who was a daughter of Patrick Leahy, a Robinson settler in Huntley Township. Some of their children included Patrick, Mary, David, John Leahy, Edward and Johanna.

Genealogists will have a little difficulty in sorting out this family because of the many different spellings of the surname. There are references to people called Doolan, Dowling, Dooling etc in other records but I do not know whether they "belong." Others with similar names came to the area in the 1840s, which further clouds the issue.

The Gaelic form of this name is O'Dubhlain, which may be translated as Doolan, Dowling or Dooling. Add to this the fact that very often officials were unable to cope with names that were strange to them, and you can see the source of the muddle.

Dooley, George, 22
Ship: Hebe, 1823
Origin: Innis, County Clare
Location: lot 4, con 4, Pakenham Twp.
Notes in 1826: "single. Has cleared four acres. At work on the Grand River."
At first, George had been allocated the west half of lot 25, concession 2, Ramsay Twp.

Doran, Martin, 40
Ship: Fortitude, 1825
Origin: Clonmel, Tipperary
Location: N lot 23, con 8, Emily Twp
Family: Mary, 40
William   23
Mary   21
Laurence   16
Catherine   13
Daniel   3

Bridget Doran, second wife of William of the Fortitude. Shown beside her is her grandson, Herman Woulff.

A copy of the ticket given to the Martin Doran family in 1825. His son ~~William~~ boarded the ship disguised as a girl, under the name of ~~Abigail~~. *Norah*
Laurence

71

Mr & Mrs Austin Doran and their son John. Mr Doran was descended from several Peter Robinson settlers, including the Dorans and the Hickeys.

When Martin and Mary Doran of Clonmel, Tipperary, boarded the ship Fortitude in 1825, they took with them their sons William and Daniel, daughters Mary and Catherine, and a third girl, Norah. Norah was really their son Laurence in disguise!

Times were hard in Ireland, and the failure of the potato crop meant that people were hard pressed to find food. There was no social security then! A family story tells us that young Laurence Doran had a hunting dog, which he had trained to retrieve game, and this dog accompanied him on some nocturnal poaching expeditions. On one such occasion the dog was caught by a gamekeeper, and the family knew that it was only a matter of time before the animal would be traced to the Dorans, and Laurence would be hauled up before the magistrates.

In those days the penalty for such offences was severe. The family knew that their son faced hanging if found guilty. The emigration scheme for Canada must have seemed heaven-sent. Martin Doran applied to Peter Robinson, and they were accepted. Some fancy footwork was necessary if they were to get their boy

safely out of the country. Their embarkation certificate clearly shows him as Norah, age 16; the ship's list records him as Laurence. Presumably he was disguised as a girl until they were safely on the Atlantic.

It is interesting to note that, while these people came from County Tipperary, Martin Doran registered for travel at Kilworth, Cork. While this is not surprising in itself as registration took place only at designated recruiting centres, it no doubt helped the deception if the presiding magistrates and landlords had no personal knowledge of the Doran family.

Reference:
We, the undersigned, know the bearers, Martin Doran and Mary his wife, together with their family which consists of seven... to be sober, quiet and strictly honest."

The Dorans were devout Catholics. Another family tradition is that there was a small chapel in their pioneer home where itinerant priests said Mass, in the days before the first log church was built in Ennismore. The original Doran lots lay on the boundary between Emily and Ennismore Townships.

Martin Doran died some time before 1840, and Mary circa 1857. Their eldest son ws William Doran, who resided with them in their early years in the township, although he immediately began to clear his own land, which adjoined theirs. He eventually had fifteen children. His first wife, Jane Meany, bore him eleven, of which two did not survive infancy. Following her death in 1855 he married Bridget Halnun, who presented him with four more children.

Laurence Doran married Bridget Finnegan and had eight children. Catherine Doran married Edmund O'Donnell, and Daniel chose Catherine Killen for his wife. While some Doran descendants still live in the Peterborough area, many more are to be found throughout the United States, their ancestors having gone there in the second half of the nineteeth century.

Downan, Robert, 34

Ship:	Elizabeth, 1825
Origin:	Mallow, Cork
Location:	E lot 1, con 4, Marmora
Family:	Eliza, 34
Ellen	14
Eliza	12
Robert	8
James	4

A reference given in Ireland described Robert as "an honest, poor man... he has got four children and his wife."

Robert Downan had "five acres chopped" by 1827. Two new births also took place by that time, and little James died.

Downie, Bartholomew, 33
Ship:	Elizabeth, 1825
Origin:	Churchtown, Cork
Location:	lot 6, con 9, Emily Twp
Family:	Margaret, 29
Mary	14
Owen	11
John	6
Ellen	5
Catherine,	born October first, 1825.

Drake, William, 23
Ship:	Stakesby, 1823
Origin:	Old Castle Town, Cork
Location:	lot 2, con 2, Ramsay Twp
Wife:	name unknown.

The 1826 report mentioned that two babies had been born in Ramsay but had died. In 1827, Drake sold this lot to Abraham Codd. Another source gives William's origin as Kildorrey, County Cork.

Driscoll, Cornelius, 47
Ship:	Brunswick, 1825
Origin:	Cape Clear, Cork.
Location:	north lot 10, con 5, Ennismore Twp
Family:	Johanna, 45
John	28
James	24
Ellen	22
Julia	17
Honora	13 ("Norry")
Cornelius,	5

Cornelius Driscoll senior and his daughter Ellen died soon after their arrival in Upper Canada. Johanna Driscoll died at the depot, October 14, 1825. Honora Driscoll married Peter Ryan.

Driscoll, Denis, 43, fisherman.
Ship:	Brunswick, 1825
Origin:	Cape Clear, Cork
Location:	S lot 11, con 8, Ennismore Twp
Family:	Mary, 40
Cornelius,	20
Mary,	18
Murtough,	15
Denis,	7
John	5
Margaret	1

Cornelius was give north lot 7, con 7.
In 1826 there were nine in this family, which included another son, who had come out separately. According to a report compiled at the time, this child was under fourteen, and a twin to one of those listed above.

My theory, for which I have no proof at all, is that this may have been the five-year-old Cornelius

Bartholomew Downey travelled on the ship Elizabeth in 1825 and settled in Emily Township in a location where the present hamlet of Downeyville grew up.

who travelled with the Cornelius Driscoll family. When Mrs Denis Driscoll came to Canada she had a baby, Margaret, who according to the ship's list would be a year old on her next birthday. It could be that her sister-in-law temporarily took one of the twins to help her out; Mrs Cornelius Driscoll had two teenage girls to assist her.

As we have seen in the previous entry, Mr and Mrs Cornelius Driscoll died when they reached Upper Canada. It was at that time that the missing twin returned to his own family.

Driscoll, Florence, 32.
Ship:	Resolution, 1825
Origin:	Castlelyons, Cork
Location:	lot 15, con 14, Otonabee Twp
Family:	Mary, 26
Denis	6
Margaret	3
Cornelius	(born Upper Canada)

Florence was a man, and Mary was his wife. (Anyone who would like an explanation of the name Florence as it applies to a man may turn to the entry for Cornelius Crowley.)

Florence was still in this township in 1851, age 63 years, along with his wife. Two children lived with them, Cornelius, 27 and Honora, 16.

Driscoll, Jeremiah, 40, mason
Ship: Amity, 1825
Origin: Manamalane (sic) County Cork.
                    Possibly Marmulland?
Location: N 21, con 4, Emily Twp.
1826: Living with John Lancaster; Driscoll travelled out to Canada with the Lancaster family.

Driscoll, Michael, 45
Ship: Brunswick, 1825
Origin: Cape Clear, Cork
Location: S lot 12, con 6, Ennismore Twp
Family: Honora 38 ("Norry")
Patrick   19
Denis   15
Ellen   11
Lawrence   2

Michael Driscoll was a brother of Cornelius and Denis Driscoll, mentioned in previous entries.
Michael's son Patrick went to the United States. Ellen Driscoll later married Patrick Brick.

Duggan, Jerry, 19
Ship: Stakesby, 1823
Origin: Watersgrasshill, Cork
Location unknown. He may have been one of the young bachelors who worked for Peter Robinson at the Shipman's Mills (Almonte) depot in 1823-1824, receiving a farm later.

Dulmage, Garret, Protestant.
Ship: Hebe, 1823
Origin: Croom, Limerick
Location: W lot 5, con 11, Ramsay Twp.
Family: Sarah, wife
Margaret   9
Richard   16
Lawrence   6

The Dulmages were descended from County Limerick Palatine settlers. This family settled near Appleton. By 1826 a new birth had occurred.
   In 1834, Garret Dulmage was living on lot 7, con 11, where he had "a well finished house." His son Richard was on lot 3 of the same concession, in place of his original holding, lot 5, con 10. The latter was held by **John Brown**, a school teacher. Brown was a relative of the Dulmages who had followed them from Ireland in the hope of getting free land, although he does not appear to have been a Peter Robinson settler. "Brown keeps school in the settlement" the government agent noted in 1834

Richard Dulmage Jr., Reeve of Arnprior and Barrister at Law.

The Dulmages did well in Canada, Some stayed in the area as farmers while others trained for professions. Richard Dulmage Jr., a grandson of Garret and Sarah, became a lawyer who later practised in Arnprior, where he was elected Reeve in 1880. Born at Appleton, he was educated at the Carleton Place grammar school, then studied the classics under Reverence James Preston, Rector at St.James' Church, and then studied law in Almonte under the tutelage of Joseph Jamieson, Barrister.

The Dulmages were often in the news, and the following newspaper clippings give examples of their life and times.
North Lanark Advance, 1867.
Prizes were awarded at the Almonte Fair to: Richard Dulmage, best pair of ducks, first and second. Best single cutter: Lawrence Dulmage. Best two bushels of peas: first, Lawrence Dulmage, second, Richard Dulmage.

Almonte Gazette, 1876.
Legal.
   Mr Richard Dulmage, for several years a student at Mr Jamieson's law office, successfully passed his examination in Toronto last week and is now entitled to write "Attorney and Solictor" after his name. Mr Dulmage will establish himself in the progressive town of Arnprior in the course of a month or two, to open an office for the practice of his profession. His natural abilities, added to his genial disposition and obliging manner will no doubt secure him a host of friends and a

An old engraving of the Richard Dulmage house at Arnprior. His grandfather, Garret Dulmage, settled with his family at Appleton in 1823. You can see a glimpse of the Madawaska River in the background.

large practice. We wish him every success, large retaining fees and many clients.

Carleton Place Canadian, 1883
At Rothsay on 11 August, Margaret Dulmage, wife of Edmond Morphy, formerly of Carleton Place, in the 69th year of her age.
(Note: Margaret's brother Richard married Mary Morphy. The Morphy family were the original settlers of Carleton Place in 1819; it was then known as Morphy's Falls.)

Carleton Place Canadian 1883.
Mr John Dulmage, commercial traveller, has instructed his solicitors, Jamieson & Greig, to enter an action against the railway for loss of baggage. He had his trunks checked at Almonte for Smiths Falls, but they got lost in the woods somewhere and came out at a small station near Montreal after a week's absence. In the meantime he had to hang himself up and he asks for compensation for the time he was on the nail.

Almonte Gazette, 1889.
An Almonte Silver Mine.
Mr John Dulmage has just added a fine well to his domestic assets. The driller, Mr Metcalfe, struck a good flow of water at 55 feet. On his way through Mother Earth some odd-looking material was encountered and the wise-heads who gathered around, after examining the soil, averred that there was a valuable mineral vein in the neighbourhood.

Mr Dulmage, having a fondness for a practical joke, helped along the idea and when the excitement was at the right heat he got some of the silvery label stuff that goes with chewing gum, cut it into small pieces and mixed it with some of the soil, and then had the local experts gather a few shovelfuls of the earth to have it assayed.

This was done, everything going through most successfully until a local jeweller tested the "ore" with aqua fortis, and a local professional man who carried a chunk of the valuable mineral deposit across town found it had evaporated by the time he reached Mr D.H.Davies' store, where the test was to be made. It had melted in his pocket!

There has been a hot time all around for a few days, and all you have to do to shut up some of the would-be Klondikers is to ask "how is that mine of Mr Dulmage's panning out?"

1898.
Mr John Dulmage has men at work tearing down the sheds and stables at the rear of his residence, and "building greater." Mr D. is one of those restless mortals the carpenters admire - he is always making changes and improvements on some of his numerous properties in town. In this respect he sets his fellow-townsmen an excellent example.

Dwyer, Jeremiah, 50

Ship:	Elizabeth, 1825
Origin:	Tipperary, County Tipperary.
Location:	S lot 12, con 10, Emily Twp.
Family:	
Richard	24
Mary	22
Thomas	20
Edmond	19
John	17
Elinor	15
Judith	14
Alicia	10
Denis	6

Richard, Mary, Thomas and John located in Smith Township. Edmond received the north half of his father's lot.

Egan, Daniel, 30

Ship:	Elizabeth, 1825
Origin:	Buttevant, Cork
Location:	E lot 14, con 10, Asphodel Twp
Family:	Mary, 34
Owen	10
Mary	6
Joseph	2

This family had the ague during the summer of 1826, but apparently survived it. They cleared four acres of land despite their illness and raised a creditable amount of produce, including 100 bushels of potatoes, 50 bushels of turnips and 60 bushels of Indian corn.

It is interesting to note that an Owen Egan was on a nearby farm some years later. This was not the boy listed above, but a man who must have been born circa 1796. i.e. someone who was about a year younger than Daniel Egan.

Egan, Patrick, 26

Ship:	Elizabeth, 1825
Origin:	Buttevant, Cork
Location:	W lot 14, con 10, Asphodel .
Family:	Honora, 20

By 1827, this family numbered three. In 1838 these people were still on this farm, and had added a fourth member to the family.

Egan, Thomas, 32

Ship:	Brunswick, 1825
Origin:	Doneraile, Cork
Location:	S lot 23, con 12, Otonabee Twp
Family:	Frances, 25
Mary	10
Anne	8
Thomas	1

The family was still on this land in 1875.

76

Egan, Timothy, 28

Ship:	Elizabeth, 1825

Timothy was a brother of Patrick Egan. Stricken with fever in the fall of 1825, he wandered into the bush in a state of delirium and was never seen again.

Elligott, Michael, 33, shoemaker.

ship:	Fortitude, 1825
Origin:	Brigown, Cork
Location:	E lot 9, con 3, Douro Twp
Family:	Abigail, 30
Mary	10
Margaret	4
Bridget	2

Abigail Elligott died at the depot, October 18, 1825. Her daughter Bridget died the same day. Two years later Michael was reported to be working as a shoemaker in Peterborough. He probably remarried for in the 1851 census for Douro there is a "Widow Cliggott" listed, age 55 years.

Ellis, John, 40, baker

Ship:	Fortitude, 1825
Origin:	Brigown, Cork
Location:	S lot 2, con 8, Ennismore Twp
Family:	Eliza, 35
Mary	9
Judith	1
Judith	30 (sister-in-law)
Ellen	20 (sister-in-law.)

1826 report: "crop failed; family sick all summer." There was one death that year. Ellis later moved to Ramsay Twp so he may have been related to some of the 1823 settlers.

English, Richard, 42

Ship:	Amity 1825
Origin:	Templetenny, Tipperary
Location:	lot 14, con 6, Asphodel Twp
Family:	Judith, 36
Nicholas	20 (Keating).
Mary	17
Bridget	14
John	11
Johanna	6
Patrick	1

Richard English was killed by a falling tree in 1828. His widow married widower Denis Hurley, whose wife had died in 1826.

Evans, John

Ship:	Hebe, 1823
Origin:	Croom, Limerick
Location:	"left at Morphy's Falls."

I do not know what became of John Evans. There was an old family of this name in Ramsay Township near Clayton, who may or may not have been connected. The 1861 census shows a William Evans there who was born in 1827 and a Richard Evans who was born in the province of Quebec. as far as I have been able to discover, this is the only old family of Irish Evanses in the district. Evans is originally a Welsh name.

Falvey, John, 34
Ship:	Regulus, 1825
Origin:	Ardagh, Limerick
Location:	unknown
Family:	Mary, 25
Daniel	14
Timothy	9
Mary	10
John	2

Field, Patrick, 22, RC
Ship:	Stakesby, 1823
Origin:	Mallow, Cork
Location:	lot 1, con 12, Huntley Twp.

Patrick's birth place was Curriglas, Cork.

Finn, John, RC
Ship:	Hebe, 1823
Origin:	Ballyghiblin, Cork
Location:	W lot 1, con 10, Goulbourn Twp

The 1826 report indicated that he was then at work in Douro Township, which may indicate that he was connected with settlers of the 1825 group.

Finn, John, 40
Ship:	Elizabeth, 1825
Origin:	Mallow, Cork
Location:	lot 8, con 8, Emily Twp
Family:	Catherine, 38

Finnegan, Daniel, 30, blacksmith
Ship:	Star, 1825
Origin:	Rahan, Cork
Location:	N lot 4, con 4, Emily Twp
Family:	Ellen, 30
Bridget	14
Timothy	12
Robert	10
Abbey	8
James	6

Rahan is a parish at Mallow, Cork. Daniel worked as a blacksmith in Emily Township. There was one death in this family in 1826.

Fitzgerald, John, 33
Ship:	Fortitude, 1825
Origin:	Affane, Waterford

Location:	unknown
Family:	Mary, 32
Catherine	13
Bridget	10
Mary	7
John	5
Margaret	2

Fitzgerald, Maurice, 40
Ship:	Brunswick, 1825
Origin:	Colemanswell, Limerick
Location:	W lot 7 , con 8, Emily Twp
Michael	16
Mary	14
James	11
Margaret	8
Sally	5

Attached to this family is a story that is repeated a number of times in the Peter Robinson group. When Maurice was being allocated land, a note was made to this effect: " No such man; came out as John Buckley." Sure enough, the ship's list shows a John Buckley on board the Brunswick and no Fitzgeralds!

If we compare the two families (refer back to the Buckley section) we see that each had the same number of boys and girls, fairly close in age. This appears to be one of those cases where one family withdrew, selling their tickets to others, who then impersonated them in order to get into Upper Canada. Michael became Timothy, Mary became Catherine, and so on. The children probably enjoyed the game.

Once safely in Canada, they resumed their own identity. A Maurice Fitzgerald and family are listed in the 1851 census for this township.

Maurice Fitzgerald did have his own reference, in which someone wrote that " I have always considered him a man of excellent character." This means that the family applied to come but did not get selected, most likely because all passages were taken before they applied

Fitzgerald, Margaret, 22
Ship:	Stakesby, 1823
Origin:	Rathcormac, Cork.
Margaret	Fitzgerald came with the **Quinn** family.

Fitzgerald, Patrick
Ship:	Hebe, 1823
Origin:	Charleville, Cork
Location:	W lot 24, con 12, Beckwith Twp.

Alias **Maurice Shea.** He travelled to Canada as Shea, but settled here as Fitzgerald. Researchers may be interested to note that some other Sheas and Fitzgeralds seem to have travelled together on the Stakesby.

Fitzgerald, Thomas, 42, Anglican.

Ship:	Star, 1825
Origin:	Newcastle, Limerick
Location:	E lot 21, con 6, Smith Twp.
Family:	Margaret, 35
Edward	18
Charles	16
Gerald	14
Millicent	11
John	9
Mary	7
Margaret	4
Harriet	2

Reference:
Courtenay Castle:

Thomas Fitzgerald, 42 years- "compelled to abandon his farm on the lands of Dually (part of the Courtenay estate) in consequence of repeated threats to his family, and injuries sustained to his property during the disturbance of 1821, engaged with me in the capacity of land steward...

His just sense of Religion, his strict moral example and very orderly habits gained for him the respect of all classes."

Alfred Furlong, J. P.
Newcastle, Limerick.

Thomas's problem seems to have been that he worked for one of the landlords, who was no doubt seen as a villain, at a time when the working people were struggling for their rights in Ireland. Mr Furlong went on to say that he did not wish the Fitzgeralds to leave, but would not stop them if they felt that they would be better off in Upper Canada.

The family became ill with the ague in 1826, but despite that they managed to clear 14 acres of land, raised 600 bushels of potatoes and other crops, and manufactured 100 lbs of maple sugar. By 1827 they possessed a team of oxen, a cow and two hogs, which earmarked them as being more prosperous than the neighbours. Perhaps since Thomas had held a job until they left Ireland, he was able to bring some capital with him.

Edward Fitzgerald was given the west half of lot 21, concession 6, Smith Township, while Gerald later owned land in Douro. Both Edward and John married Switzer girls, whose family had also come out on the Star.

Fitzgerald, William, RC

Ship:	Hebe, 1823
Origin:	Kilworth, Cork
Location:	lot 18, con 11, Huntley Twp

1826 report: "shoemaker, at work in the country." He did not live on his land, which was occupied in the

78

early days by James Buckley.
See entry for Fitzgerald, Maurice, for another Buckley connection.

Fitzgerald, William, 36, shoemaker.

Ship:	Star, 1825
Origin:	Liscarrol, Cork
Location:	S lot 6, con 8, Emily Twp
Family:	Margaret, 35
Mary	20
Ellen	19

To Peter Robinson:
Prescott, July 25, 1825.

This will be handed to you by William Fitzgerald who came with me in the Amity and in whose welfare I feel a very great interest. If any extra advantages be reserved for rectitude of conduct and strict probity, they cannot be bestowed upon a more worthy person, nor can anything give me more satisfaction than to find that this makes you acquainted with his worth should it be productive of advantage to him.

Believe me, Sir,
Very Truly Yours,
James W. Ternan, RN.

1826 report: "working at his trade in the Township of Cavan."

In 1851, a William Fitzgerald, shoemaker, was living with the Luke Connell family in Emily. These people also travelled on the Star. If it is the same William, then he was one of those who deducted a few years from his age when applying for a passage; he was 77 in 1851!

Fitzgerald, William, 30

Ship:	Amity, 1825
Origin:	Templetenny, Tipperary
Location:	N lot 13, con 6, Ennismore Twp
Family:	Bridget, 30
William	28
Mary	14
Richard	12
William	6
John	5

Ship's notes: a man of gentlemanlike behaviour. Of good principle, and to be trusted."

The whole family was sick in 1826. To judge by the ages, William Jr. was not a child of William and Bridget. Perhaps he was Bridget's brother, or some other Fitzgerald relative.

Fitzpatrick, Daniel, 40, weaver

Ship:	Brunswick, 1825
Origin:	Mallow, Cork
Location:	lot 14, con 10, Emily Twp
Family:	Margaret, 40

Denis	20
Michael	19
Mary	16
Johanna	14
Ellen	12
Elizabeth	10

Denis was given the North half of lot 12, concession 8, Emily. He is shown in the 1851 census as a weaver, accompanied by his wife Margaret, and children John, Johanna, Mary, Patrick, Margaret, Ellen, Matthew, Michael, Denis and Timothy. Living with them was Daniell, weaver, now admitting to age 70.

Fitzpatrick, John, weaver, 30
Ship:	Brunswick, 1825
Origin:	Castlemagner, Cork
Location:	E lot 20, con 1, Asphodel Twp
Family:	Elizabeth, 22
Bridget	6
Mary	5
John	3

Timothy, born November 14, 1825.
Born in Upper Canada:Sarah
Stephen
Anne
Charles.

In 1838, John was said to be living on lot 20, concession 2, with ten in his family.

Flaherty, James, 30
Ship:	Star, 1825
Origin:	Mallow, Cork
Location:	went to Ennismore. See entry for Johanna Hickey.

Flaherty, James, 50
Ship:	Fortitude, 1825
Origin:	Kilworth, Cork
Location:	N lot 22, con 9, Emily Twp.
Family:	Mary, 48
*James	30
Ellen	29
Michael	28
Patrick	22
Thomas	14
Denis	8
James	3
Edmond	

I believe James * to be the James of the previous entry. On arrival in Upper Canada the names of the whole family were given as shown above, but James Jr. and Michael were said to be "separated." This seems to be the James who went to stay with "the Widow Hickey" having travelled with her family from Ireland, although he was also allocated his own land, the

Carroll Flaherty, a grandson of James Flaherty and Catherine McAuliffe.

South half of lot 22, con 9, Emily. It appears that the two families may have been connected in Ireland.

Michael Flaherty drew the North half lot 23, con 9, and Patrick the South half of that lot. Michael married Mary Sliney and Thomas, Mary Hickey.

Flaherty/O'Flaherty, Jeremiah, 24
Ship: Stakesby, 1823
Origin: Lismore, Waterford
Location :   unknown.

Fleming, John, 66.
See the entry for <u>Allen, Edmond.</u> Mr Fleming was his father-in-law.

Flynn, Cornelius,, 43
Ship: Brunswick, 1825
Origin: Buttevant, Cork
Location: Douro Twp
Family: Margaret 40
James   24
Abby   17
Mary   12
Cornelius   5

Cornelius Sr. died before reaching Douro and his wife appears in records as a widow. James Flynn took up land in the East half of lot 10, concession five, Douro. One Mary died at the depot on September 3, 1825, but I am not sure if this was the mother or the daughter.

Flynn, James, 31, RC
Ship: Stakesby, 1825
Origin: Liscarrol, Cork
Location: W lot 9, con 12, Ramsay Twp
Family: Margaret, 28, wife
William   10
Joanna   8
Daniel   3 months

This family was well established on the land at the time of the 1834 inspection. The following year the parish priest made a note of the fact that this couple had two sons and "three or four daughters."

Flynn, Michael, 30
Ship: Elizabeth, 1825
Origin: Kilbolane, Cork
Location: S lot 10, con 9 Emily Twp
Family: Elizabeth, 28
Thomas   6
Connor   2
Mary Casey,   sister, 32

Michael Flynn was sick with the ague throughout the summer of 1826.

This is pretty Beatrice Flynn, a daughter of Kate Hickey and Cornelius Flynn. She married Joseph O'Reilly.

Flynn, William, 60
Ship: Brunswick, 1825
Origin: Mallow, Cork
Location: Emily Twp
Family: John 24
Daniel   20
Mary   16
Johanna   13
Nancy   11

William Flynn lived with his son John on S lot 11, con 10, Emily Township. William died July 12, 1826. Daniel Flynn was given the North half of lot 10, con 9.

Foley, Daniel, 38
Ship: Star, 1825
Origin: Inniscarra, Cork
Location,   N lot 2, con 8 Ennismore Twp
Family: Catherine, 34
Mary   14
Kitty   11
Margaret   8
Johanna   4
John   2
Patrick   2

Foley, Patrick, 40
Ship: Hebe, 1823
Origin: Castlelyons, Cork
Location: lot 27, con 2, Ramsay Twp
Family: Ellen, wife
Mary   17
John   15

The former Thomas Flynn house at lot 14, concession 10 is one of the prettiest houses in Emily Township.

D.W.McCuaig photo.

David   15
Patrick   11
Michael   9
Ellen   3
One birth in Ramsay.

Patrick Foley Sr. was living on this farm when it was inspected in 1834. The agent noted that Pat's brother, John, had come out with a later Peter Robinson group and was now on lot 25, con 2, belonging to George Dooley who was absent. John Foley does not appear in the 1825 group, which lends credence to the theory that more people did in fact come out under the leadership of Robinson.

Anyone who plans to work on his connections with the Foley family of Lanark County should be aware that there was more than one Foley family there in the nineteenth century. For instance, there was the Michael Foley who married Elizabeth Corkery circa 1824 (see letter written by Michael Corkery.) There is no apparent relationship between Michael and the Foleys listed above. He came here from County Carlow in 1820, and taught school in Lanark County. He was a graduate of the university at Dublin. Foleys descended from his line can, of course, count themselves as "Peter Robinson" people through his wife, Betty.

What complicates the picture is that their daughter, Catherine Foley, married Jeremiah O'Brien,

a brother of Mrs John Foley of the above group. This set up a cousinship between those of the next generation, and ties were maintained even after some members moved to the United States and to the Canadian West.

Other Foleys later moved into the Almonte area from elsewhere, who had similar first names to the Peter Robinson Foleys. Canon Foley, who was at St.Mary's, Almonte, came from the Foley's Mountain district near Westport.

Almonte Express, 1861.

For sale at Michael Foley's, Ramsay, one horse sleigh, one fanning mill, one logging chain, one box stove and stove pipes.

Almonte Express, 1862.

The subscriber, at the request of several parties both here and in Huntley, has consented to keep that three year old stallion, Young Performer, as he is often called, being sired by that approved society horse, Performer, and to accomodate all parties he will travel him as follows. From Monday noon till Friday morn at his own stables; from Friday noon till half-past three at Mr John Murphy's Almonte; en route for the stables of his son, John Foley, Huntley, there to remain overnight and Saturday. Pedigree and et cetera would be superfluous here; suffice it to say that he stands unrivalled for size, trotting and draft, by any colt of his age in these counties.

Michael Foley, Ramsay.

Almonte Gazette, 1872.
Lost and Found.
A young lady (Miss Foley) who resides near Clayton, lost a valuable gold watch in Pakenham this week. Mr James Hartney very fortunately found it near the railway station, lying in the snow, and it was returned to the owner.

Almonte Gazette, 1873.
A Narrow Escape.
A team of horses and a wagon belonging to Mr Foley, Ramsay, backed over the platform at Mr Wylie's factory last week, falling a considerable distance. They were taken out, none the worse.

Almonte Gazette, 1874.
We copy this from The Irish World, New York. (Mr Foley is a native of Ramsay and son of Michael Foley, esq.
"Mr Foley of this paper has just reached New York after a tour of eight months. He has visited about all the principal cities and towns of the United States and reports very favourably on the condition of our people, particularly in the Western States."

Almonte Gazette, 1888.
Mr Patrick Foley of the New York Irish World was called home to Almonte the other day by a telegram announcing the serious illness of his sister, Miss Annie Foley. Miss Foley has been a sufferer from paralysis for over twenty years and it ws feared that her illness was at last about to prove fatal, and her friends were sent for. We are pleased, however, to learn that a change for the better has taken place. We may add that we welcome the return to town of our old and esteemed friend, but regret exceedingly that he should be called home on such a sad errand.

Almonte Gazette, 1888.
Mr Timothy Foley, formerly of Foley Brothers of Almonte and Pakenham, who has been railroading in Minnesota for the past few years, was elected president of the First National Bank in St.Paul a few days ago. Mr Foley was born in Ramsay Township and is said to be worth about a million.

Foley, William, 44.

Ship:	John Barry, 1825.
Origin:	Listowel, Kerry
Location:	lot 2, con 4, Ennismore Twp.
Family:	Patrick 26
Ellen	24
William	22
Thomas	18
Daniel	16

Ship's notes: "a very excellent family of quiet and willing lads. They have behaved to my entire

satisfaction. Foley has two sons at Godmanchester whom he is anxious to join, provided he can have his land and allowance."

These two sons did not come out with the 1823 emigration, so possibly they came to Upper Canada under their own auspices. William Foley Sr. died in 1826. His son Patrick was given the south half of lot 2, concession 4, while William received the north half. Patrick later went to the United States.

Ellen was "rationed with John Pope", her husband. Both were from Listowel but it is not clear from the records whether they came out as a married couple, or were married in Canada. Passengers were divided into groups of people, not necessarily related, for the purpose of doling out rations on board ship. A certain amount of food was allowed per "mess" which was the name given to these groups.

John Pope travelled to Canada on the ship Regulus with his brother, while the Foleys were on the John Barry, where Ellen's name appears with her family in a ship's list. Was she actually on the Regulus with him as his wife, or did they marry on land, with the rations being supplies which they took out to the farm with them? We may never know the answer to this question.

Forrest, Richard, RC

Ship:	Hebe, 1823
Origin:	Newmarket, Cork
Location:	lot 22, con 2, Huntley Twp
Family:	Ellen (Nel) nee Harran
Catherine	(Kate) 24
Timothy	21
James	19
Richard	17
Corneius	15
Mary	12
Johanna	10

When they first arrived in Upper Canada, Timothy and James worked near Brockville, but later returned to their Huntley land. Their father, Richard Forrest, had some bad luck while getting established; his cow and calf were drowned, a serious loss for a pioneer farmer.

Richard Sr. died in 1829 and his land was farmed by his sons, Richard and Cornelius. Timothy Forrest, a co-heir, assigned his interest to them "on condition of their chopping thirty acres at his own land, which they have done." In other words, they bought him out, using the value of their labour in place of cash.

Timothy's first farm was W half lot 21, con 11. He married Catherine Herrick in 1833. The 1851 census for Huntley shows them with the following children,(ages being those of the following birthday) Michael, 18; Mary,9; Thomas,7; James,5; Eliza,3.

James drew west lot 20, con 11. His wife was Bridget Kennedy. Their children included Elzabeth, Richard, David, Honora, Bridget, Patrick, Ellen, James, Michael and John.

James Forrest later moved to Goulbourn Township, and Timothy to White Lake. Those researching Timothy are advised to be careful as the south end of Renfrew County has other Forrests with similar first names, who were of Scottish extraction.

Cornelius Forrest was too young to receive land when he came to Canada, but, as we have seen, he farmed his father's lot. Cornelius was married twice, and both wives were named Ellen. His first wife was a neighbour, Ellen Kennedy, whom he married in 1837. The couple had seven children before she died at the early age of 32 on January 25, 1849. Those children and their spouses, where known, were : Ellen m. James Brown; David; Richard; Michael m. Bridget Gleeson; Cornelius m Rosana O'Brien; John m. Elizabeth Leahy and James m Susan Manion.

When Ellen died, Cornelius faced a dilemma. His only daughter was ten years old, and his six boys included an infant and children of 2,4,5,7 and 9. Like many widowers back then, he remarried within a year. The new bride was 24 year old Ellen Connelly. Their children were Catherine, Timothy, William, Thomas, Mary, Andrew and Edward. You can find this pair in the 1851 census for Huntley Township, with their first baby, Catherine, added to the list of the first family.

Andrew Forrest, mentioned above, married into a most interesting family from the Ferguson's Falls district. His wife, Margaret Ellen Carberry, was a granddaughter of an early Irish settler who was part of a group known as "the seven bachelors."

The story goes that seven bachelors came out from Ireland together, having made a pact that, where all could not find work, none would stay. They settled in the neighbourhood of Ferguson's Falls, although James Carberry's farm was in Lanark Township rather than Drummond. Two of the brothers were Quinns, and two of their descendants were girls to married Margaret's brothers, so we can see that ties were maintained among the group.

When the seven first came to Upper Canada, the land superintendent secured a block of land for them in Lanark Township, and they built a single house, in which they "batched it" together. They had many adventures, not to mention cooking disasters; one of the crew once visited Kingston, where he purchased salt cod. Presumably they didn't know enough to soak it before it was cooked, for legend says that they had to drink a great deal of water after eating it, and they were quite ill for a time.

Not long afterwards they decided to give up their bachelor freedom. Some married local girls,

Michael Forrest, born in Upper Canada, was a grandson of 1823 settler Richard Forrest Sr.

while one of the Quinn boys sent to Ireland for a bride. It is said that he walked to Montreal to meet the boat. There are a number of descendants still in the district, and although everyone knows that these fellows were married men, they are always referred to as "the seven bachelors."

Fowke, Robert, 45

Ship:	Brunswick, 1825
Origin:	Ballyclough, Cork
Family:	Nora, 30
Michael	12
Anne	8
Catherine	7
John	4

I have been unable to trace this family. One record shows that Robert Fowke died.

Fox.
See entry for **Sheneck.**

French, John, 24, RC

Ship:	Stakesby, 1823
Origin:	Mallow, Cork
Location:	lot 8, con 5, Ramsay Twp
Family:	Mary 20
Sarah,	2 months.

John French drowned at Kingston in October, 1825.

Gahagan, John RC

Ship: Stakesby, 1823
Origin: Rathkeale, Limerick
Location: lot 17, con 10, Huntley Twp.
Family: Anne, wife
Michael,   born in Beckwith

1826: "went to work and is now sick, near Brockville."

Galeavan/ Galvin, Garrett, 44

Ship: Elizabeth, 1825
Origin: Listowel, Kerry
Location: lot 5, con 11, Ennismore Twp.
Family: Mary, 36
Patrick   20
John   18
Michael   16
Catherine   14
Garrett   12
Ellen   10
Maurice   7

The ancestors of the Galvins of Ennismore came from Listowel, County Kerry, an area where the majority of Irish Galvins can still be found today. Theirs is an old Gaelic surname, O Gealbhain, which in English has been rendered as Galvin, O'Galvan and O'Gallivane.

Yet another spelling was used when the Galvins came to Upper Canada in 1825; ship's officials recorded the name phonetically as Galeavan.

As you can see, the first representatives of this family here were Garrett and Mary Galvin and their seven children. Their eldest son, Patrick, deserves mention because among his fourteen children there were three sets of twins. A single man when he arrived in Canada, Patrick married a Miss Cadigan and they had eight children. These included twins Bridget and John, Patrick and Michael, as well as single births, Mary, Margaret, Elizabeth and Garrett.

John married Mary O'Gorman; Garrett m Alice O'Donnell; Patrick m Mary Tobin; Elizabeth m Thomas Flood.

The second set of twins was born in 1841, and Patrick's wife died then, or not long after. In those days widowers had to quickly remarry for practical reasons and Patrick had some very young children to care for. He married Catherine Moriarity, who must have been a brave woman to take on eight little stepchildren, and they added another six children to the flock, including the third set of twins, Ellen and Catherine. The others were Thomas, Margaret, Maurice and Honora.

Thomas married Mary Collins; Maurice m Ellen Young; Honora, John Crough. Margaret seems to have died young.

In the 1851 census, Elizabeth, a 66 year old widow, was living with the family. She could have been Mrs Moriarity, as Mrs Galvin Sr. was Mary.

Garrett Galeavan (Galvin) Jr, who came with his family on the ship Elizabeth, settling in Ennismore.

The agricultural census of this family gives us an interesting glimpse of the lifestyle of this family of sixteen people, made up of three generations. They lived together in a one-storey log house of lot 10, concession 6.

At that time they had 210 acres of land, of which all but 160 acres of bush were under cultivation. In 1851, 30 acres were planted in crops, 16 acres were pasture, and there was a four acre garden. In those days, field work was usually carried out by the men, assisted by the women at harvest time, and the women cared for the garden. Patrick was fortunate in having a large family to share the work load.

In that year, his family raised 100 bushels of wheat, 100 bushels of peas, 20 bushels of Indian corn, one hundred bushels of potatoes and made 20 lbs maple sugar. The women made 600 lbs of butter, salted down four barrels of beef, and cured 12 hundredweight of fish. We can see by this that they had a much better diet than many people had in Ireland at that time.

The Galvins had a large amount of livestock, including five "bulls or oxen", four "milch cows", three calves, two horses, 17 pigs and a flock of 40 sheep. Twelve tons of hay was needed for the feeding of some of these beasts.

The women of the household were skilled at spinning and weaving, and probably kept their sheep for the wool as much as the meat In 1851 they produced

30 yards of fulled cloth and 40 yards of flannel. While this was a respectable amount of material, it would not have clothed everyone in the family for a year, but then those were the days when people had two sets of garments which they "made do" for as long as possible, and it is unlikely that everyone had something new each year.

Outgrown garments would be handed down, or cut down for smaller members of the family, and the leftovers would see service in quilt patches, dolls' clothes, hooked rugs and dusters.

All in all, we have here a picture of a prosperous, hardworking family, who were probably most contented with their lot. We must remember that in 1851 the people of Ireland were still suffering terrible privation as a result of the potato famine of the 1840s and this would have been well known to the people of Ennismore. Thousands of Irish people were still coming into Canada and Canadian newspapers were full of reports of the horrors of life in Ireland.

The drive to achieve which is evidenced by the 1851 census has been handed down through the family, with many successful and prominent people bearing the Galvin name throughout the years.

Patrick Galvin's great grandson, **Clare F.Galvin**, is the author of The Holy Land, the history of Ennismore Township. Those wishing to learn more about the township and its families will find plenty to interest them in that work.

Another great grandson, **Douglas Galvin**, B.A., LL.B., was Mayor of Peterborough for 1971-1972.

Two well known Peterborough lawyers, **Sharon Murphy Gariepy** and **Marty Murphy** are also descended from Patrick Galvin, through his grandson Joseph, as is **Dr. Paul Phillips**, a history professor at St.Xavier, Nova Scotia. **Father Patrick Galvin** is another great grandson of Patrick Galvin. A number of school teachers have been numbered among the Galvin family over the years.

The people mentioned here are descended from Patrick Galvin's second marriage. A descendant of his first marriage, **Most Reverend Alden John Bell, D.D.** became Titular Bishop of Rhodopolis and Auxiliary of Los Angeles in 1956. His mother was Catherine Galvin Bell, a daughter of John Galvin, one of the first sets of twins.

Some years ago, Bishop Bell was unfortunate enough to have suffered an attack by a disturbed man, wielding a knife with a seven inch blade. The bishop received several gashes before his attacker was thrown aside by a secretary, Jean Tamaki.
Bishop Bell recovered , and at a later date was pleased to present Ms. Tamaki with a papal medal which was awarded to her, along with a special blessing from Pope John Paul II. The courageous secretary also received a citation for bravery from the Sacramento Chief of Police.

Galvin, Denis. 19
Ship: Stakesby, 1823
Origin: Mallow, Cork
Location: SW lot 5, con 3, Beckwith. Later lot 15, con 11, Ramsay.

In 1826 he was listed as "single; working on shares with another settler." By 1834 he was farming a clergy lot on the 12th line of Huntley Township. His brother John came out in 1825 and stayed with him for a while.

Galvin, John, 19.
Ship: Amity, 1825
Origin: Kanturk, Cork
Location: lot 27, con 1, Otonabee Twp.
Family: Margaret, 20

This was Denis Galvin's brother. They were not twins. Denis would have been 21 years of age by the time that John arrived. John and Margaret moved to Ramsay, where they had at least two sons. They soon moved to lot 10, con 11, Ramsay, but left there, also, purchasing a lot on the twelfth concession of Huntley from the Canada Company. These people went to Kemptville for a short time in the 1830s.

Gany/Guiney, John
Ship   Hebe, 1823
Origin   Fermoy, Cork
Location: "left at Morphy's Falls." (Now Carleton Place.)

Gardiner, Henry, 38, miller
Ship   Regulus, 1825
Origin: Ballyclough, Cork
Location: lot 23, con 4, Smith Twp
Family: Jane, 37
Eugene   16   (See Callaghan.)
Eliza   9
Bartholomew   6
Mathias   3
Bridget McCarthy 20
Born in Canada
Henry.

The following letter was written by Henry Gardiner to Peter Robinson in Ireland. It indicates that each registration centre had some sort of quota.

April 24, 1825.
Sir:
I went to Ballyghiblin as your honour desired me, but being disappointed there I am come to Mallow as you appointed me, being recommended by Lord Doneraile and Mr Freeman.
I remain, your humble servant,
Henry Gardiner, miller and millwright.

In the 1827 report we see that Henry was employed as a carpenter at "the government mill" at Peterborough.

There had been one birth and one death since the family came to Upper Canada.

Bridget McCarthy joined the family in 1825. She was one of a list of people said to have "managed to get on board after the settlers were mustered." She could have been in Canada at an earlier date, because this a statement like this often applied to people who met their families at Montreal and got themselves onto transportation within Upper or Lower Canada. Another possibility is that she was the Bridget McCarthy, 20, who sailed on the Elizabeth.

Geary, John, 41

Ship:	Star, 1825
Origin	Carrigcashel, Cork
Location:	N lot 21, con 6, Emily Twp
Family:	Ellen, 38
William	15
Michael	13
James	11
Johanna	8
Ellen	7
Margaret	2
Mary.	

Mary was born in 1826. Two conflicting dates are given, namely February 5, July 5. There was also a death in the family that year.

William Geary later went to Ennismore.

Gibbon, Maurice, 55

Ship:	Regulus, 1825
Origin:	Templetenny, Tipperary
Location:	unknown
Family:	Bridget, 39
Margaret	20
Mary	19
John	15
William	13

Gillman, Edmond, 38

Origin:	John Barry, 1825
Origin:	Magourney (Coachford) Cork
Location:	N lot 1, con 7, Ennismore Twp
Family:	Mary, 36
Rebecca	18
Ellen	16
Richard	15
John	14
Mary	13
Sylvester	9
Elizabeth	7
Edmond	3

Ship's notes: "himself a very good man."
In 1826, the Gillmans had a new birth. Unluckily they had a bad start: "crop failed, put in too late."

Gold/Gould, Daniel

Ship:	Hebe, 1823
Origin:	Charleville, Cork
Location:	unknown

Gould, James, 30

Ship:	Fortitude, 1825
Origin	Kilworth, Cork
Location:	"stopped in Montreal."
Family:	Mary, 28
Catherine,	7
James	5
John	3
Ellen	2

Gordon, John, 44

Ship:	Amity, 1825
Origin:	T ? County
Family:	Mary Anne , 42
Samuel	20
Robert	19
John	17
Mary Anne	15
Elizabeth	14
James	10
Alexander	6
Henry	3

Ship's notes "he and his family highly decent and well conducted."

Samuel Gordon was given S lot 18, concession 4, Emily and Robert received S lot 14, concession 4. Robert was sick throughout the summer of 1826, and the whole family, including Samuel, lived in a house on his lot. John Gordon must have soon died, for in one early list, Mary Anne is referred to as "the widow Gordon."

Grady/O'Grady, John, 35

Ship	Brunswick, 1825
Origin:	Mallow, Cork
Location:	lot 19, con 1, Asphodel (Later Otonabee)
Family:	Catherine 34
Judith	21
James	19
Johanna	16
Charles	12
Maria	11
Catherine	8
John	3

When the O'Grady family travelled to Canada in 1825, the list of people on the ticket was as you see it here. In actual fact, a rather different group travelled on that ticket, and the girl Johanna was really a boy named John, in disguise.

At the last moment, the John O'Grady family decided that they could not leave Ireland. They sold their ticket to a family of the same name in their

John O'Grady, Timothy O'Grady and his wife, Catherine Doherty and E lot 10, concession 9, Asphodel Township, a farm now owned by the Buck family. John O'Grady travelled to Canada disguised as a girl, called Johanna.

parish; whether they were related to them, we do not know.

Some subterfuge was necessary. With fifty thousand applicants for the few hundred places allotted, there was a huge waiting list. The second group of O' Gradys probably had little chance of getting a passage, if proper channels were used. Each family had the same number of children so the switch would be easy, but while the first family had four girls, the second only had three. Young John was persuaded to don skirts for the voyage.

Descendants of the family that I have spoken to do not know the correct names and ages of some of their pioneer ancestors. They know that Johanna was really John; he married Mary Purcell in 1833. They were the great grandparents of **Fred O'Grady** of Peterborough, who has done a great deal of work in carrying on the Irish tradition there. He and his wife Shirley are involved in the annual selection of the Rose of Tralee, where girls of Irish descent are chosen to take part in a festival in Ireland.

James married Mary Foster. There was also a Catherine, or Kitty. There were a number of Gradys in Asphodel in 1828, including an older man, Jeremiah,

and young men, Tim and Michael, but it is hard to know if there was an connection, without digging into parish records.   In any case, John O'Grady Sr. died in Asphodel in September, 1826.

Once in Canada, the family dropped the "O" from their name because they had been listed in official papers as Grady. Half a century later, some branches of the family resumed the traditional spelling.

Back in 1929, Mrs Elizabeth O'Brien, 82, spoke to a newspaper reporter about the experiences of her parents, who had settled in Otonabee. Her father was the John who was disguised as a girl. When he first settled on his farm he had an axe, a pot, a crane for the hearth, some small tools and a year's rations.
"One evening, rather late, while going through the woods, Mr O'Grady saw a small animal, and caught it. He put it under his shirt and took it home. Hailing his wife he said 'Mary, we're made forever.'
His wife said 'what luck did you have now?'
'I caught a grey fox in the woods!"
He put the animal in a trough and before morning they knew what the animal was from the scent."

The best story of all concerns the efforts of John O'Grady to put food on the table. "Once, when walking where deer had a runway he saw a deer coming. He stepped behind a tree, and when the deer passed, he threw his arms out and caught the animal. Of course, it put up a big fight, so Mr O'Grady called to his wife to bring an axe. The more Mrs O'Grady struck the animal the harder it jumped. Finally, taking the axe himself, he killed the deer."

The children of John O'Grady, and their spouses, were John m. Mary Smith; Thomas; Timothy m. Catherine Doherty; Patrick; Elizabeth, m. John Smith; Dennis O'Brien; Mary m .William Doherty; Margaret m. Timothy Sullivan; Ellen m. John Doherty; Timothy; Michael.

The Green/Greene family.

The Green(e)s who came out to the Ottawa Valley were all related despite the fact that some were Protestant and some Catholic. The ship's list is rather confusing because some of the women mentioned were sisters and others were wives of the Green men. I have broken down this list into smaller groups for the sake of clarity.

Extensive research done by family members suggests these were probably two groups of cousins, with Bustard, Thomas, Anne and John Jr. as one group, and John Sr., William, George and Abigail as another. Rose was not another sister, as one source suggests, but was Mrs John Green Jr.

The two Johns were definitely not father and son. When settlers with similar names boarded the ships, officials usually dubbed the first comer "senior" and the next, "junior." Age did not always come into it.

Green, Bustard, 25, RC
Ship: Stakesby, 1823
Origin: Castletownroche, Cork
Location   lot 22, con 8, Pakenham.
Family: Anne, 23 (sister).

The rather unusual first name of Bustard appears several times in various branches of this family; Busted and Busteed are alternate spellings. Nobody seems to know the origin of the name, except that a bustard was an old world bird; perhaps this was a variation on the old fashioned name, Buster. Descendants prefer the spelling Busteed for the man who came on the Stakesby.

1834 report: "purchased a lot on the tenth concession where he has erected a good house. Purchased a village lot and erected a good frame house." The latter might have been the site of a tavern he operated in the 1830s. He also worked as a shoemaker in that era.

In the 1840s, Busteed Green was living in Renfrew County, near Constant Creek in the Dacre area. He had married Jane Craig circa 1825; she was

Coleraine Hall, Renfrew, was the residence of the Barnet family.

The late Tom Barnet, a member of a well known Renfrew lumbering family. He was descended from the Green family of Castletownroche, County Cork.

the daughter of a Scottish settler of Lanark County. Their children were: Grace Green m. Andrew Goodry; Michael F. Green; James Green m. Arvilla Ann Carswell; Elizabeth; Thomas; George; Jane Green m. Alexander Barnet.

Of the James Green line, two descendants, father and son, have served as United Church ministers. They are **Rev. H. Irvine Hare** and **Rev. Michael Bruce Hare.**

Had Busteed Green remained in Ireland it is doubtful if any of his children would have become

This house is located at E. lot 3, con 2, Fitzroy Township and was built by John Greene in the 1850s or 1860s. He obtained the land patent in 1841. It is now the residence of descendant Merville Greene. Shown in the photo are Mr Greene's mother, Mary Lucinda (Gourlay) Greene, her daughter and some neighbours.

wealthy, but as it was, his daughter Jane became the chatelaine of Coleraine Hall, one of the finer homes in the town of Renfrew. Her husband, Alexander Barnet, was a wealthy lumberman. The couple married in 1867, and subsequently had ten children.

Jane's obituary in The Renfrew Mercury sixty years later said that "her husband ranked among the most successful lumbermen in the Ottawa Valley, and always attributed much of his success to the capable, energetic woman who presided over his household."

Although the many descendants of the Green/e families of 1823 were soon scattered throughout several Ottawa Valley counties, ties were maintained for many years. **Mr Merville Greene** of Kinburn recalls that, prior to the death of Alexander Barnet, which took place in 1917, his parents visited their Barnet cousins in Renfrew. "They went by train and were met in style and taken to the Barnet home, treated royally and had a nice visit."

William Greene

Green, George, 20
Ship: Stakesby, 1823
Origin: Castletownroche, County Cork
Location: lot 3, con 5, Pakenham Twp
Family   Abigail, 25, (sister)

According to the 1826 report, George was a single man who had been working for a year in Brockville before returning to the land. He must have married shortly after this, for when he died in 1833 he left behind a six year old daughter.

The 1834 report said that just before his death he had switched farms, now owning lot 25 in the same concession. At a later date his daughter's uncle applied to have this farm kept in reserve for the girl, but the appeal was turned down. Under the settlement scheme, only boys had this privilege. There were cases where land was allocated to widows, but this was when there were young sons who could later inherit.

Abigail Green, George's sister, is believed to have married a neighbour, **Denis Shanahan.** See entry for Shanahan.

Green, John, 32
Ship: Stakesby, 1823
Origin   Castletownroche, Cork
Location: lot 22, con 8, Pakenham Twp
Family: Catherine, 22

1834: "John Green Sr. has purchased a lot in Fitzroy, on which he resides."

Catherine Green's maiden name is something of a puzzle. Apparently she was unable to write and so her surname was spelled phonetically by officials, appearing variously as Mulshegan, Mulchey, etc.

There is a romantic story attached to the marriage of John and Catherine. The story goes that they were unable to marry in Ireland because she was Catholic and he was Protestant, so John smuggled her on board when he was leaving, and counted on his family to hide her. Every time she had to appear on deck they surrounded her so she could remain undiscovered until they were well out to sea. Although ships' officers were on the lookout for such tricks it was impossible to sort everyone out in those pre-passport days, and the ruse was successful. The pair were married when they reached Perth.

John drew land for which he obtained the patent in 1836. However, the land was too poor for farming and he did not stay there long. They moved to lot 3, con 2, Fitzroy Twp, where descendants still live. This branch of the family changed their name to Greene.

John retained his old farm, figuring that, since he had the patent and had done all the work of clearance, he might as well used the land to raise hay on. Meanwhile, another man, finding the farm unoccupied, squatted on the land and continued to improve it. This became the subject of a legal dispute between the pair in the 1840s.

On one occasion John arrived to harvest his hay, and found another man cutting out his bush. He also objected to other neighbours taking out his firewood, which he needed himself because, as he wrote in protest " my family is now increased to 13 in number." Unfortunately his claim was disallowed and he lost the farm.

The children of John and Catherine were Michael m. Charlotte Cameron; Moses m. Jane McVeity; Thomas m. Ellen Whitehead; Nancy m. Hans Ledgerwood; Catherine m. Arthur Ross; John; George; Jonathan; Elizabeth Greene m. Edward Green; Margaret m. John Switzer; William Busted m. Mary Lucinda Gourlay.

Thomas Greene moved to Eganville in the 1870s. A descendant of this branch, **Ellard Greene,** has served as Reeve of Wilberforce Township.

Jonathan Greene went to the United States and fought in the American Civil War, before settling in Portland, Oregon.

Green, John, 23
Ship: Stakesby, 1823
Origin   Castletownroche, Cork
Location   lot 21, con 7, Pakenham Twp
Family: Rose, 24 (wife)
Samuel   born Ramsay Twp

1834 report: "John Green Jr. resides on his lot but is still struggling with bad land."

These Greens were Roman Catholic. Unlike other members of the family who left the township in search of better land, this group stayed. Rose was pregnant when she left Ireland for she gave birth to their first child in Ramsay Township, en route for their land.

For part of his life John kept an inn or tavern in the district. He died in 1850 and is buried in the Indian Hill cemetery at Pakenham. Rose outlived himn by several years.

One of their children was another John Green, who married Ellen Leeney. His obituary in 1907 describes him as "an old-time lumberman of Pakenham." He served as a councillor there in the 1870s. One of their sons was **Dr. Samuel Green.**

Green, Thomas, 30.
Ship: Stakesby, 1823
Origin: Castletownroche, Cork
Location: W lot 21, con 9, Pakenham.

1834 report: "In the Township of Fitzroy. This land but lately allocated to him. Had originally drawn land in Pakenham which he had to throw up, after working considerably on it." This land was too rocky. The new farm was W half lot 1, concession 3, Fitzroy.

Thomas Green's first wife was Margaret Andrews, and the couple had at least seven children. Margaret died at the birth of the youngest child, William B. Green. Thomas later remarried; he and his new wife, Martha, had a son, James. Thomas died in 1850, leaving half the farm to Martha and half to his son George. Another son, Michael, inherited a team of horses.

James Greene (the family had by this time changed the spelling) lived for a while at Carleton Place. An older sister lived at Denbigh. Michael lived for a time at Appleton, where his daughter Jennie married Alfred Dulmage, of another Peter Robinson family. Their son, **Barnet Dulmage**, was a lawyer in Smiths Falls.

William B.Greene married Margaret Groves and he operated a cooper's shop at Mohr's Corners.

George Greene married Mary Barber and for a time they, too, lived at Appleton, where he worked at the Teskey mill. George and Mary were married in the Anglican church at Pakenham, but their granddaughter, **Dorothy McBride**, says that "somewhere along the way they became Methodists." This conversion may have occurred at Appleton, where there were only two churches, Presbyterian and Methodist.

This branch of the Greenes later attended a Methodist church at Arnprior, where they sang in the choir. George and Mary had moved to McNab Township in 1886, Their daughter Ethel, later Mrs Thomas McBride, had an organ and the family had wonderful sing-songs around the instrument, with Ethel playing by ear.

Grandpa was a talented man who could turn his hand to anything. Miss McBride says " I have a small chest of drawers that he made. He had cobbler's tools and used to do the family boot mending. He experimented with grafting and had such novelties as a gooseberry branch growing on a maple tree."

"At one time a neighbour told me that when they had a sick animal they sent for George McBride, or when anyone was sick they'd send for him instead of the doctor! He knew about green plants which could be used for food. I still marvel at how he knew all those things, living his early life in the bush as he did."

Green, William, RC

Ship: Stakesby, 1823
Origin: Castletownroche, Cork
Location: lot 1, con 6, Pakenham.

1826 report: "supposed to have traded lots with George Hanniver." "Two in family."
William Green later moved to Ramsay Township.

Gregg, Michael, 23, blacksmith

Ship: Stakesby, 1823
Origin: Conna, Cork
Location: lot 24, con 6, Pakenham Twp

Michael was a blacksmith who later moved to Ramsay township. In the 1830s he worked at his trade in Almonte, and a little later at Pakenham, where the family stayed with his nephew, William Connor. Michael's land was too poor for farming.

Michael Gregg was single when he came to Canada, but he married Ellen Barry at Perth in 1825. His parents are listed as Edmond Gregg and Mary Sexton; hers were William Barry and Helen Welch.

There are several points of interest here. William Barry, widower, who also travelled with Peter Robinson, had a daughter, variously recorded as Ellen or Helen, who was the right age to have been this girl.

Secondly, when a son of Michael and Ellen, William Gregg (born August 23, 1848) was baptised at St. Michael's Corkery, his sponsors were two Peter Robinson settlers, George Green and Johanna Leahy. The Leahy family had come from Conna, the same parish in Irish as Michael Gregg.

Thirdly, several families moved to Alumette Island from Huntley in the 1850s. Johanna's son Thomas was among them, and so were some Greggs. The two families had travelled on the same ship in 1823.

Gregg, William, 34, RC

Ship:
                Stakesby, 1823
Origin: Conna, Cork
Location: lot 23, con 6, Pakenham Twp
Family: Frances, 34 (Fanny)
William   5
Mary   4
Eliza,   born Pakenham. Died August 5,1823

The land was too poor for farming and William moved to lot 16, con 9, Pakenham Twp.

Groves, Thomas, 20

Ship: John Barry, 1825
Origin: Aghoule, Wicklow
Location: lot 17, con 7, Emily Twp.
Family;   Margaret, 46, widow
Abraham   17
Margaret   13
James   11

Cork, 1825. Petition for emigration.
I take the liberty of recommending the bearer, Margaret Groves, a widow with two sons and a daughter who are anxious to proceed to America to join a part of the family who have already gone and settled there. The woman is a Native of the County of Wicklow and bears an excellent character.

She has been all her life accustomed to the agricultural business, and her family is one of the better class of Irish tenantry.

Indeed, I may recommend her and her family as persons who came within the description of those intended to be tempted by the measure of emigrating to Canada and under these circumstances I am induced to trouble you with a line in favour of a Family who have always been considered People of excellent conduct.."

Ship's notes: "a very excellent family, Protestants, the mother a worthy kind of woman. Boys very willing and attentive. Afraid of her neighbour and has suffered ill from some on account of religion. Has two daughters in Ramsay whom she is anxious to join. She is very deserving, very industrious."

We do not know whether this young widow ever saw her daughters again. She died in Emily Township on Sept 27, 1826. The sons remained in Emily, and local historian and author Simon Connell recalls that the last of the Groves there was an elderly man who died at the time of the First World War.

I would love to know something of the two daughters in Ramsay Township. The Auld Kirk in Ramsay has a broken tombstone which gives a tantalising glimpse of a Mary Groves - Mrs James Smith! Neither the Groves nor any Smiths went out on the 1823 sailing. These women may have come separately, or have been married women whose names are not familiar to us.

The name Groves is an old one in the Carleton Place area, but I have not discovered whether it is connected with this family.

Gubbins, William, 40, RC
Ship: Stakesby, 1823
Origin: Castletownroche, Cork
Location: E lot 7, con 2, Ramsay Twp.

In 1826, William was single. He had cleared one acre of his land, and he was "working at the canal." A later report stated that he died in 1825 at the house of one Edmond Pollard, who supported him during a two-year illness. As a result, the farm was made over to Pollard "as remuneration for this care and trouble."

Guinea, Darby, 32
Ship: Elizabeth, 1825
Origin: Liscarrol, Cork
Family: Elizabeth, 30
James   4
Mary   1

James Guinea died in the bateau on July 15, 1825. On one list, Darby and Elizabeth are crossed out, to be replaced by Patrick and Ellen Shenick. Perhaps this means that they rested for a time when the settlers were being moved up to Prescott in stages.

It seems that there were more Guineas who might have come to Canada, but who did not succeed in getting a passage. A haunting letter, written by a Richard Fitzgerald who also, it seems, did not make it, is reproduced here:

His reference:
I hereby certify that I know the bearer Richard Fitzgerald these many years back to be an honest, industrious man and a good English scholar. (Signed by the parish priest of Liscarrol.)

His own letter to Peter Robinson,
I have been the seventh man you took in all Ballyghiblin, on our about the fifteenth of September last ... my two brothers-in-law (the Guineas) who have their tickets, were the next before me on the list, and indeed you desired us to prepare.

Depending on God and you I sold my little effects and bought many necessities for the voyage... I had been in Castletownroche Wednesday last...

Alas, others, more prosperous, got the preference. My wife is in a desponding condition from not going with her brothers, being an only sister. I had been a farmer but, alas, the vicissitudes of fortune have deprived me of it, but earning a little livelihood by teaching school. I humbly implore your honour for God's Sake to let me go, and in duty bound will ever pray.

Richard Fitzgerald, 43
Johanna Fitzgerald, 29
Child,   15 months.

Perhaps since these people could not go, some of the Guineas stayed behind, also. I would really like to know the outcome of this harrowing tale.

Hagarty, William, 30
Ship: Fortitude, 1825
Origin: Listowel, Kerry
Family;   Catherine, 30
Ellen   12
Catherine   10
John   6
Mary   4
Daniel   1

Notes: William Hagarty "died Monday night in the Depot." This was on November 25, 1825. What became of poor Mrs Hagarty is not known.

Hallahan, Thomas, 44
Ship: Amity, 1825
Origin: Middleton, Cork
Location: E lot 21, con 10, Otonabee Twp
Family: Mary, 30
James   17

Michael   16
Denis   13
Hannah   9

Ship's notes: a well disposed man and a good family."

Mary may have been a second wife; she was not old enough to have been the mother of most of this family. Michael Hallahan was drowned in the Otonabee rapids on May 21, 1826, and in that report he was listed as 22 years of age.

This family, one of those which remained in the township for many years, worked hard in their first season on the land. In 1826 they produced 500 bushels of potatoes, 400 bushels of turnips, 75 bushels of Indian corn, and 100 pounds of maple sugar. They possessed two cows and a pair of hogs.

O'Halloran, William, 34
Ship: Fortitude, 1825
Origin: Dungarvan, Waterford
Location: lot 14, con 10, Emily Twp
Family: Mary, 24
Ellen   6 (Nelly)
Margaret   4 (Peggy)
Catherine   1 (Kitty)

Hamilton, James, 35
Ship: Elizabeth, 1825
Origin: Charleville, Cork
Location: "disembarked at Montreal."
Family: Catherine, 24

Hanlin, John
Ship: Hebe, 1823
Alias **Daniel Callaghan.**

Handlan, James, 42, mason
Ship: Regulus, 1825
Origin: Ballyhooley, Cork
Location: W lot 30, con 9, Otonabee Twp
Family: Belle, 40
Michael   20
Maurice   18
Richard   16
Mary   10
Thomas   8
Johanna   4
Catherine   2

Michael took E lot 30, concession 9, Otonabee. Maurice had the west half of lot 29. Both Maurice and Thomas became masons.

This family had one death in 1826. In that season they produced 300 bushels of potatoes, 100 bushels of turnips, 60 bushels of corn and 300 pounds of maple sugar. They already possessed a team of oxen and a cow.

One of the elder sons of this group died of consumption (tuberculosis) in 1851 at the age of 46 years, He left a widow and nine children, including Francis, James, Michael, Maurice, John, Richard, Thomas, Ann and Daniel.

Hannon, William, 44
Ship: Elizabeth, 1825
Origin: Cobh, Cork
Location: lot 24, con 12, Smith Twp
Family: Mary, 40
Denis   21
George   19
Catherine   19
Frank   15
Mary   13

William Hannon did not draw land; he was over the age limit of 39. The whole family lived on Denis' lot, the south half of the farm listed above. George had the north half, but lived with the others in the early days. One death took place in this family in 1826.

Hanover/Hanniver, George, 21
Ship: Stakesby, 1823
Origin: Mallow, Cork
Location: W lot 26, con 6, Pakenham Twp.

George Hanover was a graduate of the University of Dublin. He came to Upper Canada as a single man, and was still a bachelor in 1826 when a census recorded him as "working at the Grand River."

He later returned to the Pakenham area, where he married. He traded lots several times before he found one that was suitable for farming.

He and Catherine had several children, who included John, Ellen, Ann, Mary, Edward, Thomas, William, Catherine and Theresa. In the absence of a suitable school in the early days, George taught his own children at home. In later years his son, Dr. William Hanover of Delaware, Wisconsin, explained that he had received all his elementary education at home.

George Hanover and his wife are buried at St.Peter's cemetery, Pakenham. He died on June 22, 1874, age 72 years and his wife in 1884, age 84.

When George died, "his affectionate daughter, Theresa" composed verses in his memory which were published in The Almonte Gazette. There were six verses in all, and the last three reflect the feelings which the first pioneers must have had when they had to leave their parents' graves behind them.

Father, the grave may long yawn between us
And if fate spread thy children far from that spot
In mind they'll return if across the wild ocean
And kneel by thy grave: oh! thou'll not be forgot.

And oft you may see looking down on the tide
Our bark tossing wildly on life's stormy seas
Oh, guide thou the helm of our frail little vessel,
Pilot us safely, for we'll call upon thee..

Farewell, death exalts, not separates ties,
For a hope breaks upon us like a heavenly spell,
That one day we'll form thy bright crown in Heaven,
Miseri Dominus, beloved father, farewell."

Hanrahan, George

Ship:	Stakesby, 1823
Origin:	Kanturk, Cork
Location:	W lot 3, con 10, Goulbourn Twp
1826 report:	"labourer, at work in the country."

Hargrove, James 27

Ship:	Brunswick, 1825
Location:	W lot 5, con 9, Emily Twp
Family:	Eliza 22
Mary	4

This family is something of a mystery as they appear in the location book- and certainly existed- but are not mentioned in the ship's list. Possibly they came under an alias, as many did, having purchased the ticket of another family who backed out.

If we scan the list of those who came out on the Brunswick, the only possibility is the Jeremiah Cronin family. Here the participants are the right age, and there is no trace of that family in the settlement book. **NB.** This is only a theory, and is completely unsubstantiated.

Hartnett, John, 46

Ship:	Fortitude, 1825
Origin:	Churchtown, Cork
Location:	S lot 23, con 10, Emily Twp
Family:	Catherine, 40
Margaret	23
Elizabeth	21
John	19
Maurice	17
Mary	14
Michael	13
Honora	12
Timothy	8
Catherine	6
Johanna	3

John Jr was given the north half of his father's lot. I cannot explain why John Sr. was given land, being over age, but perhaps it was to be held in trust for Maurice, who was close to his majority.

Everyone lived with John Sr. , who was sick throughout the summer of 1826. A death occurred in that period, which may have been his. In that season

the family raised 400 bushels of potatoes, 100 bushels of turnips, 45 bushels of corn, all from five acres, and they produced 60 pounds of maple sugar.

Healey, Daniel, 48

Ship:	Star, 1825
Origin:	Colmcille, Cork
Location:	W lot 13, con 7, Asphodel Twp
Family:	Anne, 48
Thomas	22
Ellen	20
Mary	16
Anne	14
Daniel	13

Thomas Healey drew the west half of lot 14, concession 7. In a census of 1838 he was living there as a married man with five in the family.

Healey, Patrick, 35

Ship:	Albion, 1825
Origin:	Doneraile, Cork
Location:	W lot 11, con 10, Asphodel Twp
Family:	Eliza, 36
Mary	19
Thomas	17
John	15
Judith	13
Ellen	11
Eliza	9
Margaret	2

Ship's notes: "very industrious and quiet."
"Betty, 40, died in Asphodel on Sunday, October 22, 1826."
There was a connection between this family and the James Daley family of the Albion.

Healey, Patrick, 40

Ship:	Stakesby, 1823
Origin:	Fermoy, Cork
Location:	E lot 9, con 2, Esamay Twp
Family:	Abigail, 40 (wife)
Mary	20
Denis	18
James	14
Margaret	5

Denis lived with his parents until 1831, when he moved to Lanark Township to farm lot 1, concession 7.

Heffernan, Patrick, 25

Ship:	Regulus, 1825
Origin:	Kilworth, Cork
Location:	E lot 29, con 9, Otonabee Twp
Family:	Margaret 25
Norah	3
Michael,	born August 12,1825.

One death occurred in this family in 1826.

In 1826 these people produced 200 bushels of potatoes, 100 bushels of turnips, 45 bushels of corn and 50 lbs maple sugar. In the fall of that year they sowed two bushels of wheat.

Heffernan, John
This man does not appear on any ship's list, at least, under this name. However, he was given E lot 31, con 6, Otonabee Twp as a Peter Robinson settler. A single man, he went to work on the Welland Canal during the summer of 1826.

Hennessy, Thomas, 42

Ship:	Stakesby, 1823
Origin:	Castlewrixon, Cork
Location:	E lot 7, con 6, Ramsay Twp
Family:	Thomas 19
Honora	16
Mary	15
Eliza	12

Thomas Jr. was given the adjoining farm. The two men were "turners by trade" and in 1826 were "supposed to have gone to the United States."

Hennessy, Thomas, 38

Ship:	John Barry, 1825
Origin:	Fermoy, Cork
Location:	N lot 23, con 6, Emily Twp
Family:	Nancy 30
John	17
Thomas	15
Michael	13
Bridget	11
Daniel	7
William	5
Patrick	4

Reference.
"The bearer, Thomas Hennessy, with his family of six sons and one daughter (eldest son 18, daughter 11) is desirous to go to Canada. He is an excellent labourer and has worked for me for many years. If you can do anything for him you will much oblige."

Hickey, Johanna, widow, 32

Ship:	Star, 1825
Origin:	Mallow, Cork
Location:	N lot 1, con 5, Ennismore Twp
Family:	
John	18
James	16
Patrick	15
Mary	13
Thomas	11
Michael	7

John Hickey, 1837-1917. Mr Hickey was a son of two 1825 settlers, Patrick Hickey and Margaret Sliney.

This well dressed child was Charlie Hickey, a descendant of Patrick Hickey whose widowed mother, Johanna, brought her children to Upper Canada in 1825.

A delightful picture of Leo and Marion Carroll. On their mother's side they are descended from the Hickeys and Slineys.

Reference:
We, the undersigned gentlemen, do hereby certify that we know the bearer, Johanna Hickey, widow, to be an independent, honest woman, and know her sons to be good labourers.

James Flaherty Jr., age 30, travelled with this family, although he later took up land in Emily near his family, who had come out on a different ship. It seems probable that he was a male relative, helping Johanna to get through the ordeal of moving to a foreign country.

James Hickey married Jane O'Donnell; Patrick married Margaret Sliney; Mary married Thomas Flaherty; Thomas married Elizabeth Lynch.

Hickey, William, RC
Ship: Hebe, 1823
Origin: Mitchelstown, Cork
I ocation: lot 11, con 12, Ramsay Twp

1826: "single. Took a farm on shares at Brockville but is now on his land."
1834: William was still on the land. He purchased wheat from a neighbour, Michael O'Keefe, and at the latter's request gave the cash to the parish priest in settlement of church dues.

ELECT
JOHN W. (BILL)
CARROLL
STATE SENATOR
FOURTH DISTRICT

⊗ **VOTE REPUBLICAN**

United States Senator Bill Carroll is a descendant of the Hickey family who came with Peter Robinson in 1825. A veteran of the U.S. army, he once worked as an accountant and he also owned his own newspaper. He spent twenty years as a member of the state legislature and served in the Senate for eight years. He is a resident of Chicago.

Hoare, Patrick, 24, RC
Ship;   Stakesby, 1823
Origin: Fermoy, Cork
Location: E lot 2, con 10, Goulbourn Twp.
This was a young bachelor, who was located on his farm on October 25, 1823. At the time of the 1826 inspection he was said to be "at work in the country as a labourer."

Hodge, John
This man received land as a Peter Robinson settler on East lot 19, concession 11, Otonabee Township. However, he does not appear in any of the ship's lists. The most likely explanation for this is that he was a brother-in-law or cousin of one of the heads of families, and so appeared under that name.
1826: "working with a farmer near his land."

Hogan, David, 29
Ship: John Barry, 1825
Origin: Cork City

Location: lot 32, con 9, Otonabee Twp
Family: Sarah, 23
Catherine   6
Mary   1

Ship's notes: "An old soldier, wrought hard and behaved well on voyage, acting as cook. Has since committed himself."

<u>Reference, Kingston, August 7, 1825.</u>
I have known David Hogan, private in the 48th Regiment, on his passage from New South Wales. His conduct was correct and his character excellent. I do believe him to be a good and honest man.
John Ternan, RN. Ship's surgeon.

Hogan, John, 35
Ship: Elizabeth, 1825
Origin: Carrigdonan?? Cork
Location: N lot 11, con 6, Emily Twp.
Family: Johanna 32
Michael   15
Daniel   13
Ellen   2
Margaret   born Emily Twp, June 13, 1826.

<u>Reference July 22,1825.</u>
The bearer, John Hogan, is as good a man as can be found. He is hard working and industrious and honest.

John Hogan was ill during the summer of 1826, yet the family raised 200 bushels of potatoes and 45 bushels of corn.

Hogan, William, 35, sawyer.
Ship: Resolution, 1825
Origin: Mitchelstown, Cork
Location: W lot 2, con 8, Douro Twp
Family: Alice 34
Thomas   9
Francis   7
Mary   4
Ellen   1

Ship's notes: one child dead.
In 1826, the family produced 150 bushels of potatoes, 200 bushels of turnips, 60 bushels of corn and 150 lbs maple sugar.
This family was in Asphodel in the 1830s.

Horan, Michael, 30
Ship: Hebe, 1823
Origin: Mallow, Cork
Location: lot 25, con 1, Ramsay Twp
Another document gives his place of origin as Freemount, Cork.

1826 report: Single. Has been at work upon the canal." Michael Horan did not occupy this land, and when another inspection was made in 1834, the agent said that nobody knew where he might have located. However, the parish priest had Horan down in his diary as living on lot 25, concession 1.

Horney, William, 45.
Ship: Brunswick, 1825
Origin: Mallow, Cork
Location: Montreal.
Family: Anne, 40
Edward   16
William   9
John   7
Anstey   2

Houlihan, Denis, 42
Ship: Elizabeth, 1825
Origin: Charleville, Cork
Location: W lot 8, con 10, Emily Twp
Family:
William   20
James   18
Margaret   17
Michael   15
Johanna   13
Denis   11
Thomas   8

James Houlihan died during the trip to Upper Canada. William Houlihan drew the east half of his father's lot.

One of the saddest aspects of life years ago was the fact that women often died young, either in childbirth or from one of the many infectious diseases which were then prevalent. While this was a tragedy for the bereaved families, it must also have been hard for mothers to accept the fact that they would not be there to guide their children as they grew up.

The Houlihan family had to cope with this. When Denis brought his family of seven to Canada in 1825, their mother was already dead. His youngest daughter, Johanna, grew up to marry a neighbour, William Lehane, (whose family came out from County Cork in 1830) but, sadly, she also was destined to die in her thirties, leaving eight children behind her.

Her eldest girl died young. The rest of the family did well. One daughter became Sister Thecla; another was Sister Antoinette.

Johanna's great-great-grandson is **Father Sean O'Sullivan** who is well known in Canada at the time of writing. At the age of twenty he was the youngest person ever to be elected to Parliament in Canada. Later he entered the seminary and was subsequently ordained to the priesthood. In 1986, his book <u>Both My Houses</u> was published, in which he told the story of his two careers.

Father Fergus O'Brien, 1883-1946 was also a Houlihan descendant.

Howard, Patrick,
This man received the west half of lot 10, con 7, Douro Twp. He is not listed under the name Howard in the ship's lists which probably means that he was a brother of one of the married settlers and travelled under his or her name. In 1826 he was a single man, employed by Robinson at the Peterborough depot.

Howernan, Cornelius, 33
Ship:	Brunswick, 1825
Origin:	Kilmeen, Cork
Location:	N lot 6, con 7, Ennismore Twp
Family:	Mary, 32
Daniel	13
Denis	10
Mary	4
Connor	2

1826 report: Cornelius was "sick during the summer."

Hurley, Denis, 40, boatman
Ship:	Star, 1825
Origin:	Kilmurrough, Cork
Location:	lot 19, con 5, Asphodel Twp
Family:	Catherine, 40
Bridget	19
Michael	17
Margaret	15
John	8
Honora	4
Ellen	2 months.

Catherine Hurley died in Asphodel Sept 24, 1825, possibly as a result of childbirth complications. Denis is said to have later married a widow, Judith English.

In their first season on the land, the Hurleys raised 400 bushels of potatoes, 100 bushels of turnips, 105 bushels of maple sugar. The family also owned a cow and a pig.

Michael Hurley farmed lot 15, con 7. He later married Bridget English, PR.

Hurley, James, 35, carpenter.
Ship:	John Barry, 1825
Origin:	Kilfinaghty, Clare
Location:	S lot 6, con 10, Emily Twp
Family:	Mary, 30
Jane	9
Thomas	7
Patrick,	3 (died at Kingston).

In 1826, James Hurley was listed as a "carpenter, working at Peterborough."

98

Hurley/ Herlehy, Patrick, 42
Ship:	Brunswick, 1825
Origin:	Mallow, Cork
Location:	S lot 14, con 12, Emily Twp
Family:	Ellen, 36
Patrick	18 (north half same lot)
Timothy	16
William	13
Mary	11
Jeremiah	8
Ellen	3

In their first season on the farm, these people produced 200 bushels of potatoes, 200 bushels of turnips, 60 bushels of corn and 150 pounds maple sugar. They owned two hogs.

In old records, the name of this family alternates between Hurley and Herlehy. In the nineteenth century these were interchangeable translations of an old Gaelic surname. People with this surname originally came from one of two groups, the O' Muirthile of County Cork and the O'hUirthile of County Clare.

Jessop, Francis, 25, Protestant.
Ship;	Hebe, 1823
Origin:	Kilfinane, Limerick
Location:	W lot 14, con 12, Ramsay Twp.

Francis Jessop was a native of Kinsale, Cork. He must have moved to Kilfinane at a later date. He received his ticket to come to Canada at Michelstown, Cork.

Single when he arrived in Upper Canada, Jessop acted as an agent for Peter Robinson. He inspected the settlers on several occasions, reporting on their progress, and he also administered the sale of Crown lands, for which Robinson was commissioner. Jessop's full name, with which he signed some of these reports, was Francis William Kinnear Jessop.

The 1861 census for Ramsay Township shows him to be an Anglican, born circa 1791 (note the age discrepancy) with a wife Frances (Fanny) who was born in Jamaica. This probably indicates that she was the daughter of one of Lanark County's military settlers. Children living at home in 1861 were John, 24; William, 21; Francis, 19.

Keane, Michael, 35, barber.
Ship:	Fortitude, 1825
Origin:	Brigown, Cork
Location:	W lot 9, con 3, Douro Twp
Family:	Ellen, 30
John	16
James	14
Margaret	11
Michael	5
Mary	2

1826: "all this family had ague in the summer, except for two children."
Despite their illness, this family produced 200 bushels of potatoes, 100 bushels of turnips and 35 bushels of corn in that year. They made 25 pounds of maple sugar in the spring.

Keane, Timothy, 42

Ship:	Regulus, 1825
Origin:	Listowel, Kerry
Location:	N lot 11, con 8, Ennismore Twp
Family:	Margaret, 40
Mary	20
Thomas	19 (N lot 12, con 7)
Catherine	17
Patrick	15
Timothy	12
Johanna	8

There was one death in this family in 1826

Kearney, Dennis 26

Ship:	Amity, 1825
Origin:	Templetenny, Tipperary
Location:	E lot 31, con 3, Otonabee Twp
Family:	Mary, 30

Ship's notes "an honest, well meaning creature."

In 1826 this couple grew 200 bushels of potatoes, 100 bushels of turnips and 60 bushels of corn. They also possessed a cow.

Kearney, Patrick, 36

Ship:	Resolution, 1825
Origin:	Castlelyons, Cork
Location;	E lot 14, con 14, Otonabee Twp
Family:	Catherine, 30
Denis	10
James	8
Mary	3
Patrick	1

One birth in this family in 1826.

Keating, Nicholas, 20

Ship:	Amity, 1825
Origin:	Templetenny, Tipperary.
Location:	E lot 25, con 2, Otonabee Twp

This man was listed with the Richard English family; he was Richard's brother-in-law.
1827 report: "Has lived with R.English; now chopping on his own lot."

Keefe/O'Keeffe, Cornelius

Ship:	Hebe, 1823
Origin:	Clogheen, Tipperary
Location:	Not given, but located October 1, 1823.

Keefe, Denis, 33

Ship:	Regulus, 1825
Origin:	Castlemagner, Cork
Location:	W lot 20, con 1, Asphodel Twp
Family:	Mary, 30
Nancy	12
Patrick	10
William	7
Mary	5

There was a new birth in 1826. In that year, Denis was found to be "absent without leave" which probably meant that he was working out for pay. He may well have felt the need to do so, with four youngsters and a fifth on the way.

Keefe, James, 38

Ship:	Albion, 1825
Origin:	Doneraile, Cork
Location:	E lot 17, con 1, Otonabee Twp
Family:	Ann, 29
Catherine	18
James	17
Ellen	13
Eliza	12
Timothy	9
Mary Ann	5

Timothy died at Rice Lake, December 30, 1825. Ship's note on James: "tidy, but I fear not fit for hard work."
This was probably a composite family. Ann may have been a second wife and the elder children her stepchildren, or alternatively, the latter may have been siblings of the married couple.

Keeffe, Jeremiah.

Ship:	Hebe, 1823
Origin:	Mitchelstown, Cork
Location:	unknown

Keeffe, John

Ship:	Stakesby, 1823
Origin:	Watersgrasshill, Cork
Location:	unknown.

O'Keeffe/Keeffe, Patrick, 35, RC

Ship:	Stakesby, 1823
Origin:	Lismore, Waterford
Location:	lot 20, con 11, Ramsay Twp
Family:	Mary, 48
Thomas	18 (E lot 13, con 11.)
Mary	15
John	13

Patrick O'Keeffe came out in 1823 with his son Thomas. Mary, with their two younger children, followed on the ship Albion in 1825. The ship's surgeon described Mary as "very decent and quiet; wife to Pat, taken out in 1823."

Mary had no sooner arrived on the farm then her menfolk "went rafting on the St.Lawrence." After they returned the family moved to another Ramsay farm, and at a still later date, to Huntley Township.

At the time of the 1834 inspection, Patrick had "erected an excellent dwelling house and barns." His son Thomas died in 1831 and Patrick petitioned to keep the land for another son.

According to the parish priest of the day, these people had four sons and three daughters living with them in 1835. In view of Mary's age it is possible that other children remained in Ireland, joining them later, or that the single young O'Keeffes mentioned earlier may have belonged to them. It is believed that other members of the O'Keeffe family came out to Huntley at the time of the potato famine of the 1840s.

It is unlikely that Mary was eleven years older than her husband. He may have deducted a few years from his age when coming to Canada, in order to get below the magical cut-off point of 39 years, to be eligible for land. According to his tombstone, Patrick was probably 47 in 1823.

Keily, Owen, 35
Ship: Brunswick, 1825
Origin: Kilbehenny, Cork
Location: S lot 15, con 11, Emily Twp
Family: Mary,   37
Ellen,   14
Timothy   13
Margaret   12
David   9
Mary   5
Owen Keily died in 1838.
In the 1851 census for Emily Township we can see Timothy Keily with a wife, Isabella, and children Owen, John, David and Mary. His widowed mother, Mary, was with them, her age given as 75.

Keeler, James
Ship: Hebe, 1823
Origin: Clogheen, Tipperary
Location: lot 19, con 10, Huntley Twp
Family: Mary
Ellen

James Keeler, alias **James McGrath.**

Kelleher, John, 28, fisherman
Ship: John Barry, 1825
Origin: Dingle, Kerry
Location: S lot 14, con 6, Ennismore Twp
Family: Ellen, 28
Denis   18 (brother. S lot 13, con 6.)
Mary   9

Jane   6
Michael   2

Ship's notes on John: "an excellent and willing man and deserving of every recognition and encouragement from his good conduct, with which I am fully satisfied in every particular. Assisted the third mate with the provisions, and took care of the dogs on the passage." (These dogs were being brought out from Ireland for Peter Robinson.)
Later note for John :"not living on the land." Denis drowned at Mud Lake May 31, 1826. However, I have seen another source which says that this was John.

Kelly, Christopher, RC
Ship: Hebe, 1823
Origin: Buttevant, Cork
Location: E lot 18, con 4, Ramsay Twp

1826:" absent without leave, but supposed to be in Canada."
Kennedy.

Three Kennedy brothers came to Canada with the Peter Robinson settlers. Timothy came first; he drew land in Pakenham Township but went to work at Brockville for a time, returning to the area later. He later moved to Huntley. Timothy was single when he came out here.

In 1825, his brothers David and John also came out. There is no record of where David settled; perhaps he lived with one of his brothers. John and his family also settled in Huntley. In 1825, John was 29, David 28 and Tim 27.

Dr. Dunn's book on the history of St.Michael's parish says that the trio came from County Tipperary. This could well be so, in which case their Cork origins might be the locations where they registered for tickets.

Kennedy, David, 28
Ship: Regulus, 1825
Origin: Kilbolane, Cork

Kennedy, John, 29
Ship: Regulus, 1825
Origin: Kilbolane, Cork
Location: lot 19, con 10, Huntley Twp
Family: Margaret, 30
Ellen,   10
Mary,   6
Honorah,   1

Kennedy, Timothy, 25
Ship: Stakesby, 1823
Origin: Charleville, Cork
Location: W lot 1, con 5, Pakenham Twp. Later traded land with Patrick Mealey for E lot 21, con 11, Huntley Twp.

Timothy Kennedy eventually married and his children included sons, Thomas and David.

John's daughter Ellen maried Cornelius Forrest. Mary Kennedy married Con Mahoney, but died at the age of 27 years.

Researchers should be aware that there were other Kennedys in this township who came in at an even earlier date. There was a John Kennedy whose wife was Margaret Manion; this family also intermarried with the Peter Robinson Forrests. A member of this Kennedy family has done considerable research and feels that this John and Margaret are not the couple who came here in 1825. Whether there was any relationship in Ireland is unknown.

Kennelly, John, 34

Ship:	Amity, 1825
Origin:	Kilbenny, Limerick
Location:	Lot 19, con 3, Otonabee Twp
Family:	Ellen, 35
William	12
Patrick	8
James	3
John	1

Ship's notes: "an honest, well disposed and industrious creature."
William Kennelly died on the way to his new home.
This was a hard working family. Within a year of their arrival they had cleared eleven acres of land. In 1826 they produced 400 bushels of potatoes, 200 bushels of turnips, 105 bushels of corn and 50 lbs maple sugar.

Kennelly, Bartholomew, tailor.
Alias **Michael Maddigan.** See entry for Owen Maddigan.

Kenny, John, RC

Ship:	Hebe, 1823
Origin:	Fermoy, Cork
Location:	E lot 7, con 5, Ramsay Twp
Family:	Bridget, wife
Jeremiah,	5

1826 report. Ten acres cleared. Four in family; one birth, one death.
1834 report: "resides on his lot and is doing well."

Kenny/ Kerny, Michael, 30

Ship:	Albion, 1825
Origin:	Kilworth, Cork
Location:	lot 17, con 10, Ops Township
Family:	Mary, 32
James	28
Margaret	20
John,	5

Ship's notes: "a hard working family."

Kent, Lawrence, 43

Ship:	Fortitude, 1825
Origin:	Templetenny, Tipperary
Location:	lot 19, con 4, Otonabee Twp
Family:	Mary, 30
Bridget	17
Michael	15
Mary	15
Margaret	13
Kitty	8
Maurice	6
Honora	2

To judge by the ages of the children, Mary Kent may have been a second wife, unless the older children were other young relatives.

Lawrence Kent suffered with the ague in the summer of 1826, yet this group cleared six acres of land and grew, among other things, 500 bushels of potatoes.

Lancaster, John, 40

Ship:	Amity, 1825
Origin:	Marmulland? Cork
Location:	S lot 22, con 5, Emily Twp
Family:	Mary Anne, 40
Eliza	16
Jonathan	15
Louisa	14
Mary	12
Michael	10
John	8 (died Sept 7. 1825.)
Daniel	7
Richard	1

Ship's notes: " a useful and well conducted man with a decent family." On arrival in Canada, they were joined by a son who had already been in Canada.

Among the passengers on the Amity were a pair of dogs which had been purchased in the old country by Peter Robinson. Presumably they were among the first residents of the embryo town of Peterborough.

During the voyage, John Lancaster helped care for these dogs and as a result his name was mentioned in a letter written by the ship's captain to Robinson. "Your two dogs ...were in excellent condition and as promising as ever visited Canada. Much of their good state they owe to a man who came out with me in the Amity."

In the absence of Robinson, who was travelling back to Upper Canada via New York, the dogs were collected by his brother, John Beverley Robinson, who was supervising the settlers at Kingston, pending Peter's arrival.

Landrigan/ Lonergan, James
Ship: Hebe, 1823
Origin: Clogheen, Tipperary
Wife: Mary.
Alias **Luke McGrath**. (See Ballyghiblin riots.)

Landrigan/Lonergan, Patrick.
Ship: Hebe, 1823
Origin: Clogheen, Tipperary.
Family: Mary
Alias **McGrath**, a brother to Luke McGrath.

1826 report: "at work on the canal."

Lane, John, 46, shoemaker
Ship: John Barry, 1825
Origin: Aghada, Cork
Location: E lot 39, con 13, Smith Twp
Family: Ellen, 42
Cottrell   22 W.lot 39, con 13. Shoemaker
Catherine   20
Ellen   18
Helena   10

Ship's notes: "a good family, instrumental in saving the ship when on shore, thereby avoiding additional expense and delay."

Lane, John, 23
Ship: Resolution, 1823
Origin: Castlelyons, Cork
Location: "left at Lachine."
Family: Mary, 24
Patrick   1

Langane/ Leonard.
Some families in the Peter Robinson group have been known by either or both of these surnames. The original Gaelic name was O'Leannain or O'Lionnain. These have been variously anglicized as Lennon, Linnane, Langane, Leonard and so on. After some years in Canada the more easily pronounceable Leonard was often used.

Langane/ Leonard, Bartholomew, 36
Ship: Albion, 1825
Origin: Doneraile, Cork
Location: N lot 2, con 1, Ennismore Twp
Family: Ellen 18
Mary   16 (Mrs Martin McAuliffe Jr.)
Jeremiah   13
David   12 (m. Ellen Mills)
Patrick   10 (m. Ellen McAuliffe)
Eliza   6 died May 23, 1826
Margaret   3 died June 13, 1826
Ship's notes: " a quiet family"
1826: Bartholomew "worked at the canal this summer."

Tragedy touched this family in the 1850s when Patrick Leonard's wife and three of his children, Daniel, Teresa and John, died in a diphtheria epidemic. This family can be seen in the 1851 census as follows:
Bartholomew Leonard, widower, 70
Patrick Leonard, 45
Ellen Leonard   33
Jeremiah   13
Martin   12
Mary   11
Bart   7
Ellen   6
Catherine   5
Daniel   4
Teresa   3
John   1

Langane/Linguane, Edmond, 26
Ship: Albion, 1825
Origin: Doneraile, Cork
This was a brother of Bartholomew of the previous listing.
An 1826 report said "has gone to the USA to see his brother." This must have been a third brother, as Bart was in Canada at that time, although he, too, went to the USA at a later date.

The Leahys.
The Leahys of County Cork were a large family who came out with Peter Robinson in both 1823 and 1825. Most, possibly all, were related. However, there is no apparent connection between these people and the family of Michael Leahy of Asphodel, an 1825 settler who hailed from County Limerick.

Because many of the Christian names are similar, this group needs some explanation . In 1823, twelve Leahys travelled to Canada aboard the ship Stakesby. All were from the Conna-Brigown-Mitchelstown area. They were Mr and Mrs Patrick Leahy and their family of five; two brothers and a sister named John, William and Mary, and two men in their twenties who were also named William and John. They received land in the adjacent townships of Ramsay, Pakenham and Huntley.

Two years later, another group travelled out on the Fortitude, settling in Douro Township. They were Mr and Mrs Michael Leahy, their family of seven and Mrs Leahy's mother, and a widower with twins, Patrick Leahy. While modern Leahys do not know of a relationship between Michael and this Patrick, there may have been a connection. Patrick's wife was a Lonergan; another Michael Leahy on the Fortitude travelled under the alias Lonergan. The two groups settled next door to each other in Douro.

We do know that there was a connection between Michael and the 1823 settlers. William, John and Mary were his children. The boys later joined him in

Douro; it is hard to trace Mary because presumably she married and changed her name.

When Michael Leahy came to Canada he was 56 years old, and too old to receive land, the upper age limit being 39. Peter Robinson allowed him to emigrate for a reason.

"In 1823 the brother, two sons and one daughter of this man accompanied me, when the feeling was rather against emigration, and I have promised if it was ever in my power to bring out the old people I would. William Leahy the son was of great use to me in Canada and in consideration of his services and good conduct, as well as the circumstances of the old man's having a family of fine children, and withal a reduced farmer, I selected him."

The question is, which of the 1823 settlers was Michael's brother? I put my money on Patrick, who was closer to him in age than the young lads, William and John. I think that the latter may have been nephews.

William assisted Mrs Patrick Leahy on the farm after her husband died; John was embroiled in the Ballyghiblin Riots and soon left the area.

We will now look at the individual Leahy families.

Leahy, Michael, 41, carpenter.

Ship:	Brunswick, 1825
Origin:	Kilfinane, Limerick
Location:	W lot 17, con 4, Asphodel
Family:	Catherine, 36
David	20 (W 19, con 5)
Ellen	18
Catherine	17
James	15 (lot 17, con 4)
Bridget,	9
Honorah	7
Mary	2

One death occurred soon after their arrival.

Leahy, Michael, 50

Ship:	Fortitude, 1825
Origin:	Brigown, Cork
Location:	lot 10, con 7, Douro Twp
Family:	Mary, 50 (nee Burgess.)
Patrick	23 (m Bridget Condon)
Timothy	19 (m. Catherine Sullivan)
David	17 (m. Johanna Connors)
Dennis	15 (m. Mary Moher)
Ellen	14
Abigail	13 (m. Patrick Sheehan)
Judith	6 (m. Henry Sheehan)
William	28 (m. 1. Anne Meehan; 2.Ellen Walsh)
John	25 (m. Johanna Tobin.)

Ellen Burgess, Mary's widowed mother, also came to Canada.

Patrick Joseph Leahy,1912-1962 A descendant of Douro pioneer Michael Leahy and his son John, this man was descended from other Robinson settlers, including the Allens and the Tobins.

Michael Leahy's sons were given lots in Douro Township but they all lived with him at first. By 1826 they were able to clear 12 acres of land, where they harvested 600 bushels of potatoes, 700 bushels of turnips and made 100 pounds of maple sugar. They possessed three oxen, three cows and two hogs.

At least three of Michael's children married other Robinson settlers who had come from their home parish of Brigown. John Leahy married Johanna Tobin who had also come on the Fortitude. Descendants include **Father Harold Leahy, Sister Rosemary Leahy** and the late **Sister Helene Garvin,** Superior General of the Sisters of St.Joseph at Rochester, N.Y.

Patrick Leahy's wife was Bridget Condon of the ship Brunswick. She lived to be well over 100 years of age.

William Leahy married Anne Meehan, the daughter of a neighbour, Daniel Meehan, and after her death, Ellen Walsh, whose parents had come to Canada in the 1840s. A descendant of William and Ellen is **Gerald O.Leahy,** administrator at Sacred

The family of Thomas Leahy Jr. at Allumette Island in 1892. Thomas was born in Huntley Township, a son of Thomas Leahy and Mary O'Connor.

Heart Hospital, Spokane, Wash.

Brother Marcellus, (**Leo Leahy**) a descendant of David Leahy and Johannah Connors, joined the De Lasalle Christian Brothers in 1921. He held the position of Director General of the motherhouse between 1933 and 1955.

Dennis Leahy's family motto appears to have been "community service and music." Three doctors have appeared in this line, including **Carl Leahy, Philip Leahy** and **W.H.Leahy.** The latter served in England, France and Egypt during the First World War, and in civilian life practised in the United States and at Sault Ste Marie. **Father Leo Leahy** is also a descendant of this line.

Frank and Kevin Leahy have music in their souls, apparently inherited from their musical father, **F.D.Leahy,** who was Reeve of Douro and also Township Clerk for many years. Kevin is profiled in another section of the book. His brother Frank, a well

known fiddler, and his equally gifted wife, have produced a unique family of eleven who perform in a family group as singers, dancers and musicians. They have performed in several countries and are the subject of a National Film Board movie. The youth of the participants, their obvious talents and the fact that they are a fine looking crowd, makes a winning combination.

Leahy, John, 20
Ship: Stakesby, 1823
Origin: Conna, Cork
Location: W lot 2, con 12, Huntley Twp

Leahy, John, 25
Ship: Stakesby, 1823
Origin: Mitchelstown, Cork
Location: W lot 15, con 12, Ramsay Twp.
                             Later to Douro Township.

Leahy, Patrick, 40, RC
Ship: Stakesby, 1823
Origin: Conna, Cork
Location: W lot 7, con 12, Huntley Twp
Family: Joanna, 34
Thomas   11 (m. Mary O'Connor)

A view of the pleasant cemetery at the four corners, Douro. In the foreground is a well preserved tombstone put up in 1860 after the death of five year old Dennis Leahy Jr. His parents, Dennis Leahy and Mary Mawher (sic) were born in Mitchelstown, Cork and Calvert, Cork, respectively.

D.W.McCuaig photo.

John	9	(m.Elizabeth Nagle)
Mary	7	(m. Edward Dowling)
Elizabeth	5	
Katherine	2	(m.Patrick Nagle.)

Unfortunately, Patrick Leahy died in 1825. He is believed to have been buried on his Huntley farm, a cemetery not yet being open. Left with five children under twelve, his widow was assisted on the farm for a time by William Leahy, who may have been a nephew.

Technically this land should have been inherited by the elder son, Thomas, but for some reason he signed it over in 1831 to his mother and younger brother, John. The Thomas Leahy family moved to Allumette Island in 1857. He and other members of this line are buried at Chapeau. Descendants of this branch include **Father Thomas Leahy Lynch**, OMI; **Sister Grace Martin**, and **Frank Martin**, who is Executive Director of the Social Planning Council of Ottawa-Carleton.

John Leahy remained in Huntley, where relatives can still be found. His sisters married other Peter Robinson descendants.

Leahy, Patrick, 40
Ship:	Fortitude, 1825
Origin:	Convamose? Cork
Location:	E lot 6, con 7, Douro Twp
Catherine	14
John	13

Patrick Leahy was a widower when he travelled to Canada with his children in 1825. The children are shown as being of different ages, yet family records show that they were really twins, born in 1811. Furthermore, ship's records say that these people came from County Cork, yet their tombstones say that they were natives of County Waterford.

Two younger children, Bartholomew and Mary, came out from Ireland later. Circa 1827, Patrick Leahy remarried. His new bride was Mary Lonergan. The couple had two more children, James and Michael.

John's first wife was Elizabeth Magher; after she died in the 1840s he married Mary Tobin. Catherine was Mrs Crowley. Bartholomew Leahy married Ellen Sharkey; Mary was Mrs Condon.

James married Margaret O'Leary. Among their children were **Dr.Bartholomew Leahy**, **Father T.J.Leahy** and **Sister Loyola** (Elizabeth Leahy.)

Michael Leahy married Bridget Torpey. The pair went to the United States. Their children included **Dr Bart Leahy** and **Father Bill Leahy**. Grandchildren included **Monsignor Bartholomew Leahy**, **Dr Paul Leahy** and two talented athletes, **Eugene Leahy** and his famous brother **Frank Leahy**, the football coach of Notre Dame University. Eugene and Frank are featured elsewhere in the book.

Leahy, William, 28
Ship:	Stakesby, 1823
Origin:	Mitchelstown, Cork
Location:	lot 22, con 10, Ramsay Twp
Family:	Mary , 22 (sister)

(These were children of Michael Leahy of Douro.)

Leahy, William, 30
Ship:	Stakesby, 1823
Origin:	Conna, Cork
Location:	lot 1, con 3, Pakenham Twp.

This is the William who assisted Joanna Leahy on the farm.

O'Leary, John, 40
Ship:	Amity, 1825
Origin:	Kilbehenny, Cork
Location:	lot 29, con 3, Otonabee Twp
Family:	Margaret, 38
Mary	22
Margaret	20
Daniel	18
Patrick	16
John	14
Fanny	8
James	4

Ship's notes: "an honest creature and a very deserving family."

Two members of this family had died by 1827. Despite these troubles the survivors had cleared seven acres by that time and had raised a great deal of produce, including 600 bushels of potatoes. They also owned two hogs.

Leary, Timothy, 50
Ship:	John Barry, 1825
Origin:	Liscarrol, Cork
Location:	S lot 1, con 5, Emily Twp
Family:	Norah, 35
John	30 (son) N lot 1, con 5
Mary,	28
Patrick	14
Norah	12
Timothy	7
Judith	3

1827 report: "from his sickness, late on his land."
This is probably a case of a second marriage. We know that John Leary was Tim's son, yet Norah was too young to have been his mother.

O'Leary, William
| Ship: | Brunswick, 1825 |

No other details.

Lee, James, 30, shoemaker
Ship:	Elizabeth, 1825
Origin:	Charleville, Cork
Location:	"deserted, taking bag and baggage."
Family:	Honora, 27
John	16
Peter	12
Judith	6
James	4

Lewis, Patrick, 30
Ship:	Brunswick, 1825
Origin:	Mallow, Cork
Location:	"deserted at Cobourg"
Family:	Bridget, 30
Catherine	5
Patrick	2

Linehane, Denis, 54
Ship:	Star, 1825
Origin:	Doneraile, Cork
Location:	Ennismore Twp
Family:	Patrick, 28 (N
Mark	20 (N lot 3, con 3)
Margaret	21
Denis	17

Denis Linehan Sr. died in Ennismore July 30, 1826 and his son Patrick on August 26. Mark was described in 1827 as being "absent."

Lonergan/ Londergan, Michael, 40
Ship:	Fortitude, 1825
Mary	35
Michael	25
John	22
Margaret	20
Honora	25

This name is derived from the Gaelic O'Longargain. Recognized derivations include Lonergan, Londrigan, Londergan.

The people in this group appear to have been travelling under assumed names. They may have taken the tickets of friends or relatives who changed their minds about coming.

It is believed that Michael, senior, was actually Maurice Lonergan who settled in Otonabee Township. A Peter Robinson settler of that name located on lot 29, concession 8, with three in his family.

John Lonergan was an alias for Michael Leahy, a single man who settled in Douro. Since he settled near the other Michael Leahy family he was known as Michael Leahy Jr, although apparently not a son of the older man.

The younger Michael Lonergan and Honora were a married couple. They settled in Douro, where several children were born to them, including twins, John and Margaret. The family moved to Asphodel around 1835, where additional children were born, including Nicholas, Johanna, Michael and Lawrence.

Long, David, 35, shoemaker.
Ship:	Regulus, 1825
Origin:	Inniscarra Cork
Location:	W lot 18, con 9, Otonabee Twp
Family:	Abigail, 27
John	9
David	7
William	3

This family suffered with the ague in the summer of 1826. In that year they grew 300 bushels of potatoes, 100 bushels of turnips, 30 bushels of corn and made 15 lbs maple syrup.

Lowes, George, 40
Ship:	Albion, 1825
Origin:	Nantinant, Limerick.
Family:	Hannah, 37
Zacariah	20
Rebecca	8
George	6

Ship's notes: "a most worthy man, wife very industrious. He is brother to Michael Lowes and they wish to be together. They are Protestants."

George Lowes died very soon after his arrival in Canada and his widow, left with young children, remarried on March 28, 1826. Her new husband was James Best, "an old settler."

George Lowes Jr can be seen in the 1851 Emily census, with a wife and two little girls, Margaret and Maria.

Lowes, Michael, 44
Ship:	Albion, 1825
Origin:	Nantinant, Limerick
Location:	Emily Twp. (Later to Ennismore).
Family:	Sarah, 42
Michael	28 N lot 23, con 3, Emily Twp
Richard	24 N lot 17, con 5, Emily.
Dorothy	20

Ship's notes: "an excellent family, worthy of favour."
One member of this family died in 1826.

Lynan, Patrick, 22
Ship:	Albion, 1825
Origin:	Monanimy, Cork
Family:	Ellen, 21
Note:	"deserted at La Chine."

Lynch, Daniel, 20
Ship:	Stakesby, 1823
Origin:	Watersgrasshill, Cork

Location: Unknown. He may have been one of the young bachelors retained at the Shipman's Mills depot to work for Peter Robinson, and located later, as there was a Daniel Lynch family in Ramsay Township for many years.

Lynch, Michael, 25
Ship: Stakesby, 1823
Origin: Castletownroche, Cork
Location: lot 18, con 7, Pakenham Twp
Family: Julia, 22 (wife)
Thomas   8 months
Katherine Lyons, 18 (sister)

1826 report: "a millwright by trade. Supposed to have gone to the United States.

Lynch, Patrick, 32
Ship: Hebe, 1823
Origin: Killarney, Kerry
Location: lot 8, con 3, Ramsay Twp

This man was Roman Catholic when he first came to Canada, but later became Anglican. He died in 1876 at the age of 98 years and is buried at St.James' cemetery, Carleton Place.

Like many others who at first drew bad land, Patrick changed lots several times. An inspector noted that "he declined to take a deed after his first crop-barren rock" He subsequently purchased land from the Canada Company.

A story is still recalled in Ramsay Township concerning an experience of Patrick Lynch in pioneer times. Once, when he was rounding up his cattle, he met a pack of wolves, and he prudently climbed the nearest tree. Unfortunately the wolves killed his dog and two cows, a serious loss to a farmer.

Bathurst Courier, 1835

A house belonging to Patrick Lynch of Ramsay was entirely consumed by fire last week. We understand that the greater part of the furniture was lost. The fire broke out in the absence of Mr Lynch, and his wife, while endeavouring to rescue the children, was severely burnt.

Lynch, Patrick, 32
Ship: Albion, 1825
Origin: Churchtown, Cork
Location: N lot 1, con 3, Ennismore Twp.
Family: Deborah, 30
Mary   14
Catherine   12
James   10
Eliza   8
Ellen   6
Thomas   3
Deborah   " born at Lachine"

Ship's notes: "hardworking, though poor."
There was one death in 1826.

108

Lynes, Catherine, 44 (widow)
Ship: Elizabeth, 1825
Origin: Liscarrol, Cork
Family:
Edmond   25 (W lot 8, con 8, Emily)
Patrick   19 (E lot 7, con 8, Emily Twp)
Margaret   16
Cornelius   13

Edmond and Patrick also went by the alias **Callaghan**. It may be that their mother was married and widowed twice. Two interesting references from Ireland have survived, the first rather ambiguous!

Reference:
"The bearers Edmond Lyne and brother have every wish to be taken to Upper Canada... you would serve this country very materially to take them away".

Reference:
"I know the Callaghans, three men, two women, with their mother Catherine Lyne. They always conducted themselves honestly and industriously."
Thomas Barry,
Mallow, 1825.

Also listed on this ship were a widowed Johanna Lynes, 32, and children Andrew,10, and Kitty, 7.

Lynes, Cornelius, 35
Ship: Brunswick, 1825
Origin: Mallow, Cork
Location: N lot 20, con 11, Emily Twp
Family: Sarah, 30
Johanna   19
Eliza   16
Patrick   14 (brother to Con)
Margaret   14

One death in 1826.

Madden, Thomas, 38, RC
Ship: Stakesby, 1823
Origin: City of Cork
Location: lot 6, con 6, Ramsay Twp
Family: Ellen, 32 (nee Danahy)
Jeremiah   16
Mary   9
John   7
Thomas   5

In the Peter Robinson papers the City of Cork is given as the place of origin for this family. However, they cannot be located in church records there, which makes their descendants suspect that Cork was merely the place where they obtained passage for Canada.

The Madden family in 1914. The older couple are William Madden and his wife, Margaret Powell (centre). He died not long after the photo was taken. In the back row are Julia, Laura, Margaret and Maude. In front are John Madden, Lily Egan (a friend), Etta Madden and Mary Carty (a niece.)

Four children came to Upper Canada with their parents. Jeremiah Madden was promised land in due course, but he had to wait until his father traded lots, moving to lot 11, con 12. The original lot was described as being of little value, and Thomas had to try several farms before finding a satisfactory place.

According to an 1834 inspection report, Thomas Madden had erected "an excellent dwelling house" in the twelfth concession. The family must have done well, for in 1831 they were able to give ten shillings to the parish priest, and even Jeremiah could afford half a crown, which was one quarter of that sum.

Joseph Madden, a great great grandson of Thomas, lives on the family farm, lot 11, concession 12. His children are the sixth generation to live there.

Two of the Madden children married into other Peter Robinson families. Mary Madden married Garrett Nagle's son Richard, while Timothy O'Brien's daughter Julia became John Madden's bride.

John Madden was a faithful supporter of St.Mary's church, Almonte. In 1867 this church burned down, and the congregation had to raise the funds for its rebuilding. A local story says that John mortgaged his property in order to make his contribution to the building fund. Great granddaughter Mary Madden Oikle is puzzled by the story because land records do not show an official mortgage. However, she says, "the Maddens must have done something to help as it seems to be a fairly well known story which we were

told as children, even having to sit in the very front pew, which doesn't help if you are a little bit late getting in from the country!"

Information which has just come in as this book goes to press - literally stop press news! - shows how Thomas Madden and William Slattery lent money when the original wooden church was being built in the 1840s! It is, of course, possible that the Maddens also contributed to the fund which was begun in 1869 but it seems to me that this document of the 1840s may be the answer to the Madden's mystery.

"On or before the 1st January, 1847. We the undersigned Roman Catholic inhabitants of the Townships of Ramsay and Packingham (sic) do acknowledge and bind ourselves to pay Thomas Madden and William Slattery the sums put opposite our respective names for the purpose of lathing and plastering the R. Catholic Church in Ramsay Ville. Dated this 22 day of May, 1846."

The average amount pledged was one pound sterling, then about four dollars, and most of the money was repaid by 1848. On the list were a number of "Peter

Wedding picture of Laura Madden and Charles Newton, January, 1915. They were attended by the bride's sister Maude, and the groom's cousin, J.Sherlock. The bridal couple were described in the local newspaper as "a prosperous young farmer and a popular young teacher."

The Nicholas Bawlf residence in Winnipeg. Mrs Bawlf was formerly a Madden from Ramsay Township.

Robinson" names, such as O'Brien, Corkery, White, Bresnahan, Nagle, Dooling, Riordan, Connors and Foley.

John Madden has many interesting decendants. His son Timothy was Chief of Police at West Superior, Wisconsin, in the 1890s. A daughter, Catherine, married Nicholas Bawlf, who became a millionaire in Winnipeg. **Judge C. James Newton** of Lanark County is a descendant, as is **Raymond Madden**, a history teacher at the Smiths Falls & District Collegiate Institute. Both these men are profiled elsewhere in the book.

A Millionaire's Wife.

Catherine Madden, a granddaughter of pioneers Thomas and Ellen, married Nicholas Bawlf in Almonte in 1877. The bridegroom was a Smiths Falls man whose parents had come out from Ireland at the time of the potato famine, a year or two before his birth.

Nicholas had trained as a moulder in a Smiths Falls foundry, but he found the job boring. After their marriage the newly-weds went to Winnipeg, where Nicholas founded the Bawlf Grain Elevator Company. By 1910 his name was listed in *The Winnipeg Telegram* as one of nineteen millionaires of that city.

He was one of the founders of the Winnipeg Grain Exchange and was later a partner in the Northern Elevator Company, a firm which became one of the largest corporations in the west. Bawlf was one of the first traders to ship grain from west coast ports, and at one time he was said to have shipped more wheat to Japan than any other Canadian entrepreneur.

With his wealth and business acumen, Nicholas Bawlf became part of the elite of the Winnipeg business community. He took part in an amazing number of community engagements, and he contributed generously to charity. At the time of the First World War he was a director of Winnipeg's fund-raising drive for the war effort.

A devout Catholic, Nicholas Bawlf was among those who opposed the Manitoba School Act of 1890 which advocated a secular school system for the province. He also campaigned to have more Catholics appointed to the Canadian Senate.

Catherine Madden Bawlf raised the couple's eight children, and she was a gracious hostess at the lovely family home, where the elite of Winnipeg came to dine. She, too, was active in charitable work, taking a special interest in St. Joseph's orphanage. Her obituary published in the *Manitoba Free Press* just a few days after the Armistice of 1918, bears this out.

"She had a genius for being a good neighbour...she was always a welcome addition to committees, her executive ability and sense of humour making her easy to work with. She was capable, reliable, resourceful, and her place in the community she loved so well and served so faithfully will not be easily or quickly filled."

Despite her wealth and her place in society, Catherine had her sorrows. Three of her sons served overseas during the First World War, and her youngest boy, David, was killed in action. Her daughter Josephine served as a V.A.D in European military hospitals, and this, too, must have caused anxiety at home. Nicholas Bawlf died in 1914, and the war must have been an anxious and lonely time for his widow, as it was for the thousands of others whose children were serving at the front.

The mighty Bawlf empire was a casualty of the Great Depression. Fortunately neither Nicholas nor Catherine were alive to see the collapse of their dream. Their success was remarkable when we consider that both were the children of poor Irish immigrants. Theirs is the classic story of climbing the ladder of success in the New World.

Maddigan, Owen, 60

Ship:	Elizabeth, 1825
Origin:	Colemanswell, Limerick
Location:	W lot 13, con 12, Emily Twp

Family:	Michael	29	(N lot 1, con 11)
	James	27	(E lot 13, con 12)
	Benjamin,	24	(N lot 1, con 11)
	Mary	22	
	Owen	20	(E lot 1, con 12)
	Denis	18	(W lot 1, con 12)
	Matthew	15	
	Bridget	13	

This appears to be one of those cases where a family of in-laws travelled together. Michael Maddigan was listed as "alias Bartholomew Kennelly, and Mary Maddigan "married Kennelly. " It is possible that there was a Michael Maddigan, who stayed behind in Ireland; the man who actually travelled to Canada was Owen's son-in-law.

In 1826, Benjamin Maddigan was sharing a house with Bartholomew Kennelly. The rest of the group were living with their father, with the exception of Owen Jr. who spent the summer of 1826 working on the Welland Canal. Those who stayed home on the farm raised, among other things, 400 bushels of potatoes.

Barthomew Kennelly was a tailor. He and Benjamin raised 300 bushels of potatoes and 45 bushels of corn; they also kept a pig.

Maher/ Meagher

People of this name have lived in Huntley Township for many years, and some of their descendants have worked on their family history. To date, I have not been able to tie in some of their research with the information given in the Peter Robinson papers. At the same time there is a very strong family tradition that these people were Peter Robinson settlers.

A few years ago, a descendant from the Ottawa Valley was hunting in Michigan when he met a man named Meagher. This man explained that three brothers had gone from Ireland to Canada under the auspices of Peter Robinson and that one of the trio, his ancestor, had gone to the United States.

I haven't found three Meagher families in my research, yet we do know that one of the 1823 settlers of this name left very soon for the USA! This is documented in the government reports.

Another researcher tells of her ancestor, John Meagher Sr., who "married Mary Fox in Ireland and came out on the Peter Robinson expedition." People of both those surnames came out in 1825; could there have been a connection?

I am mentioning this for the sake of other researchers who may have come across a similar roadblock. Many of the Peter Robinson settlers did travel under different names, taking up their own again on landing here. This is one possibility.

I do not entirely rule out the possibility that Peter Robinson may have brought out other settlers in addition to those of 1823 and 1825. It is only by sheer chance that the Peter Robinson papers survived - they were stored in a trunk and discovered at Peterborough a century later.

What if he brought out another group later, whose papers did not survive? I have seen one reference to a group that came in 1826, settling along the banks of the Rideau, but so far have been unable to substantiate this.

I should very much like to hear from anyone who feels that his ancestor, not mentioned in this book, did in fact come to Canada with Peter Robinson!

Yet another possibility is that families, possibly connected to Peter Robinson settlers, may have come out later under their own auspices, purchasing land here. Robinson was Commissioner for Crown Lands for a number of years, and his signature could have been on their deeds.

The following are the Meagher families who came in 1823 and 1825.

Magher/Meagher, David 32
Ship	Resolution, 1825
Origin	Kilworth, Cork
Location:	E lot 24, con 11, Otonabee Twp
Family	Mary, 32
John	15
Catherine	11
David	9
Mary	4

1827 notes: "one man dead." David died in Otonabee May 31, 1826.

Magher/ Meagher, James
Ship:	Hebe, 1823
Origin	Mallow, Cork
Location:	lot 28, con 11, Huntley Twp
Family:	Ellen (wife)
Mary	
Jude	

1826 report: "labourer, in the USA."

Magaurin, Michael, RC
Ship	Hebe, 1823
Origin	Liscarrol, Cork
Location:	E lot 25, con 1, Ramsay Twp. Later, lot 25, con 2 (behind Clayton.)

Michael was located on his land on October 24, 1823. He was given one blanket, an axe, a pick axe, an "English axe", a hoe, a saw, a wedge and some nails.

1826 report: single; six acres cleared.
1837: married, with four boys. The family now owned a cow.

Mahoney, Daniel 19
Ship	Fortitude, 1825
Origin	Mallow, Cork
Location:	S lot 14, con 11, Emily Twp.

This young man travelled out with the Doogan or Dorgan family and is listed as Daniel Dorgan. However, he was actually a first cousin to Timothy Dorgan. In 1826 he was living with the John Sheehan family. These people had the farm next to the Dorgans and had also travelled out on the ship Fortitude.

Mahoney, Denis. 23
Ship:	Stakesby, 1823
Origin:	Blarney, Cork
Location:	unknown

Mahoney, Henry, 26
Ship	Stakesby, 1823
Origin	Mallow, Cork
Location:	lot 27, con 6, Pakenham Twp
Family:	Bridget, 30
Child	(born Pakenham)

1826 report: "two in family; one born, one died."
"Worked out at his trade, saddler."
This family later went to Montreal.

Mahoney, James, 36
Ship:	John Barry, 1825
Origin:	Knockacappel, Kerry
Location	lot 11, con 4, Ennismore Twp
Family	Nancy, 34
Denis	15
James	13
Julia	10
Nancy	7
Daniel	5
Jeremiah	1

Ship's notes: "a quiet family. All very sickly."
James Mahoney died in 1826.

Mahoney.
There was another Mahoney family in Huntley Township who had a family tradition of having come out with the Peter Robinson settlers. This was the family of Patrick Mahoney, whose son Con was a well known figure in the township in the nineteenth century. He kept a tavern there and was also a postmaster. However, if the ages of Patrick's children are to be believed (and the censuses are not always correct) then this group could not have come out before 1826. Another small link in the story that indicates that a third group could possibly have come out in 1826.

Mahoney, William, 26, carpenter
Ship: Resolution, 1825
Origin: Brigown, Cork
Location: E lot 4, con 6, Douro Twp
Family   Mary, 50 (widowed mother)
Michael   24 (W lot 4, con 6)
Ellen   23

In 1826 the whole family lived in a house on William's lot. In their first year, the family cleared 7 1/2 acres of land and had produced 150 bushels of potatoes, 200 bushels of turnips, 75 bushels of corn and 7 lbs maple sugar. They had also been able to purchase an ox.

Maloney/Molony, Daniel, 41
Ship   John Barry, 1825
Origin: Roscrea, Tipperary
Location: W lot 9, con 9, Douro Twp
Family: Catherine, 36
Mary   15
John   14
Roger   13
Sarah   12
James   7
Daniel,   born October 1, 1825.

Ship's notes: "a very excellent family. Behaved entirely to my satisfaction during the passage. Was instrumental in saving the ship"
(This refers to some impending disaster which happened in the Gulf of St.Lawrence. A number of the men were obliged to "man the pumps.")
    This family soon managed to clear 10 acres of land, where they raised 400 bushels of potatoes, 200 bushels of turnips and other produce. They also owned a cow.
    Unfortunately John Molony was "drowned in the rapids of the Otonabee" on May 21, 1826.

Malony, Henry, 32
Ship   John Barry, 1825
Origin   Sixmilebridge, Clare
Location   unknown
Family   Hannah, 3

Ship's notes: "Youngest child died at the Cascades on passage up the River. Buried at the Cedars."

Maloney/Molony, John, 40
Ship   Fortitude, 1825
Origin   Ballyhooley, Cork
Location   S lot 5, con 5, Ennismore Twp
Family   Maria 30
Ellen   13
Mary   11   (m. Pat Sullivan)
Francis   7   (m. Johanna McCarthy)
Hester   5   (m. Michael O'Reilly)
Margaret   2
1826 report on John "lately returned from the canal."

(See under **Moloney** for John Moloney/Mollowney.)

Mann, Timothy, RC, 35
Ship: Hebe, 1823
Origin: Charleville, Cork
Location: E lot 23, con 12, Beckwith Twp.
Family: Joanna (wife)
James
Bridget
Martin

Timothy's actual birthplace was Newcastle, Limerick. By 1826 this family had cleared 12 acres of land. There were seven people in all living on this property. They included Timothy's son Patrick, who had come out with Peter Robinson in 1825, being given land on lot 2 in the same concession. There is no sign of Patrick Mann in any of the ships' lists of 1825 - although he might well have travelled under an alias, as so many did - but this information was gleaned from a report of 1834, following an official inspection.

Mansell, Lawrence, 26, RC
Ship: Stakesby, 1823
Origin: Mitchelstown, Cork
Location: lot 27, con 10, Huntley Twp.

In 1826, Lawrence was single and "at work with his brother." In that year the Mansell brothers owned two horses, the first among the Peter Robinson settlers of 1823 to do so.

Mansell, Martin, 28, RC
Ship: Stakesby, 1823
Origin: Mitchelstown, Cork
Location: E lot 23, con 11, Huntley Twp

This was a brother of Lawrence Mansell. His birthplace was actually what seems to be "Kilnafree". (Writing unclear.)
By 1826 Martin was married. He and his wife had a child, which died.

Mantil/Mantle, James, 19, RC
Ship: Stakesby, 1823
Origin: Rathcormac, Cork
Location: E lot 25, con 5, Pakenham Twp

This was a son of John Mantil. James later left his Pakenham land and settled in Huntley. He obtained the Crown patent to W lot 27, concession 10, in 1836.

Almonte Express, 1860.
Land for sale.
100 acres of valuable land, East half lot 23 on the ninth concession in the Township of Huntley. Thirty acres cleared and fit for tillage. For particulars of sale and

terms of payment, apply to James Mantle, Huntley. October 5, 1860.

Mantil/Mantle, John, 45, Rc

Ship:	Stakesby, 1823
Origin:	Rathcormac, Cork
Location:	W lot 25, con 5, Pakenham Twp.
Family:	Ellen , 40 (nee Horgan)
Mary	16
Ellen	12
Margaret	10
Robert	6
Katherine	2

John Mantil died in 1831, leaving his farm to his widow and to his second son, Robert, who was not yet old enough to take up his own land. According to his tombstone, John may actually have been 52 when he arrived in Canada, and his wife 48. However, another child was born to the couple after they came to Canada, so it is hard to judge the accuracy of these dates. In any event, Ellen outlived her husband by 40 years.

Their daughter Mary married Benjamin Finner. A descendant is **Paul Finner,** Deputy Reeve of Ramsay Township and a long-time member of the Almonte Town Council. Another descendant, Lucy Finner, became **Sister Gervase.**

Margaret Mantil married Richard Coady, a native of County Cork. They raised a large family in Fitzroy Township. **Charles Coady,** a well known lawyer in Arnprior, is a descendant.

Robert Mantil married Ann (Nancy) Finucane and they have a number of interesting descendants. Their daughter Jane married **John Fenlon,** who operated a hotel at Rosebank, now Blakeney. Modern descendants of Robert Mantil include **Angus Mantil,** a long-term employee of The Almonte Gazette; **William Mantil,** who owns a computer-oriented business in California, and **Tony Hickey,** a great grandson who at the time of writing is the Canadian light-heavyweight wrist wrestling champion.

In 1835, a Fitzroy Township pioneer, Edward Lunney from County Fermanagh, Ireland, married a

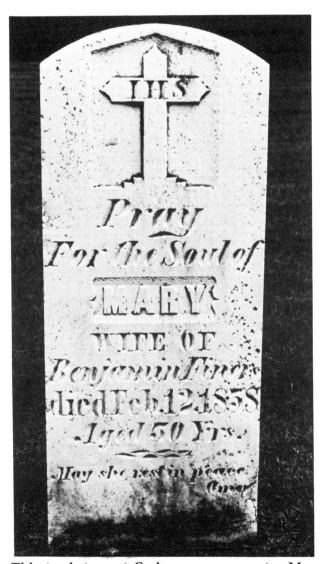

This tombstone at Corkery commemorates Mary Mantil, the wife of Benjamin Finner. Note that the age on the stone does not agree with the age given on the ship's list.

John Fenlon and his wife, the former Jane Mantil, and their daughters. The girls were Catherine (Mrs Tims), Anne (Mrs J.L.Meehan), Mary Veronica (Mrs M.J. Gannon) and Rosemary.

Seven Lunney brothers, circa 1938, sons of James and Mary (Ryan) Lunney. There are also three sisters in this family. Left to right: Lawrence (school principal); Leonard, now Father Lunney of Holy Rosary, Ottawa, principal of St. Pius X and co-chaplain of the Ottawa Fire Department; Alphonse, Renfrew; William, now Father Lunney of Fitzroy; James, Renfrew; Hugh; Edmund (retired school principal.) This is a very musical family, and some of these men are also antique car buffs.

widow, Johannah Fitzgerald, nee Mantil. It is believed that this girl was connected with the other Mantils .(Mantil is a most uncommon name in these townships, and all of them are descended from the Rathcormac group).

There is no proof of this and I debated leaving her out of the book in case it is incorrect. However, since this section of the book is for the use of genealogists I have decided to include her, for the simple reason that a great number of people who married in to this family tree belong to Peter Robinson families. This means that certain later generations of this Lunney family are descended from Peter Robinson settlers.

Mara/OMara, James (mason.)
Ship:	Stakesby, 1823
Origin:	Cork City
Location:	E lot 13, con 10, Goulbourn Twp
Family:	Frances (wife)
Anne	14
Mary	2

This family arrived on their lot on October 31, 1823, receiving rations for four, plus three blankets, a camp kettle, one pan, an axe, a spade, an auger and two pounds of nails.

In 1826, James went to work as a mason at the Rideau Canal, but later returned to his farm, obtaining a Crown patent in 1836. A report of 1834 said that "he chiefly follows his trade of a mason."

In 1839, James sold this land to Michael Foley.

Mara/O'Mara, John, 42, RC
Ship:	Stakesby, 1823
Origin:	Rathcormac, Cork
Location:	lot 4, con 4, Ramsay Twp
Family:	Joanna, 36 (wife)
Mary	15
John	12
Joanna	8
Bridget	6
Thomas	5
Ellen	3

By 1826, two more births had occurred in this household. John certainly worked hard at establishing himself. By 1834 he had occupied three different farms "which he improved but had to give some up."

By 1835 he was living on lot 9, concession 9, Ramsay. The parish priest noted that the couple then had "two sons and four or five daughters". Mrs O'Mara was evidently an accomplished knitter, for in 1831 she presented a pair of "stockings" to the priest.

Mason, Ellen, 20
Ship:	Brunswick, 1825
Origin:	Charleville, Cork. (Castletownroche also given.)
Nicholas,	1

This girl presents something of a mystery. It is unlikely that a young widow, or a girl with a small brother, would have come to Canada alone. Possibly she was a sister of another family on the same ship.

Another Mason family travelled out on the ship Fortitude in 1825 but she did not appear to settle with them.

Mason, George, 48
Ship:	Fortitude, 1825
Origin:	Brigown, Cork
Location:	Asphodel Twp
Family:	James 23 (E lot 20, con 3, Asphodel)
Charles	21 (N lot 20, con 11, Asphodel)
Michael	19
Bridget	15

One member of this family died in 1826.

Meade, Richard, 38
Ship:	Fortitude, 1825
Origin:	Brigown, Cork
Location:	lot 7, con 4, Douro Twp
Family:	Julia 30
Ellen	10
Johanna	7
Mary	3

In some records, this name appears as Maid, a phonetical spelling of the Irish pronunciation.

Having managed to clear three acres of land in their first year, this family produced 150 bushels of potatoes, 50 bushels of corn and 30 lbs of maple sugar in 1826.

Mealey/ Maley, Patrick, 32, RC
Ship:	? 1823
Origin:	Castlelyons, Cork
Location:	E lot 21, con 11, Ramsay Twp.

In 1826, this man was single and "at work with a settler." He married Catherine Nelligan, the widow of another Peter Robinson settler. They are believed to have moved into Huntley Township at a later date.

Little Joe Duffus, who was descended on his mother's side from the Dorans who came on the Fortitude and the Meany family of the Brunswick.

Meany/Mearny, William, 49
Ship:	Brunswick, 1825
Origin:	Churchtown, Cork
Location:	E lot 29, con 11, Otonabee Twp.
Family:	Ellen, 19
Jane	17
John	16

Meehan, John, RC, 24
Ship:	Hebe, 1823
Origin:	Churchtown, Cork
Location:	lot 18, con 10, Huntley Twp.
Family:	Honorah (wife)
Mary	

By 1826, a second child had been born to this couple, and there had been one death. In due course John Meehan sold his farm to Timothy Forrest, and purchased another from Patrick Nelligan.

Meehan, Michael, RC, 19
Ship: Hebe, 1823
Origin;   Churchtown, Cork
Location: lot 19, con 9, Huntley.

Michael Meehan was John's brother. He stayed with that family for a time. Michael was the subject of a land dispute in the 1820s when he attempted to obtain a lot which had earlier been awarded to one William Brook. He eventually obtained lot 19 in the ninth concession.

Michael Meehan married Esther Manion. Their children and their spouses were as follows: John: 1. Johanna O'Neil; 2. Kitty O'Connell. Lawrence m. Elizabeth Lindsay. Andrew m. Ann Lindsay. Patrick m. Jane O'Keefe. Edward; Michael m. Ellen Lunney. Esther m. Richard O'Connell. Margaret m. Michael O'Connell. Mary m. James Whelan; Ellen m. James Quinn.

Father John Meehan was a son of Patrick and Jane Meehan. **Father John Lawrence Meehan** was a grandson of John and Kitty.

In this family, three of the children of Michael Meehan married three of the children of another Peter Robinson settler, William O'Connell.

Miles/Myles, Thomas, 35, shoemaker
Ship   Brunswick, 1825
Origin   Doneraile, Cork
Location   lot 19, con 6, Asphodel

This tombstone in St.Michael's cemetery, Corkery, shows the surnames of several families who came from Ireland in 1823.

Memorial to John Meehan and his wife, Kitty O'Connell. Both were the children of Peter Robinson settlers.

Family   Honorah, 30
Michael   11
Anne   9 (m. Michael Shea)
Jeremiah   3
Catherine   2

In the spring of 1826, these people made 25 pounds of maple sugar. That year they raised several types of vegetables, including 200 bushels of potatoes. They were still on the same lot in 1838, including Michael, who owned his own farm, and there were now seven in this family.

117

Once the home of Edward Morrissey, this house is on lot 14, concession 9, Emily Township. One of the oldest houses in the township, it is now the home of Mr and Mrs Harold Lynne.

John Sr. suffered with the ague in the summer of 1826. At that time, Thomas was still living with his parents. There was one birth and one death in 1826, the death listed as "John, 14, drowned in the rapids May 21, 1826." Two years later, Thomas was working as an assessor in Douro.

Miller, George, 31

Ship:	Star, 1825
Origin:	Adare, Limerick
Location:	N lot 18, con 4, Emily Twp
Family:	Anne, 28
Eliza	5
Catherine	2

These people were most likely the descendants of the Palatine settlers of County Limerick.

Molony, John, 50

Ship:	Fortitude, 1825
Origin:	Brigown, Cork
Location:	W lot 10, con 1, Douro Twp
Family:	Margaret, 40
Thomas	24 (E lot 10)
Catherine	19
Mary	17
Denis	14
Michael	12
John	10
James	8
Edmond	4

Morrissey, John, 40

Ship:	Star, 1825
Origin:	Croom, Limerick
Location:	N lot 14, con 9, Emily Twp
Family:	Catherine, 34
John	17
Mary	13
Bridget	11
Edward	8
Margaret	5
Daniel	5
Anne,	baby.

John Morrissey Sr. died in Emily September 9, 1826. His baby daughter Anne was born on St.Patrick's Day of that same year.

Mulcahey, William, 39

Ship:	John Barry, 1825
Origin:	Caherlogga? Cork
Location:	W lot 1, con 6, Emily Twp
Family:	Mary, 38
David	17 (E lot 3, con 5)
Michael	15

Patrick   12
Elizabeth   8
William   4

Ship's notes: "a good, quiet family."

Mullane, Jeremiah, RC
Ship: Hebe, 1823
Origin: Ballyghiblin, Cork
Location: lot 13, con 10, Ramsay Twp
Family: Johanna (wife)

1826 report: "gone to the USA."

Mullane, Michael, 43
Ship: Star, 1825
Origin: Adare, Limerick
Location: W lot 15, con 10, Asphodel
Family: Catherine, 42
Maurice   20, E 13, con 10
William   18 , E lot 15, con 10
Michael   16
Thomas   13
Mary   11
Denis   9

In 1826 this family produced 400 bushels of potatoes, 100 bushels of turnips, 90 bushels of corn and an incredible 220 pounds of maple sugar.

Some years later, Nicholas Keating (listed earlier under his own name and also with the English family) was "living with Mr Mullins" (sic) perhaps as a hired man?

Murphy, Bartholomew, 22, RC
Ship: Stakesby, 1823
Origin: Clogheen, Tipperary
Location: E. lot 13, con 6, Ramsay Twp

"Batt" Murphy was the leader of the Ballyghiblins in 1824. His land was in the Wolves' Grove area of Ramsay, and later owned by Michael Foley, son-in-law to Michael Corkery. Batt Murphy went to work on the canal at Kingston and was drowned there in October, 1825.

Murphy, Denis,
Ship: Hebe, 1823
Origin: Doneraile, Cork (born Churchtown)
Location: W lot 6, con 10, Goulbourn Twp
Family: Margaret (his mother)
Patrick   (his brother) W lot 6, con 11
Joanna   18
Bartholomew   16
Margaret   14

All this family lived with Denis in the early days, with the exception of Patrick, who had his own place.

Murphy, Edmond, 55
Ship: Fortitude, 1825
Origin: Templetenny, Tipperary
Location: Marmora Twp
Family: Mary, 52
Denis   27 (S lot 1, con 2, Marmora Twp
Patrick   25
Jeremiah   22
Margaret   20
Mary   18
Alicia   16

In 1826, five members of this family were living on the farm allocated to Denis Murphy. Three people had died since coming to Canada. One of these deaths was Edmond who died in Ennismore soon after their arrival; another may have been Patrick, as he was not allocated land in the district.

Murphy, Jeremiah, 35.
Ship: Brunswick, 1825
Origin: Kilbehenny, Cork
Location: W lot 19, con 11, Emily Twp
Family: Susan, 30
Charles   8
John   5

Murphy, John.
Location: N lot 3, con 7, Emily Twp.
No other information, except that in 1826 he was a labourer, living with the Richard Sullivan family.

Murphy, Patrick, 32
Ship: Elizabeth, 1825
Origin: Newmarket, Cork
Location: lot 8, con 9, Ennismore Twp
Family: Ellen, 40
Thomas   7
Ellen,   baby

Patrick died within a few years of his arrival and Thomas eventually inherited this farm. The family was still in the township at the time of the 1851 census, with Ellen shown as a 60 year old widow, living with Thomas and his family.

Murphy, William, 44
Ship: Brunswick, 1825
Origin: Buttevant, Cork
Location: lot 19, con 1, Asphodel Twp
Family: Ellen, 40
Honora   20
John   16 (Sw 1/4, lot 19, con 2)
Anne   12
Catherine   9

In 1851, Ellen Murphy was a widow, living with her son John and daughter, Catherine.

Margaret Carroll, who became Sister St. Wilfred. A daughter of Wilfred Carroll and Elizabeth O'Donoghue and a descendant of Martin McAuliffe who came on the Fortitude.

Tombstone of Martin McAuliffe Jr. He came from Ireland in the ship Fortitude in 1825.

Murray, Thomas, 35
Ship:	Amity, 1825
Origin:	Templetenny, Tipperary
Location:	lot 32, con 8, Otonabee Twp
Family:	Honora, 30
Judith	14
Margaret	12
Mary	9
Catherine,	born August 9, 1826, Otonabee.

Born in Canada:
John
Honora
Ellen.

Ship's notes: "a well disposed, honest, indolent man."

In 1826 this family raised 200 bushels of potatoes, 200 bushels of turnips and 60 bushels of corn; they made 40 pounds of maple sugar, and they owned a cow.

McAuliffe.

In years gone by, the name McAuliffe was seldom found outside County Cork. Long ago, their chief resided at Castle McAuliffe at Newmarket, Cork, and it is interesting to note that some of the McAuliffes who came out with Peter Robinson were from that part of Ireland.

McAuliffe, Cornelius, 32
Ship:	John Barry, 1825
Origin:	Churchtown, Cork
Location:	lot 20, con 9, Emily Twp
Family:	Ellen, 26
Johanna	15
Mary	13
James	12
Owen	6

Cornelius McAuliffe, alias **John Leary.**
Ship's notes: "a quiet family."

McAuliffe, Garrett, 22
Ship:	Hebe, 1823
Origin:	Newmarket, Cork
Location:	No record. He may have been one of

the bachelors hired by Robinson to work out of the Shipman's Mills depot, and located later.

For many years there were McAuliffes in the Almonte area. Also, a man named Garrett McAuliffe was an early settler in Bastard Township, where he first lived in the eighth, and later the tenth concession.

McAuliffe, Martin, 44
Ship:	Fortitude, 1825
Origin:	Kilworth, Cork
Location:	W lot 20, con 9, Emily Twp
Family:	Catherine, 44

Martin	24	E lot 20, con 9
Michael	22	W lot 20, con 9
Catherine	20	
Margaret	18	
John	14	
Ellen	5	

Martin McAuliffe Jr. later moved to Ennismore. He married Mary Leonard and had nine children. Michael also had nine children; his wife was Mary Madden. Catherine married Daniel Boyle; Ellen married Patrick Leonard and had twelve children.

Martin McAuliffe Jr.

How often do we wonder just what our ancestors were really like? Sometimes a tantalising glimpse may be afforded through some item of family folk-lore, yet this does not give us a three dimensional picture. However, the character of Martin McAuliffe comes vividly alive through a notation made by Father Keilty in the register of St.Martin's church, Ennismore, when he buried Martin in 1886.

"March 28th the undersigned priest interred the remains of Martin McAuliffe aged 87 years. During all his life he commanded the respect and goodwill of all who knew him. He was a magistrate and as such, or in his private capacity, all his efforts made for peace among neighbours. He acted as treasurer of the committee when the church was being built under Father Coyle, and the priest's house under Father Keilty.

There was a very large funeral - people coming from Peterborough, Emily and Omemee. Father Keilty passed a glowing eulofium on the deceased, saying that every priest who had known him, loved him, and that the parish would hardly ever look on his like again." W.J.Keilty.
"Martin McAuliffe: in every sense of the word patriarch of the parish - peace to his ashes!"

McCann, John
Ship:	Hebe, 1823
Origin:	Croom, Limerick
Location:	lot 2, con 2, Lanark Twp
1834 report: "absent."

McCarroll/Carroll John, 45
Ship:	Star, 1825
Origin:	Adare, Limerick
Location:	S lot 18, con 3, Emily Twp
Family:	Eliza, 38
James	24 (S lot 10, con 5, Emily Twp.)
Rebecca	22
Eliza	20
Catherine	18
Martha	16
William	15

Jane	13
Vaisey	11 (boy)
John	5

John died In Emily September 30, 1826. I am not sure whether this is the father or the son.

McCarthy, Charles, 27
Ship:	Stakesby, 1823
Origin:	Rathkeale, Limerick
Location:	W lot 4, con 10, Goulbourn Twp

1826: "at work in Kingston, his lot let upon shares." Soon afterwards, this man moved to "Peterborough, Newcastle District."

Later, a man of this name is shown as a Peter Robinson settler at East lot 19, concession 6, Asphodel Township. This is something of a mystery if it was the same Charles as five people are listed in the family.

McCarthy, Denis, 50
Ship:	Fortitude, 1825
Origin:	Brigown, Cork
Location:	W lot 8, con 6, Douro Twp
Family:	Johanna, 42
Mary	21
Owen	17 (died Douro, 1826)
Patrick	16
John	14
William	12
Joanna	10
Ellen	8

This household was one of the stations where mass was held in the township before the church was built.

In 1826 this family produced 500 bushels of potatoes and 75 bushels of corn. They owned a cow.

McCarthy, James, 35
Ship:	Resolution, 1825
Origin:	Glounthane, Cork
Location:	W lot 10, con 5, Douro Twp
Family:	Mary, 34
James	9
Thomas	6
John	4
Mary	2 (died on land.)

There were three deaths in this family by 1827, and one new birth.

McCarthy, Jeremiah, 45
Ship:	Elizabeth, 1825
Origin:	Abbeymahon, Cork
Location:	N lot 25, con 12, Smith Twp
Family:	Elizabeth, 45

Catherine   19
Elinor   17
Abigail   15
Mary   13
Eliza   10

1827 report: "ague during the summer" of 1826. One of the girls may have married soon after arriving, as only six people are listed in that 1827 report, and nobody had died.

In 1825, the family was met at the boat by a woman, name not given, who had already been in Canada and who travelled with them to Smith. This could have been one of the elder girls listed here as we know that some of the ships' notes were completed some time after the people arrived here. Some of the surgeons, whose job it was to write these reports, travelled to Peterborough with the 1825 group.

If this daughter was already married, or working elsewhere, it would account for the missing person.

McCarthy/ Carty, John, RC
Ship: Hebe, 1823
Origin: Kilfinane, Limerick
Location: W lot 9, con 8, Goulbourn Twp
Family: Ellen "Nelly" (sister)

In 1826, this man was working s a labourer at Richmond, which is in Goulbourn Township.
1834 report: "also occupies a clergy reserve lot. Cleared 20 acres and has erected some good buildings."

McCarthy, John
Ship: Brunswick, 1825
Origin: Kilshany? Cork (hard to read.)
Location: W lot 13, con 10, Emily Twp
Family: Margaret 35
Florence   20 (W lot 13, con 11, Emily)
Michael   15
Charles   11
James   9
Owen   7
Margaret   2

Florence was a man. An explanation of this name is given earlier in the book. In 18126 there was a birth and a death in this household, and these people had ague all summer.

McCarthy, Michael
Ship: Hebe, 1823
Location: "stopped at Montreal"
Family: Catherine

McCarthy, Owen, 38
Ship: Amity, 1825

Origin: Caheragh, Cork
Location: S lot 7, con 4, Ennismore Twp
Family: Margaret, 36
Margaret   16 (m. Herlihy)
Catherine   15 (m.Costello)
Mary   14 (m. Gorman)
Michael   13
Jeremiah   9 (m. Mary O'Donoghue)
James   6
Johannah   2 (m.Moloney)

Ship's notes: "a good, industrious man, and a very well-conducted family."

Other children were born to this family in Upper Canada. This home was visited by Sir Peregrine Maitland when government dignitaries went to view the Peterborough settlement soon after the families located.

This family worked hard in their first year on the land.In 1826 they produced 200 bushels of potatoes, 100 bushels of turnips, 60 bushels of corn, and 50 lbs of maple sugar. This is far more than we would think of growing for one family today, but we must remember that these vegetables formed the staple diet of the Irish pioneers. They had to have produce that would keep from one growing season to the next.

Letter to Peter Robinson, 1824.
Sir:

I beg leave to solicit your attention to the application of the bearer, Owen Carthy and Patrick Twomey, who are candidates for emigrating to Upper Canada with their families under your protection.

The excessive population of this little island from many causes induces me to forward the wishes of these poor people, and indeed, Sir, you have yourself from your kindness to those persons who went from hence last year very much increased the anxiety of the people here to embark under your auspices, and for each conduct I am with many others most thankful.

The persons I have recommended in this letter are orderly industrious men and I think would be useful characters in the establishment of a young colony.

I am Sir
Your very obedient Servant,
S.W.Hoare, Capt. RN, Justice of Peace, County of Cork.

McCarthy/ Carthy, Thomas, 28
Ship: Fortitude, 1825
Origin: Kilworth, Cork
Location: W lot 21, con 8, Smith Twp
Family: Mary, 24
Ellen   2
Michael   1
Jane   17 (sister to Mary McCarthy.)

Weekly Despatch, 1847.
Married Thursday January 28, 1847, by the Rev. J.Butler, Mr Redmond McGrath of Ennismore to Ellen, eldest daughter of Mr Thomas McCarthy of Emily.

McCarthy, Thomas, 40

Ship:	Elizabeth, 1825
Origin:	Abbeymahon, Cork
Location:	S lot 23, con 11, Smith Twp
Family:	Johanna 40
Denis	19 (N lot 27, con 11)
Catherine	16
Jeremiah	13

One member of this family had died by 1827.

Denis McCarthy initially resided with his parents. This often happened in the case of young single men who had come out with families. Houses were put up under the guidance of experienced men, and probably the rule was one to a family at first, time and labour being in short supply.

McCarthy, Timothy, 26

Ship:	Elizabeth, 1825
Origin:	Knockatemple, Cork
Location:	unknown.
Family:	Bridget, 20

Could this be the Bridget McCarthy who was living with the Henry Gardiner family in Smith Township in 1827?

McConnell, James,

Ship:	Stakesby, 1823
Origin:	Rathkeale, Limerick
Location:	E lot 4, con 11 Goulbourn Twp

"Drowned in June, 1825"

I am going to mention something here which strikes me as strange, because it may be of use to researchers. In 1825, a family named O'Connell (Connell in the ship's list) settled on lot one, concession 10, Goulbourn Township. This is very close to the land allocated to James.

An official record says that their son Michael was drowned circa 1825. There is also a record which says that James drowned at this time. This seems to be a curious coincidence. It leads to some speculation. Could James have been a son of William O'Connell? Was there one drowning, or two? James and William did not originate from the same place, although this is not significant because as I keep pointing out, people registered at official centres which were not necessarily in their home districts.

James McConnell has appeared in some modern lists as McDonnell, but I have checked the original location lists and it is clearly the former.

McDonnell, William, 34, shoemaker

Ship:	Albion, 1825
Origin:	Doneraile, Cork
Location:	N lot 21, con 4, Smith Twp
Family:	Mary, 32
John	16
William	14
Alexander	11
Charles	8
Patrick	5
Michael	3
Deborah	born at Lachine.

Ship's notes: "well behaved"
In the summer of 1826, these people suffered from the ague.

In the 1851 census for this township we can see Patrick and William Jr, with wives and young families.

McGrath, James

Ship:	Brunswick, 1825
Origin:	Kilworth, Cork
Location:	unknown

McGrath, James, RC

Ship:	Stakesby, 1823
Origin:	Clogheen, Tipperary
Location:	W lot 19, con 10, Huntley Twp
Family:	Mary

James McGrath, alias **James Keeler**. Birthplace Ballyghiblin, Cork.
1826 report: "at work on the canal."

McGrath/ McCraith, John, 37

Ship:	Resolution, 1825
Origin:	Brigown, Cork
Location:	E lot 15, con 16 Otonabee
Family:	Mary, 34
Ellen	14
John	12
Daniel	10
Mary	8 (died Oct. 12, 1826)
Catherine	4
Baby	

This family remained in the township, and John and Mary, age 66 and 60, may be seen in the 1851 census. Daniel and his family lived nearby.

McGrath, John , 28

Ship:	Brunswick, 1825
Origin:	Kilworth, Cork
Location:	N lot 23, con 7, Emily Twp
Family:	Ellen, 25
John	4
Redmond	1 (m. Ellen McCarthy)

In 1826 this family grew 200 bushels of potatoes, 100 bushels of turnips and 15 bushels of corn. They made 80 lbs of maple syrup.

McGrath, Luke, RC
Ship: Stakesby, 1823
Origin: Clogheen, Tipperary
Location: E lot 19, con 11, Huntley Twp.

Luke McGrath, alias **James Landrigan or Lonergan**, was a brother to James McGrath.
Luke played a leading role in the Ballyghiblin riots of 1824. In 1826 he was listed variously as "at work on the canal" and "labourer, at work in the country."

McGrath/McCraith, Thomas, 35
Ship: Resolution, 1825
Origin: Castlelyons, Cork
Location: W lot 15, con 16, Otonabee Twp
Family: Margaret, 28
Redmond   3
Catherine   Neville, 18 (sister)

Ship's notes: "one child born, two children died. " Thomas died on Monday, July 10, 1826, in Otonabee. The family had cleared one and a half acres of land but did not plant a crop that summer.

McGuire, James, carpenter
Ship: Brunswick, 1825
Origin: Mallow, Cork
Location: E lot 17, con 11, Ops Twp
Family: Hannah 32
Margaret   12
Hannah   6
William   3

By 1826 another child had been born, and one had died.
James had not cleared any land at that point, but had been "working at his trade."
Note for researchers: Hannah was usually a short form of Johanna.

McKoy, John, 27
Ship: Resolution, 1825
Origin: Doneraile, Cork
Location: E lot 28, con 4, Otonabee Twp
Family: Catherine, 24
Ellen   7
James   5
Catherine   2

Ship's notes: "one woman, one child dead." John not only suffered this bereavement, but he also suffered with ague during the summer of 1826. Despite these handicaps he was able to clear eight acres of land and he harvested a creditable amount of produce, including 40 pounds of maple sugar.

McMahon, Denis, 42
Ship: Star, 1825
Origin: Newmarket, Cork
Location: E lot 16, con 3, Asphodel Twp
Family: Mary, 38
Matthew   20
Timothy   17
Murtough,   14
James   12
Catherine   19
Mary   6

A report of 1827 states that "Martin" was living with his father. He and Matthew were probably one and the same. In 1826 this family was quite prosperous. They owned two cows, two pigs and a team of oxen. They raised a large amount of produce in that year, including an amazing 800 bushels of potatoes.

McNamara, Matthew, 22
Ship: Stakesby, 1823
Origin: Mallow, Cork
Location: unknown. Possible one of the single men employed by Robinson at the Shipman's Mills depot and located later.

Nagle, David, 37
Ship: Albion, 1825
Origin: Monanimy (Mallow district) Cork
Location: lot 17, con 5, Bathurst Twp.
Family: Julia, 30
Richard   16
Patrick   15
Ellen   13
John   10
Garrett   7
Margaret   5

Ship's notes: "well behaved." Re Patrick: "found on board after we sailed, but not victualled at sea." In other words, a stowaway who had to share his family's rations. Note that if 30 was Julia's true age, she could not have been the natural mother of the older children.
David Nagle was a brother of an 1823 settler, Michael Nagle, and he settled within two farms of him in Bathurst Township, in what is now Lanark County.

Nagle, David
Ship: John Barry, 1825
Origin: Mitchelstown, Cork
Family: Wife.
Location: not given. It is possible that he was the David Nagle who settled in the same concession of Bathurst Township as the David Nagle just listed, and Michael Nagle who settled in 1823.

David's problem was that he had worked as an agent for a landlord. This was honest work, which he had no doubt accepted in order to feed his family, but agents were unpopular people in Ireland because they collected the rents for the landlords, and were sometimes required to evict those whose rent was in arrears.

When applying to come to Canada, David Nagle had explained that the Whiteboys were after him, and he was afraid that he or his family would be harmed by them. This was no idle fear.

The Whiteboys were a secret society, basically an agrarian movement, in the province of Munster. The members, bound by an oath, abhorred a system where the majority of people were labourers or tenant farmers, at the mercy of landlords who were often unscrupulous. They had no faith in the law as a means of seeking redress for wrongs done to them, and their activities ranged from simple non-co-operation to occasional bouts of intimidation and arson.

As an example of the wrongs done to tenants, we can consider the case of one man who applied to Robinson for passage to Canada. Despite the fact that he had paid his rent, he was evicted from his home because the landlord wanted to extend his own lawn, and the man's cottage was in the way.

The Whiteboys were denounced by the Catholic Church and some members were excommunicated, but it did not make much difference to their activities. Indeed, in difficult times, people tended to obey the law of the Whiteboys rather than the law of the land.

While landlords and agents were often the target of the Whiteboys, they were even more militant against the tithe proctors, men who had to collect a tax for the Church of Ireland from all citizens, regardless of religious affiliation.

Nagle, Garrett, RC

Ship:	Hebe, 1823
Origin:	Fermoy, Cork
Location:	lot 27, con 10, Ramsay Twp.
Family:	Honorah, wife (nee Monaghan)
Gerrard	18 E lot 26, con 9
Richard	16
John	13
Patrick	10
Michael	8 (later lot 21, con 10)
Mary Anne	6
James	3

Born in Canada
Onagh Teresa (Sister St.Gregory)

1826 report: 11 in family, including two births. In their first two years on the land this family produced, among other things, 800 bushels of potatoes.

By 1834, Garrett was found to be "in prosperous circumstances" and his son Gerrard had moved to his own farm and had built "an excellent frame house."

At least seven nuns were descended from Garrett and Honorah. They include **Sister St.Gregory** of the Holy Cross (Onagh Nagle) a daughter of Garrett; four daughters of Gerrard Nagle: **Sister Mary Gabriel** of the Holy Names of Jesus and Mary (Mary Teresa Nagle, 1841-1879) **Sister Marie Ange,** Presentation Order (Ellen Teresa Nagle, 1845-1867); **Sister Geraldine of St.Joseph** of the Holy Names of Jesus and Mary (Louisa Geraldine Nagle, 1849- 1893) and **Mother St.Agnes** OSU of the Ursuline monastery at Quebec City, (Grace Marie du Rosaire Nagle, 1856-1946.)
Sister St.Joseph, Order of the Daughters of the Cross, St.Norbert, Man., who died in 1930, was the daughter of Mr and Mrs J.J.Nagle.

Then there is **Sister Nano Nagle,** PBVM, the former Nano Nagle of Saskatoon, who is a great-great granddaughter of Garrett Nagle. These Nagles are related to Nano Nagle, 1719-1784, foundress of the Presentation Order.

Father Terence Gallagher, SFM, is another descendant of this family, a son of Edmund Gallagher and his wife, the former Mary Nagle McGuire. Father Gallagher was ordained a priest of the Scarborough Foreign Mission Society on August 6, 1966, at Our Lady Queen of the World Cathedral, Montreal, and he celebrated his first Mass at Pointe Claire the following day.

Father Gallagher, a graduate of the University of Ottawa and of St.Mary's, Halifax, has six years' mission experience in the Phillipines and has also served in the Dominican Republic. He is now working in a Toronto parish, and until recently he was co-ordinator of a team which was responsible for the training of both lay people and priest candidates for missions in third world countries

Honorah Monaghan Nagle.

It is interesting to note that Honorah Monaghan Nagle was related to Patrick Sarsfield, Earl of Lucan. For this reason, many Nagle descendants have been given the name Sarsfield. At the time of the War of the Two Kings, another high-ranking officer in King James' army was one Sir Richard Nagle, who certainly knew the Earl well. Whether there was also a family connection at that point, we cannot say.

Gerrard Nagle was about 18 years of age when he left Ireland with his family. For the first few years he lived with his parents in the Blakeney district, but he moved to his own lot, just across the Mississippi from their farm, shortly before marrying a neighbour, Margaret Stevenson, another Robinson settler. Margaret died after they had established a large family, and he then married her sister Mary.

Within a few years Gerrard Nagle was working as a surveyor, establishing a road through the

Some members of the first generation to be born in Canada: Jack, Gerald, Edmund and Parker Nagle, grandsons of Garrett Nagle.

Upper Ottawa Valley, an area which was rich in white pine, valued in the lumber trade. In 1845, for example, one T.C.Keefer noted that " Mr Nagle is engaged in chaining and marking the new line of road established by me between Bytown and the Boncher. (Sic. This is the Bonnechere River in Renfrew County.) He has reached the Madawaska and will probably abandon it on account of the deep snow and frost."

Having made his way up almost to the limits of what today is Algonquin Park, Gerrard established himself at Calumet Island, from where he supervised the construction of timber slides on the Ottawa River. His family lived with him there, and a stone house was built for them, which was still there until a few years ago.

Next, these Nagles moved to Ste. Hyacinthe, where Gerrard served as a Crown land agent. Before his arrival in the Eastern Townships he had served as Superintendent of Public Works under the Baldwin ministry. He was a man of many talents. He once worked as an undertaker, and he must also have possessed some medical skill for he was listed as a

doctor on the baptismal certificate of one of his daughters.

Came the day when Gerrard Nagle turned 66. Most of us retire at that age, but, having moved to Rock Forest near Sherbrooke, Gerrard turned to other things. As his obituary later recorded: "here, although advanced in years, he did not remain idle. Opposite his dwelling was a magnificent water power. To build a dam and erect there a sawmill and a flour mill was the most natural thing in the world."

" Later, fire destroyed the establishment, but quite a bit of it remains much the same; some fine cleared farms, satisfied colonists, a post office, a school house and soon, we hope, the colony will have a church bestowed on it by the Diocesan Bishop. This is what our old friend has accomplished in Orford...it was he who put the schools of the district on a decent footing. How much effort, how many nights did he give over to this task, pleasing to a good natured man, but so often thankless!"

"Such has been the career of this brave Irishman, whose name will live on for a long time in the memory of his generation, and for whom it is fitting that he be placed in the front ranks of self-made men of our own times. It is not essential to be a prince or a politician to be useful to one's country."

This is the story of Gerrard Nagle. He died in 1884, at a time when ethnic and religious differences often caused hostility. When he died, the editor of an area newspaper reported that the six pallbearers included "two English Protestants, two Irish Catholics and two French Canadians. The deceased united us, perforce, and in spite of ourselves. May we learn how to live united and as brothers."

The other children of Garrett and Honorah Nagle married as follows: Richard m. Mary Madden, PR; William m. Eliza Jane Nugent; Patrick m. Katherine Leahy, PR; Michael Dominic m. 1. Helen O'Brien; 2. Ellen Burke; James m. Mary Anne Cavanaugh; Mary Anne was a Mrs MacGregor. John Nagle died at the age of 25 years.

William Nagle, newspaperman.

Like his famous countryman, Thomas D'Arcy McGee, William H.Nagle was a newspaperman. Like McGee, he died an untimely death, although it was consumption which carried him off, rather than an assassin's bullet.

William was a son of Richard Nagle and Mary Madden, a grandson of four Peter Robinson settlers. At one time, he published The Ottawa Herald. Then he went out to Manitoba, where he ran The Winnipeg Sun. During the boom days he became a wealthy man, well known in Winnipeg.

At the time of William Nagle's death, an American newspaper commented that "he made heaps of money... money flowed in upon him with little exertion and it was a common thing to see him strolling down Main Street with his pockets full of twenties." When he was on the point of becoming a millionaire his luck changed, and soon he had little to show for his years of hard work.

He contracted tuberculosis and so moved to Denver, Colorado, in the hope that the climate would improve his health. While there, he was connected with the Hotel Bulletin and the Denver Evening Star. He died in 1890.

Nagles in the news.
Bathurst Courier, 1835.
Mr Garret Nagle of Ramsay has a ewe that had two lambs on the 24th of March and then on the 29th of June (three months) had another, which are all alive and thriving.

Almonte Gazette, 1874.
Saw mill for sale.
The undersigned offers for sale his saw mill with three acres of land, situated on lot two, concession 11, Huntley. For further particulars, apply to the undersigned, Michael Dominic Nagle, Huntley, March 24.

Miss O. Nagle proposes opening a select school, to commence on or about the third day of August, provided she succeeds in obtaining a sufficient number of scholars, say 20 or 25. She will also continue her music class as heretofore. Terms, one dollar per month, music extra. Parents who do not wish to send their children to the overcrowded public or separate schools will no doubt embrace this opportunity. Miss Nagle is in every respect competent for the position of teacher.

Miss O.Nagle will commence school on Wednesday, the fifth of August. Rooms on Bridge Street opposite the Catholic Church. In addition to her day school she will also hold night school, commencing at 7.30 p.m.

Almonte Gazette, April 1898.
Mr R.F.Nagle has had several letters from his son, Charles, who is on his way to the Klondike. They show that he is making good progress, and the world through which he is passing is an entirely new one to him.

Nagle, John, 40

Ship:	Elizabeth, 1825
Origin:	Tullow, Cork
Location:	N lot 8, con 9, Emily Twp
Family:	Catherine, 40
Catherine	24
Patrick	19 (S lot 8, con 9)
Mary	14

1826: Patrick was living with his father; John was "very ill."

Nagle, Michael, 35, RC

Ship:	Stakesby, 1823
Origin:	Mallow, Cork
Location:	lot 19, con 5, Bathurst Twp
Family:	Mary, 32 (wife)
David	10
Ellen	8
Mary	6
Maurice	3

Michael was a brother of David Nagle, an 1825 settler.

1834 report: "East half lot 19, concession 8, Bathurst Township. This is a mistake as it is the E 19 on the fifth he has occupied. He also occupies a clergy lot which he has improved considerably but had to give it up, it being disputed land."

This was evidently a family with a good garden as in the fall of 1835 Mary was able to give the parish priest a gift consisting of " six cabbages, about a peck of onions and carrots and some beats." sic.

That spring they had paid their church dues with Mary donating five and a half pounds of maple sugar and two dozen eggs, and her husband handing over "224 pounds good wheat."

Nelligan, Patrick, 23
Ship: Stakesby, 1823
Origin: Doneraile, Cork
Location: lot 18, con 4, Ramsay Twp
Later, lot 17, con 10, Huntley Twp

Patrick came out as a single man, but must have married soon after his arrival, for the 1826 report shows him as one of a couple. By 1834, his Huntley lot was occupied by John Meehan, another Robinson settler.

Nelligan, Thomas, 32, wheelwright.
Ship: Brunswick, 1825
Origin: Doneraile, Cork
Location: lot 22, con 10, Ramsay Twp.
Family: Catherine, 27
William   6
Mary   4

This man appears to have been a relative of Patrick Nelligan. Thomas died in 1826. His widow, left with young children to support, married another Peter Robinson settler, Patrick Healey, and they continued to reside on the Nelligan farm, which later went to William Nelligan.

Nunan, Charles, 45
Ship: Brunswick, 1825
Origin: Kanturk, Cork
Location: Verulam Twp
Johanna   21
Ellen   19
James   17
Jeffrey   15
Margaret   13
Nancy   10
William   6
Jeremiah   3

Nunan, John, 22
Ship: Stakesby, 1823
Origin: Mallow, Cork
Location: lot 18, con 9, Huntley Twp
Family: Katherine ,22
Mary,   3 months.

1826 report: "absent without leave, but supposed to be in Canada."

Oakley, William, 30
Ship: Amity, 1825
Origin: Templetenny, Tipperary
Location: lot 22, con 7, Verulam Twp
Family: Catherine, 24
Grace   24
John   22

Reference, written at Kingston, July 14, 1825 by ship's surgeon James McTernan, RN, to Peter Robinson:
"Dear Sir:
    Hearing that you have it in contemplation to give employment to shoemakers of good character, I beg to recommend William Oakley who came with me in the Amity, as one deserving encouragement and every indulgence which upright conduct and honest principles can give him claim to."

Ormsby, Andrew, 40, shoemaker.
Ship: Elizabeth, 1825
Origin: Liscarrol, Cork
Location: lot 3, con 5, Emily Twp
Family: Margaret, 40
George   20 (lot 6, con 5)
Margaret   12

Owens, David, 45, carpenter.
Ship: John Barry, 1825
Origin: Tomfinlough, Clare
Location,   E lot 19, con 12, Emily Twp
Family: Bridget, 36
John   20 (W lot 19, con 12)
Richard   18 (S lot 18, con 12)
Robert   16
Boyle   12
David   8 (m. Bridget Brennan)
Anne   6
Thomas   1
Richard Owens was also a carpenter.

1826 report: "family sick all summer."
They grew 200 bushels of potatoes and 30 bushels of corn that year, and made 30 lbs maple sugar.

    When David Owens applied to bring his family to Upper Canada in 1825, he stood a good chance of being accepted. He was a discharged soldier, with proven allegiance to the Crown. In his application he explained that he had served as a private soldier, rising to the rank of sergeant, under "the present Governor of Canada." (Sir Peregrine Maitland was Lieutenant-Governor of Upper Canada at that time.)

    Many Irishmen of Owens' generation had served in the British army, some in regiments which had been specially raised in Ireland. Owens said that he had left the army when numbers were reduced "during the rebellion."

    What rebellion could this have been? The great insurrection of 1798 comes first to mind, but this could hardly have been what Owens was talking about because, according to his age, he probably joined up at about that time. It could have been the rising of 1803, when Robert Emmet organized Irishmen to protest the Act of Union which had bound Ireland to the United Kingdom in January, 1801.

    In April, 1825, Owens was given a recommendation by his employer, Lt.Col. John

Vandeleur of Newmarket-on-Fergus, County Clare, which said that Owens had "worked on my estate for the past twenty years, understands farming and is honest and sober." (Incidentally, some of the Owens children were born at Newmarket.)

In 1826, the Owens family had a miserable introduction to their new country; a government report, sent to England in 1827, noted that the family was sick all summer. Dogged persistence enabled them to raise 200 bushels of potatoes and 30 bushels of corn, and they made 30 pounds of maple sugar in the spring.

When you consider that it takes approximately 40 gallons of sap to make one gallon of syrup, and that sugar is made by boiling the syrup down still further, it is clear that the manufacture of so much sugar entailed a great deal of walking about with heavy pails; hard work, even for so large a family. At that time, the Owens family had no oxen to help them, so all the hauling was done by hand, a mammoth job for healthy people, let alone those suffering from the ague.

Some descendants of this family now live in Saskatchewan, while another is the Dean of a college in the State of Michigan.

Phelan, John, 37

Ship:	Stakesby, 1823
Origin:	Killmore, Tipperary
Location:	lot 18, con 1, Ramsay Twp
Family:	Katherine, 35 (wife)
Denis	14
Michael	9
Ellen	7
Joanna	5
John	4
Patrick	2

1826 report: one birth, one death. Sixteen acres cleared. One thousand bushels of potatoes raised in the first two growing seasons.

1834 report: "has not lived on this lot these five years. Am informed he resides in Pennsylvania. Am told he sold his lot to Mr Graham, a merchant of Perth. This is a hard case when many of our industrious settlers are struggling to make out a livelihood on some of the worst of lands. Michael Corkery petitions the Hon. Peter Robinson to get this lot for a younger son."

Pigott, William, 46

Ship:	Elizabeth, 1825
Origin:	Churchtown, Cork
Location:	E lot 5, con 11, Emily Twp
Family:	Honora, 40 (widow)
Maurice	25
Bartholomew	23 (W lot 5, con 11, Emily)
Julia	21
Ellen	19
Edmond	18 (N lot 4, con 10)
Daniel	15 (E lot 5, con 11)
John	13

William Pigott died soon after his arrival here, and his son Maurice "died on land." William's lot was reserved until Daniel should come of age, and the remaining members of the family settled on it. In 1826 they raised 500 bushels of potatoes, 250 bushels of turnips and 60 bushels of corn, and made 100 pounds of maple sugar.

This family remained in Emily Township.

Pope, James W. 36, school teacher.

Ship:	Regulus, 1825
Origin:	Listowel, Kerry
Location:	lot 9, con 4, Ennismore Twp
Family:	Catherine, 27
Alexander	19
Eliza	17
Frances	14
William	12
John	10

Some, or all, of these young people may have been siblings of the married couple, as was:

Pope, John, 26

Ship:	Regulus, 1825
Origin:	Listowel, Kerry
Location:	N lot 14, con 6, Ennismore

John's wife was Ellen Foley, another settler of 1825. From the ships' lists it is unclear whether they came out as a married couple, or married in Canada.

Power, Richard, 40

Ship:	Brunswick
Origin:	Churchtown, Cork
Location:	N lot 23, con 12, Otonabee
Family:	Frances, 40 (nee Leahy)
Ellen	21
Mary	19
Elizabeth	16 (m. Lawrence John McGuire)

Richard Power was born in Ireland circa 1785, a son of Andrew Power and Ellen Barry. In 1803 he took part in a rising led by Irish patriot Robert Emmet, protesting the Act of Union, passed two years earlier, which made Ireland part of the United Kingdom. The rebellion was short-lived and its leader was executed. Richard probably headed home immediately the trouble died down, for he then married Frances Leahy, a daughter of Thomas Leahy and Frances Byton of Buttevant. Their daughter Ellen appeared a year later.

Richard and Frances settled in Otonabee Township; three additional children were born there. Richard is said to have lived to be 108.

Their daughter Elizabeth married Lawrence McGuire, The McGuires had come to Otonabee from County Fermanagh a year before the marriage. Several of their descendants have served either Church or State. These included **Sister St.Gertrude CND (Margaret McGuire,) Father Michael McGuire** and **Senator Will McGuire.**

Purcell, Nancy, 40 (widow)

Ship:	Resolution, 1825
Origin:	Churchtown, Cork
Location:	W lot 14, con 6, Asphodel Twp
Family:	
Thomas	24
Eliza	22
Patrick	17
Margaret	15 (m. Thomas Fallon)
John	14
Daniel	13
Mary	
10 (m. John O'Grady.)	

Ship's notes: "one child dead."
Nancy Purcell was still in the township at the time of the 1851 census, still a widow, listed as being age 62 years.

Quinlan, John, 35, fisherman

Ship:	Resolution, 1825
Origin:	Affane, Waterford
Location:	E lot 21, con 4, Marmora Twp
Family:	Margaret, 28
Michael	12
James	10
Catherine	6
Nancy	1

Ship's notes: "one child born." This was probably Nancy, as the "age next birthday" was usually given when ages were being noted. By 1827, however, the family numbered eight people. At that time, John was "living on land which they have engaged for."

Quinlan, Patrick, 34, sawyer

Ship:	Regulus, 1835
Origin:	Newmarket, Cork
Location:	lot 15, con 4, Asphodel Twp
Family:	Susan, 34
John	13
Ellen	11
Daniel	9
Honorah	2

One new birth in 1826.

Quinlan, Patrick, 44

Ship:	Elizabeth, 1825
Origin:	Newmarket, Cork

Location:	W lot 16, con 3, Asphodel Twp.
Family:	Johanna, 40
John	18
Patrick	16 (W lot 18, con 2)
David	14
Michael	5
Mary Brien	8 (orphan)
Judith Brien	6 (orphan)

In 1851, Patrick Quinlan Sr. was still alive, living in Asphodel with his son, Patrick Jr. His age was given as 75 years, which indicates that he docked a few years from his age when signing on to come to Canada. He would have been 49 in 1825, too old to have obtained land.

At home in·1851 were Patrick Jr. and his wife, Honora; seven sons: Patrick, William, David, John, Michael, Cornelius and Thomas, and daughters Johannah and Mary Anne. It is interesting to see how these names parallel those of the earlier generation.

Also in Asphodel at that time was David Quinlan with his wife Maria, and their children, John, Patrick, Michael, Johannah, Alice and Bridget. David may have married twice, as Alice was not old enough to have been the natural mother of John and Patrick. Furthermore, there was an eight-year age gap between Patrick and the next child, Johannah.

A distinguished decendant of this family is **Edgar Boland** of Peterborough, whose maternal grandmother was Hannah Quinlan. After he retired from teaching in 1967, Mr Boland assumed the position of historian and archivist for the Roman Catholic Diocese of Peterborough, which he held for 15 years. Some years ago, at the request of the then bishop he wrote a history of the diocese, entitled " From the Pioneers to the Seventies." It was published in 1976, and I recently saw a copy, offered for sale at the price of thirty dollars, in the catalogue of an antiquarian bookseller in Toronto. It was immediately snapped up.

Quinn, John , 40

Ship:	Fortitude, 1825
Origin:	Kilbehenny, Cork
Location:	E lot 9, con 5, Douro Twp
Family:	Johanna, 25 (died April 20, 1826)
Thomas	7
James	4
David	3
Ellen	2

David Quinn is said to have lost his eyesight while on the journey to Canada.

Quinn, Timothy 40, RC

Ship:	Stakesby, 1825
Origin:	Rathcormac, Cork
Location:	lot 4, con 4, Ramsay Twp
Family:	Mary, 28 (wife)

Katharine   5
John   3
Patrick   1 (died.)

1826 report: "Five in family; one birth, one death.
1834 report: "doing well, considering the badness of his land."

Rahilly, Thomas 36
Ship: Brunswick, 1825
Origin: Rathkeale, Limerick
Location: W lot 31, con 8, Otonabee Twp
Family: Margaret, 30
Patrick   8
Johanna   6
John   1

In 1826 there were four people in this family, one death having occurred.

Rahilly, Timothy, 40, RC
Ship: Hebe, 1823
Origin: Newmarket, Cork
Location: lot 7, con 4, Ramsay Twp
Family: Honora (wife)
Jeremiah
Patrick
Mary

In 1826 there were six in the family, including a new birth. Ten acres of land had been cleared by Timothy. The family was still on the lot at the time of the 1834 report.

Ray/Rae, James RC
Ship: Hebe, 1823
Origin: Doneraile, Cork
Location: W lot 21, con 5, Ramsay Twp.
Family: Mary (wife)
Margaret   1 year.

1826 report: four in family. Six acres cleared.
1834 report: "sold to a man named Booze (sic- Bowes) and occupied a clergy lot, hoping to better himself. Has since attempted to retract but Booze will not give it up."
1837 census: the family was still on the land, but the name was now spelled "Rae." The family consisted of the parents, four boys and three girls. Ten acres had been cleared, and the family owned a cow. Later, these people moved to Pakenham.

Researchers please note that another Irish James Rae family later came into the township, but they are not connected. Those people are buried in the old Methodist cemetery on highway 29.

Regan, Daniel, 48, RC
Ship: Stakesby, 1823

Mary Rand of Renfrew does exquisite needlework. Her beautiful quilt, made in the "violets in snow" pattern, was judged grand champion of the quilt exhibit at the 1986 Renfrew Fair, and in 1987 it was one of the finalists in the annual Canada Packers quilt competition.

Her prize-winning quilt is sure to become a treasured heirloom of the future. Its colours are mauve and green on a snow-white background, set off by a backing of deep purple. Mary has been quilting for about eight years, making both full size and crib quilts, and her work has won a number of awards, including several first place ribbons and two grand championships. Mary is a descendant of Daniel Regan, and she is married to George Rand of Renfrew.

Origin: Mallow, Cork
Location: W lot 22, con 4, Ramsay Twp
Family:
John   18
James   17
Mary   14
Katherine   12
Daniel   8

Daniel Regan was a widower when he came to Upper Canada. In 1826 there were seven people in the family, including John, a landowner in his own right who resided with his father.

The 1837 census showed them on lot 19, con 5, Ramsay Twp, with a cow, and three acres cleared. At that point the family consisted of a boy, two sons over sixteen, and one woman, who was probably Mary or Katherine. Some of this family later moved to Pakenham Township.

Included among the descendants are the well known step dancers, **Kim McWatty** and **Debbie McWatty Reid**, and there are a number of descendants in the Renfrew area who are the family of the late Patrick Regan of Ferguslea.

Regan, John, 32
Ship: Albion, 1825
Origin: Churchtown, Cork
Location: W lot 7, con 11 Emily Township.
Family: Norry, 30
Abigail   16 (alias William)
Mary   6

Researchers will have to totally disregard this list and turn to the entry for **Thomas Shenick**. This is plainly a case where people purchased tickets from another family who had changed their minds about coming. William made the voyage disguised as a girl and was quite successful at the ploy for a while The ship's surgeon later made a note : "William, victualled as a female." .

Oddly enough, he did better by drawing rations as a girl. The men received cocoa, which they heartily disliked, and cheddar cheese, which was so foreign to them that they continually threw it overboard. The women were given tea, which was much more popular.

Regan, Michael, 28, RC
Ship: Stakesby, 1823
Origin: Mallow, Cork
Location: lot 4, con 2, Ramsay Twp
1826:   "labourer, at work in the country."

Regan, Timothy, 35
Ship: John Barry, 1825
Origin: Donaghmore, Cork
Family: Catherine, 32
Patrick   16
Norah   13
Mary   10
Michael   6
Daughter,   newborn.

Ship's notes: "Timothy Regan came on board sickly. Took fever on second of June. Died at Lachine hospital. Wife took sick shortly after and produced a child on the eighth, Monday. Convalesced at Quebec. Hurried off to Lachine. Arrived Saturday evening. Took dangerously sick on Sunday and died at twelve on Tuesday. Child died, and was buried at Kingston. Two boys and two girls - very fine children - are left

orphans. I left eight dollars between them in Mr Reade's charge. Their chest, by some mistake, has been left at Quebec.

Reilly, Brian, 33, RC
Ship: Stakesby, 1823
Origin: Dundrum, Tipperary
Location: W lot 20, con 5, Ramsay Twp.

Located Sept 20, 1823; died before 1826, "killed by the fall of a tree."

Reilly, John, RC
Ship: Stakesby, 1823
Origin: Dundrum, Tipperary
Location: E lot 20, con 5, Ramsay Twp
Family: Eliza 24
Bridget   23   (Brian's sister)

At the time of the 1834 report, Mr Jessop noted that Brian Reilly, deceased, "had a brother and sister in this country of whom I can learn nothing."

These were Michael and Bridget. I don't know whether John was another brother, or perhaps a cousin.

Reilly, Michael, 28
Ship: Stakesby, 1823
Origin: Dundrum, Tipperary
Location: He lived with his brother until Brian died. He then inherited the farm, and he was still there at the time of the 1833 inspection. The adjoining farm, which had been the property of John Reilly, was owned by a Patrick Reilly in 1833.

Michael Reilly died on August second, 1865, at the age of 70 years.

Reilly/ Riley, William, 35, shoemaker
Ship: Albion, 1825
Origin: Ballyclough, Cork
Location: W lot 10, con 1, Asphodel Twp
Family: Elizabeth, 30
Thomas   13
Joseph   11
John   8
Mary   4
Jeremiah   2
Johanna   1 (died May 13, 1826)

Ship's notes: "well behaved"
Another person apparently died in 1826.
1827: "absent without leave."

Riordan/Reardon, John, 38
Ship: Brunswick, 1825
Origin: Charleville, Cork
Location: E lot 19, con 2, Asphodel Twp

Family:	Catherine,	36
Richard	19	
Catherine	17	
John	15	
Michael	12	
William	9	
Thomas	4	
Patrick	2 months.	

Despite the fact that the ague struck this family in the summer of 1826, they raised 600 bushels of potatoes, 100 bushels of turnips and made 80 lbs maple sugar. They kept a cow and two pigs.

At a later date, John Riordan had a team and he would hire out for work at a fee of seven shillings and sixpence per day.

Riordan/ Reardon, William, 22, RC
Ship:	Stakesby, 1823
Origin:	Mallow, Cork
Location:	E lot 23, con 5, Ramsay Twp

In 1826, William was still single, and he had cleared five acres.

1834 report: "had married Widow Curran and lived on and improved her son's lot, W lot 13, con 11, Ramsay until 1833, when he returned to his own." At that time, young James Curran would have been 19 years old, and eligible to own his own land. His parents were John and Sarah Curran, who had come on the Stakesby in 1823, as did his stepfather, William Riordan.

In 1837, the spelling of this name was now changed to Reardon. William had cleared sixteen acres, and had a cow and two calves.

The family now numbered eleven, and included four boys under 16, three males over 16, one girl and three women.

Ring, John, 23
Ship:	Stakesby, 1823
Origin:	Kanturk, Cork

It is not known where John Ring settled. However, at least two families called Ring, not necessarily related to him, settled in Fitzroy Township later. One of them came before 1830 and went to Huntley first, then Fitzroy, while the other came at the time of the potato famine of the 1840s.

Roche, Cornelius, RC
Ship:	Hebe, 1823
Origin:	Doneraile, Cork
Location:	lot 10, con 9, Pakenham Twp.
Family:	Bridget (wife)
John	
Denis	

Cornelius Roche was a blacksmith. Soon after his arrival he practised his trade at Shipman's Mills, now Almonte. He was unwittingly caught up in the Ballyghiblin riots of 1824; in fact it was in his house that Mass was being celebrated on the fateful Sunday when the sheriff's men from Perth fired shots through the cabin wall, killing one man and injuring others.

Both Mr and Mrs Roche were required to give evidence at the subsequent investigation of this outrage. Soon afterwards, their family moved to Montreal.

Roche, James, 20, RC
Ship:	Stakesby 1823
Origin	Doneraile, Cork
Location:	W lot 25, con 6, Ramsay Twp
Family	none

Roche, James, 39, RC
Ship:	Hebe, 1823
Origin	Clogheen, Tipperary
Location:	lot 19, con 12, Huntley Twp
Family	Nora (wife)
Ellen	9
Maurice	7
Joanna	5
Michael	2

This man's origin is also given as Doneraile, Cork.

1826 report: "seven in family, including one birth."

1834 report: "James Roach, formerly of Pakenham, patent of lot 15, con 9, Huntley Twp. Roach has since been murdered, leaving his widow the charge of a young family, the eldest of whom, a daughter, is only about 12 years old."

Roche, John, 27
Ship:	Stakesby, 1823
Origin	Charleville, Cork
Location:	lot 16, con 9, Lanark Twp.

Roche, Michael, 44
Ship:	Fortitude, 1825	
Origin	Brigown, Cork	
Location:	lot 14, con 16, Otonabee Twp	
Family:		
Maurice	23	W lot 14, con 16
Ellen	21	
Patrick	19	E lot 12, con 17
Kitty	17	
James	15	

In 1826, there were five people listed in this group; one death had occurred.

The 1851 census for this township includes a Patrick, 44, a tollkeeper, with his wife, age 32, and other family members from age 25 on down: Michael, Catherine, Ellen, Thomas, James, Mary, Patrick, Margaret and Julia.

Roche, Thomas. 26
Ship	John Barry, 1825
Origin:	Kilmoylen, Tipperary
Location:	W lot 26, con 5, Otonabee Twp
Family	Mary, 24
Catherine	5
Judith	3
John	1

Ship's notes: "a quiet family. Youngest child died at Lachine." Another member of the family died by 1827.

According to the settlement report, Thomas Roche's name was an alias; he settled under the name **James Slattery.**
Researchers may like to investigate the fact that the 1851 census does show a Thomas Roache family of the right age, including six children who were all born in Canada from about 1828 on.

Rochfort, James, 34, weaver.
Ship	Brunswick, 1825
Origin	Killhaney? Cork
Location	N lot 23, con 5, Emily Twp
Family	Bridget, 30
Peter	10
James	6
Michael	3

1826: four in family; one death.

Rourke, Patrick, RC, 24
Ship:	Hebe, 1823
Origin	Newcastle, Limerick
Location:	W lot 19, con 3, Ramsay Twp
Family	Ellen

1826 report: "three in family. Three acres cleared. Has been at work on the canal."
1834 report: "Has sold, Has always been engaged in teaching school in the neighbourhood." Patrick then located on lot 5, concession 8, Lanark Township.

Ruby, John, 17
Ship:	Stakesby, 1823
Origin:	Mallow, Cork
Location	lot 3, con 5, Pakenham Twp.

Listed as "a boy" in the 1826 return. John Ruby went to the United States. One wonders if John came out with other relatives, as it seems unlikely that a lone teenager would be considered suitable material for carving a farm out of the bush singlehandedly.

Russell, Ellen, 22
Ship	Fortitude, 1825
Origin:	Brigown, Cork

Listed with the Sargent family on the voyage.

Russell, William, 43
Ship:	Star, 1825
Origin	Charleville, Cork
Location:	W lot 18, con 7, Emily Twp.
Family:	Anne, 38
Hester	18
Cornelius	15
Anne	11
Sarah	8
Jane	6
William	2
David,	

born at Cobourg August 15, 1825.

Reference.
Maryland.
"The bearer of this, William Russell, has been in the Marquess of Thomond's employ as Gatekeeper for upwards of twelve years, during which time he has conducted himself strictly honest, and now wishes to leave his situation for the purpose of taking his family to America as a Settler."

The Russells worked equally well in Canada. In their first year on the land they produced 400 bushels of potatoes, 100 bushels of turnips and 60 bushels of corn. They made 100 pounds of maple sugar. They owned an ox and a cow.

Ryan, Cornelius, 39
Ship	Stakesby, 1823
Origin:	Mitchelstown, Cork
Location	lot 4, con 2, Ramsay Twp

This man's birthplace is given as Aylesborough, Limerick.

1826: "single, has four acres cleared. Has been at work on the canal."
1834 report: W half lot 4, concession 2. Has sold part to William Bailey. Though Ryan does not live on this lot he has always remained in the country, working for others." In that year he married Mrs Ward, the widow of David Ward.

Recommendation:
Ramsay Township, July 1827.
I came to this country from Ireland with Mr Robinson, and received rations for one year. I have now seven acres cleared, a yoke of steers, a cow and a calf. I certainly think that an industrious man may repay to the Government the expense attending his location, if they do not require it to be paid sooner than five years,

and then by installments in produce at five pounds per year. I do consider my farm worth now 80 pounds.
Cornelius Ryan X (his mark.)

Ryan, Daniel, 37

Ship:	Stakesby, 1823
Origin	Kanturk, Cork
Location	E lot 7, con 8, Ramsay Twp
Family:	Mary, 35 (wife)
Mary	12
Bridget	8

Another birth occurred after this, at which time Mary Ryan apparently died, for not long afterwards Daniel married the Widow Connor. Both had a young family to care for so no doubt the arrangement was a good one. However, it was unfortunate that Daniel was convicted of theft in 1828, and his sentence was banishment from Upper Canada. This family then went to the United States.

He may have been a brother of Cornelius Ryan, as the parish priest reported in 1825 that Mrs Cornelius Ryan was living on "Tim Connor's land, Pakenham."

Ryan, Martin, 36, RC

Ship	Stakesby, 1823
Origin	Sixmilebridge, Clare
Location	lot 22, con 2, Ramsay Twp
Family	Margaret, 30 (wife)
Michael	12
Mortimer	10
Martin	8
John	6
Katharine	4
James	2

<u>Bishop Ryan</u>

A baby boy, born in Ramsay Township to an immigrant family, grew up to become the Roman Catholic Bishop of Buffalo, New York. He was a son of Martin and Margaret Ryan, who first farmed the land around which the present village of Clayton grew up. His parents carried him to Shipman's Mills (now Almonte) for baptism.

The Ryans were hard working people, and they were fortunate enough to have two teenaged boys among their brood of seven when they arrived in Canada. Within three years of their arrival they had cleared 25 acres of land, on which they kept cattle and hogs and raised grain and garden produce.

Robinson's inspector, submitting his report in 1826, noted that there was a grist mill and a saw mill on this lot, and thereby hangs a mystery. Historians usually credit Edmund Bellamy with being the founder of Clayton; he was a Vermont man who is supposed to have built such mills on the site. For a time, the growing community was named Bellamy's Mills in his

honour, and a contemporary road, once a pioneer trail, is still known as the Bellamy Road.

What actually happened here? Ryan was on the land in 1823; Bellamy is supposed to have arrived in 1824. Did Ryan actually build the mills which Bellamy later operated, or did the American erect the buildings by mistake, not realising that Ryan owned the land?

Francis Jessop, inspecting the farm on behalf of Peter Robinson in 1834, wrote of Ryan: "left for Pennsylvania in 1828, having been induced to sell his land to Edmund Bellamy on account of a saw mill and grist mill thereon." This cryptic remark seems to indicate that the mills belonged to Bellamy, but in the meantime Ryan must have been working in good faith, for by 1828 he had cleared sixty acres of the original seventy.

In those days, farms were often the source of bitter disputes because it was sometimes hard to prove ownership before a Crown patent had been issued. Whatever the truth of the story, the Ryans moved on. Neighbours told Jessop that Martin Ryan was concerned for the future of his children because there was no means of getting an education for them in Ramsay at that time.

After they moved to the United States, ties were maintained with Lanark County. More than half a century later, Bishop Ryan paid a summer visit to Almonte, where he said Mass at St. Mary's church and reminded the congregation that he had been baptised in that same community in the days when the visiting missionary priest, Father John MacDonald of Perth, visited periodically.

In a sermon given that August day, Bishop Ryan had this to say:
"Ireland has many reasons to feel a blessed joy in the fact that her poor children, driven from their native land, have yet in all nations and places clung with fervour and devotion to the holy faith of their fathers. But if this be so, it is due almost entirely to the devotion and unselfish labours and sacrifices of the Irish priesthood. It is because Irishmen or the descendants of Ireland , endowed with those loyal and ennobling attitudes with which God, in His goodness, has blessed you... have worn out their lives in working for the ancient faith."

Ryan, Patrick, RC

Ship	Hebe, 1823
Origin	Mitchelstown, Cork
Location	lot 11, con 12, Ramsay Twp
	1826: "absent without leave."

Ryan, Patrick, 32, schoolmaster

Ship	John Barry, 1825
Origin	St. John's, Limerick

Location   S lot 7, con 10, Emily Twp
Family:
Elizabeth   21
Timothy   21 (S lot 12, con 11)
John   19
William   14
Bridget   25
Elinor   18
Patrick   2
James   1

Ship's notes: "a good man. Instrumental in saving the ship. Brothers Tim and John very troublesome."

Ryan, William
Ship: Hebe, 1823
Origin: Croom, Limerick
Location: "left at Morphy's Falls." (Now Carleton Place.)

Ryan, William, 30, weaver.
Ship   Albion, 1825
Origin   Kanturk, Cork
Location   S lot 27, con 1, Otonabee Twp
Family   Catherine, 30
Michael   13
William   5
Ellen   3
Catherine "born on land."

Ship's notes "well behaved." This family later left the settlement.

Sargent, John, 40
Ship: Fortitude, 1825
Origin: Templetenny, Tipperary
Location: W lot 28, con 10, Otonabee
Family: Alicia, 34
Thomas   17
Margaret   15
Philip   14
John   12
Jane   7
William   5
James   2
John Jr.   36
Ellen Russell,   22

In 1826, this family had one new birth, making eleven in the group. John Jr. had his own farm, but he was absent at the time. This John was a brother-in-law of John Sargent, who had come to Canada at an earlier date, joining the family in 1825.

Sayward/Seward, James, 21
Ship: Stakesby, 1823
Origin: Castletownroche, Cork
Location: E lot 4, con 4, Lanark Twp

James Sayward was a shoemaker, who left his land to work at his trade in Perth. He later took up a farm at lot 26, concession 5, Pakenham Township, for which he received a Crown patent in 1836. A government inspection report of 1834 said that he was "mostly engaged in shoemaking."

Single when he came to Canada, he later married Hannah Grady. They had six known children, whom they named Martha, Margaret, Eliza, William, James and Mary. Some of these people used the spelling Seward for their surname. Family research shows that Margaret married Robert Rob of Pakenham (I have seen a record where she was apparently Mrs Robert Boyle) and James married Mary Jane Bingham of Ramsay. Mary Ann married John Towey.

The family of James Seward and Mary Jane were among the many who headed for the Canadian west in the 1880s. Accompanied by their first five children (they eventually brought the total to ten) they went to Ridgeville, Manitoba in the spring of 1881.

Life in the west was just as hard for these pioneers as it had been for the early settlers of the Ottawa Valley; perhaps harder because of the cruel winter temperatures and the isolation. Although Mary Jane's brother also went to Manitoba, she suffered great loneliness on the homestead and sometimes walked out to a neighbouring Indian camp, just to be able to speak to another woman.

Money was scarce, and the little Seward girls wore boys' boots instead of girls' footwear, because their father believed that the boots would last longer. A few years later this family operated a post office in their home, and they received the grand sum of ten dollars per annum for their work.

Life was not all work, and Sunday was the highlight of the week. Dressed in their best (did this include the boys' boots?) the family hitched their team of work horses to the grain wagon and went to church. This was a Methodist congregation which later became part of the United Church of Canada.

Summer picnics were a treat, and the annual Orangemen's picnic was looked forward to by all the neighbours. Dances were held in the settlers' homes, and after a school was built, special events were held there.

Before the school was built, Mary Jane Seward held a school class in her kitchen. There she taught her own children as well as those of the neighbours.

There is no doubt that she also spent many anxious hours in that kitchen as she waited for her husband and sons to return from the bush. In order to get wood for cooking and heating they had to leave home for a week at a time, travelling across country by sleigh, often running into blizzard conditions. While doing this work they stayed in tents, a miserable existence in a Manitoba winter.

Remarkably for those days, all ten children grew to adulthood, although one daughter died as a young woman, in a typhoid fever epidemic. Others lived to a good old age, such as Lydia May, the youngest, who died in 1977 at the age of 88.

James and Mary Jane Seward, as well as a number of their children, are buried in the Greenridge cemetery.

Scanlon, James, RC

Ship	Hebe, 1823
Origin:	Rathkeale, Limerick
	(Signed on at Mitchelstown, Cork.)
Location	W lot 2, con 12, Goulbourn Twp
Family	Ellen, wife
James	7
Bridget	3

1826 report: "at work near Prescott." He did not return to this lot.

Scanlon, Jeremiah

Ship:	Hebe, 1823
Origin:	Kilfinane, Limerick
Location	"left at Morphy's Falls." (Now Carleton Place.)

Scanlon, William, 42

Ship:	Brunswick, 1825
Origin:	Brury, Cork
Location:	lot 13, con 10, Asphodel Twp
Family	Catherine, 36
Patrick	21
Mary	18
John	15
Thomas	12
Bridget	8
William	6

Catherine Scanlon died soon after their arrival in Asphodel. Since a new birth was listed in that period, she possibly died in childbirth.

Scully, Daniel, 31

Ship:	Amity, 1825
Origin:	Newmarket, Cork
Location:	S. lot 3, con 7, Emily Twp
Family:	Catherine, 29
John	8
Daniel	6
Bartholomew	4
Catherine	2

This was the first brick house built by a Peter Robinson settler in the Peterborough area. Erected at lot 2, con. 7, Emily Township by John Scully, it was made of brick which was made on the farm. It is now the home of Mr and Mrs Harry Peeters.

Ship's notes: "a quiet, industrious man."
There was one death in this family in 1826.
In that year, the family raised 200 bushels of potatoes, 100 bushels of turnips and 15 bushels of corn.

Shanahan, Denis, 22, RC

Ship	Stakesby, 1823
Origin	Charleville, Cork
Location:	W lot 24, con 8, Pakenham Twp
Family:	Abigail, wife.

By 1826, a child had been born to this couple. A report tabled in that year said that Denis " worked last year on the Ottawa, but is now on his land."

This land proved to be useless, and by 1834, agent Jessop reported "declines to take a deed. Prays to get East lot 21, concession 9, Huntley in exchange." However, Denis and Abigail were still in Pakenham Township for the 1871 census, where they were shown to be 68 and 63 years of age respectively.

In 1834, the parish priest noted that this couple then had four children. Researchers in the Green family believe that Abigail Shanahan was the former Abigail Green who came out with the Robinson settlers of 1823.

Shanahan, Denis, 33

Ship	Amity, 1825
Origin	Listowel, Kerry
Location:	N lot 6, con 4, Ennismore Twp
Family	Honora, 25
William	15
Daniel	13
Florence	8 (m. Mary Murray)

Florence was, of course, a boy, that being an English translation of a Gaelic saint's name.
Ship's notes: "an honest, well disposed man."

1826: Denis "worked this summer at the canal." Honora and her children nevertheless raised 300 bushels of potatoes. Note the ages: the older boys were obviously not the natural children of Honora, and possibly not Denis's children, either. They may have been siblings. A man who had already been in Canada joined this family when they arrived. His name was not given.
A tavern was operated on this lot at one time.

Shanahan, Patrick, 34, carpenter

Ship:	Regulus, 1825
Origin	Listowel, Kerry
Location	N lot 12, con 6, Ennismore Twp
Family	Bridget, 34
Patrick	20 (see **Patrick Brick**)
Daniel	15
John	12 (died Sept 10, 1826)
Paul	9
Patrick	6
Norah	2

In 1826, this family was sick all summer, and one death took place. That spring the family had made 200 pounds of maple sugar! This maple sugar was used by the pioneers as we would use ordinary sugar today. It was their main source of sweetening.

Shea, Daniel, 34

Ship:	Albion, 1825
Origin	Doneraile, Cork
Location	unknown
Family	Catherine, 32
Mary	14
Daniel	12
Jeremiah	9
Nancy	2

Ship's notes: Daniel "quick but indolent; the wife industrious."

Shea, Edward, 32

Ship	John Barry, 1825
Origin	City of Cork
Location:	lot 1, con 6, Emily Twp
Family	Ellen, 31
Edward	12
Mary	5
Patrick	4

Ship's notes: "a good, quiet family."
One death by 1826.

Shea, Maurice

Ship:	Hebe, 1823

"Alias **Patrick Fitzgerald**." (See earlier entry.)

Shea, James, 23

Ship:	Stakesby, 1823
Origin:	Newmarket, Cork
Location:	not known. However, he may not have been a Shea at all, as the following letter shows.

Ramsay Township, July 1827.
I came to this country with Peter Robinson, and have now about twenty acres cleared, a yoke of steers, one cow, three calves, pigs, poultry, etc. I did not receive rations. I am well contented with my lot, and consider it worth one hundred pounds.
James X Sheil (his mark.)

James appears to have been one of the single men who did not take up farms until 1824, being employed as labourers by Peter Robinson during the winter of 1823-24. They assisted with the building of log shanties and in allocating rations. They stayed at a camp beside the Mississippi at what is now Almonte.

You will note that James could not read or write, so he had to rely on someone else to spell his name correctly. It may have been wrongly spelled in the ship's list. The names Sheil and Shail, belonging to two quite different families, are well known in the Carleton Place area today.

Shea, Patrick, 40

Ship	Star, 1825
Origin	Newmarket, Cork
Location	W lot 16, con 9, Emily Twp
Family	Mary, 38
Mary	16
Cornelius	14
John	12
Jeremiah	3

Baby, born Emily Twp August 11, 1826.

Patrick Shea died within a few years of their arrival in Upper Canada.

Shea, Robert, 36, RC

Ship	Stakesby, 1823
Origin	Mallow, Cork
Location:	W lot 15, con 11, Lanark Twp
Family	Mary, 28 (wife)
Simon	10
Ellen	3
Mary,	born in Ramsay Township.

By 1826 there were six in this family, one more birth having taken place.

In the 1834 report this man is listed as Michael Shea, which must have been an error, as the parish priest made a note of him in that same year as Robert. The government agent wrote: "had worked hard for the first year on a lot which proved to be another's, whereby he lost his labour. Has been particularly unfortunate, having been three times burned out."

Shea, Thomas, 44

Ship	John Barry, 1825
Origin:	Coolacappagh, Cork
Location	E lot 12, con 7, Asphodel Twp
Family	Bridget, 39
Jeremiah	18 ("Darby", m. Ellen Brennan.)
Michael	16 (m. Ann Myles)
John	14
Mary	12 (m. Michael O'Grady)
Thomas	9 (m. Mary Jane Doris)
Johannah	6
Denis	2.

Mr and Mrs James B. Walsh of Douro. Mr Walsh is a descendant of the Thomas Shea and the Thomas Myles families who settled in Asphodel in 1825.

Poor Bridget Shea had a miserable introduction to her new country. Denis, her youngest child, died within sight of land as their ship came up the St.Lawrence. As the family headed for Asphodel, her husband was drowned at Rice Lake. These are the two deaths which are mentioned in the 1827 report.

Fortunately, Bridget's eldest son, Darby, was old enough to qualify for land, Bridget, listed as "Widow Shea," received one cow, two blankets, three axes, meat, flour etc. The three axes were probably meant for her sons Darby, Michael and John, who as teenagers, considered to be men, would have borne the brunt of the land clearing chores.

Darby Shea and his wife Ellen can be seen in the 1851 census with four young children, Thomas, Mary Ann, Michael and John.

His brother Michael also appears in that census, with his wife Ann and their children: Mary, Thomas, John, Catherine, Honorah and William. Five other children were also born to them. Ann was a daughter of Thomas and Honorah Myles, who had come to Canada on the ship Brunswick in 1825.

Reverend Joseph Walsh, 1904 - 1984.

Several of Michael's children grew up to become farmers; William was a clerk, Honorah, Johanna and James became teachers, and James also ran a hotel. Johanna married John O'Keeffe in 1873, and her youngest daughter, Catherine, entered St.Joseph's Convent in Toronto in 1907. Another daughter, Anne O'Keeffe, married James M.Walsh, a descendant of a family who had come from County Tipperary at the time of the potato famine, settling in Asphodel.

There were three sons of this marriage. **Father Joseph Walsh,** ordained in 1934, served the Church at Kinmount, Peterborough, Wooler, Campbellford and Downeyville. Raymond Walsh was an employee of Quaker Oats Ltd, Peterborough. James B.Walsh, the father of two married daughters, resides in Douro with his wife, the former Hilda Lynch of Mount St.Patrick. She is a retired school teacher.

Sheehan, Daniel, 40
Ship	Albion, 1825
Origin	Kanturk, Cork
Location	E lot 1, con 6, Douro Twp
Family	Ellen, 39 (nee Walker)
Mary	21
Elizabeth	17
Daniel	15
Patrick	10

Judith	9
Daniel	1

Ship's notes: "an industrious family."
In 1826 this industrious family grew 266 bushels of potatoes, 25 bushels of turnips, 75 bushels of corn. They made 15 pounds of maple sugar.

Sheehan, Daniel, 34 schoolmaster
Ship:	Star, 1825
Origin:	Mallow, Cork
Location:	W lot 1, con 5, Douro Twp
Family	Mary, 31
Henry	13 (m. Judith Leahy)
John	10
Patrick	7 (m. Abigail Leahy)
Mary	3
Ellen	11 days.

Ship's notes: "Ellen was born after the ticket was given."
One member of this family died in 1826.

In the 1851 census we can see Henry Sheehan still living in this township, with his wife Judith and their children, all under ten, who were Daniel, Mary, Abigail, Johanna and Michael. Also living with them was Judith's mother, Mary Leahy, the widow of Michael Leahy of Douro.

Sheehan, Denis, 38
Ship:	Star, 1825
Origin:	Newmarket, Cork
Location	W lot 19, con 3, Asphodel Twp
Family:	Honora, 37
James	9
Honora	8
Denis	4
Ellen	1

Sheehan, Edward, 25
Ship:	Stakesby, 1823
Origin	Mallow, Cork
Location	unknown.

Sheehan, James, RC
Ship:	Hebe, 1823
Origin	Buttevant, Cork
Location:	lot 11, con 4, Ramsay Twp
Family:	Mary, wife
John	16
James	16
Patrick	12
Margaret	10
Mary	7

Two more births took place between 1823 and 1826. The family was still living on this farm in 1834, but it was concluded at that time that "the land is not capable of sustaining the occupants."

Sheehan, John, 32

Ship	Fortitude, 1825
Origin	Ballyclough, Cork
Location	W lot 13, con 11, Emily Twp
Family:	Mary, 26
William	7
John	6
Jeremiah	2

Sheehan, John, 39

Ship	Regulus, 1825
Origin:	Mallow, Cork
Location	N lot 17, con 11, Emily Twp
Family	Honora, 35
Daniel	20 S.lot 17
Julia	17
John	14
Margaret	8
Michael	6

John Sheehan Sr. died in Emily September 10, 1826. His is one of the oldest tombstones at St.Luke's cemetery.

Sheehan, John, 39

Ship:	Albion, 1825
Origin:	Churchtown, Cork
Location	E lot 2, con 4, Douro Twp
Family:	Bridget, 36
Cornelius	21 (E lot 1, con 4)
Timothy	18 (W lot 3, con 3)
Mary	16
Patrick	14
Michael	8
John	6

Ship's notes: "an industrious, good family". John's sons, Cornelius and Timothy, were described by the ship's surgeon as "hard working, good young men."

In case readers wonder what sort of work the passengers did aboard ship, I should explain that some of the ship's surgeons also had charge of passengers in Canada, as they travelled to the area where they would locate. Such remarks, then, often refer to the time when the travellers were making their way to the Peterborough area via water and wagon trail. Supplies had to be loaded, boats had to be paddled, and so on.

There was one birth in this family in 1826. In that year the group raised 300 bushels of potatoes, 300 bushels of turnips and made 50 lbs of sugar. They possessed a cow and two hogs.

In the 1851 census we can see Cornelius Sheehan and his wife Norry (Honora O'Brien) living with their eight children, whose ages ranged from 17 down to 2: Patrick, William, Honora, Cornelius, Maurice, Catherine, Timothy and Ellen. Also with

them was his mother, Widow Sheehan, 77, whose age does not equate with that given when she came to Canada.

In that year, one 19 year old member of the household died; cause given: "sudden death."

Sheehan, Joseph, 32

Ship:	Brunswick, 1825
Origin:	Cape Clear, Cork
Location:	S lot 2, con 8, Ennismore Twp
Family	Margaret, 22
Mary	14
Margaret	11
Bartholomew	9
Michael	5
Mary	3
Catherine	19

Obviously a composite family. Here we seem to have some children of a married couple, plus some younger brothers and sisters of one or both of them.

Sheehan, Timothy. RC, 37

Ship:	Hebe, 1823
Origin	Liscarrol, Cork (born Mallow)
Location	E lot 17, con 2, Ramsay, then lot 16, con 3.
Family	Mary, wife
Mary	14
Joanna	12
Maurice	8
Honora	7
Cornelius	3

A birth occurred between 1823 and 1826. Fourteen acres of land had been cleared by 1826, and the family had four head of cattle, two hogs, and had raised plenty of produce, including 300 bushels of potatoes.

In 1829 this family sold out and moved to York. (Toronto.)

Sheehan, Timothy, 34

Ship	Regulus, 1825
Origin	Fermoy, Cork
Location	lot 3, con 3, Douro Twp
Family	Ellen, 32
Judith	14
Timothy	11
Ellen	7
Michael	5

Sheneck/Shennick

There is something very interesting about the surname of this family. Shennick is a phonetical English spelling of the Gaelic Sionnach, which is the word for Fox. After some years in Canada these Shennicks dropped their Gaelic name and adopted the surname Fox.

There were other families in Ireland called Fox, who were originally from England. They have no connection with this group, whose ancestor bore the nickname, The Fox.

Sheneck, James, 31
Ship	Albion, 1825
Origin	Liscarrol, Cork
Location	E lot 6, con 11, Emily
Family	Johanna, 28
Mary	2

In 1826, this family grew one hundred bushels of potatoes on the one acre they had cleared. Presumably this work was done by Johanna because her husband spent the summer working at the Welland Canal.
This family remained in the township, and they can be seen in the 1851 census, now using the name Fox.

Shenick, Patrick
Location	N lot 7, con 10, Emily.

Not listed on any of the ships, but definitely located as a Peter Robinson settlers, with three in his family. Possibly travelled under an alias.

Shenick, Thomas, 32
Ship	Albion, 1825
Origin	Churchtown, Cork
Location	W lot 7, con 11, Emily
Family	Honora, 30
William	16
Mary	6

This family travelled under an alias, possibly having obtained tickets from the John Regan family, whose name they adopted. (See Regan, John.)

We know that William's name is correct; this was noted by the ship's surgeon when it was discovered that Abigail Regan was in fact a boy in disguise. It is possible that Honora and Mary were also temporary names. Researchers should take this into account when searching church records. By the same token, it is also possible that these people were not natives of Churchtown.

It is my belief that there are some errors in the 1851 census concerning the Fox families. If the ages and country of birth of some of the children are to be believed, then these people could not have come to Canada until a later date. However, they most definitely were Robinson settlers, being well documented under more than one name.

Shine, Daniel, 46
Ship	Brunswick, 1825
Origin	Mallow, Cork
Location	lot 3, con 3, Smith
Family	Ellen, 45
Mary	24

Michael	19 (W lot 3, con 3)
Daniel	17
John	15
Denis	14
William	12
Ellen	10

In 1826, Daniel Shine suffered with "ague during the summer." At that time, Michael was living at home.

Shouldiss, Adam, 44, Anglican
Ship	Star, 1825
Origin	Newcastle, Limerick
Location	S lot 22, con 3, Emily
Family	Eliza, 33
Catherine	20
John	19 (N lot 19, con 6)
Sarah	16
George	14
Samuel	10
William	6
James	2
Adam	1

A George Shouldiss, probably the one listed above, appears in the 1851 census for this township, with a family of two boys and four girls. Interestingly enough, in the section for "place of birth" his wife, Ann, 34, is listed as "born at sea."

Slattery, James, 35
Ship	Fortitude, 1825
Origin	Mitchelstown, Cork
Location	lot 22, con 13, Otonabee
Family:	
Mary	16
John	14
Norah	12
Bridget	10
Alicia	7

In 1826, this family raised 350 bushels of potatoes, but as the government inspector noted: "Indian corn failed; all the family sick during the summer."

Slattery, James, 26
Ship	John Barry, 1825
Origin	Kilmoylen, Tipperary
Location	W lot 26, con 5, Otonabee
Family	Mary, 24
Catherine	5
Judith	3
John	1

James Slattery travelled to Canada under the alias **Thomas Roche.**
Ship's notes: "a quiet family. Youngest child died at Lachine." Another child died in Upper Canada by 1827.

Slattery, Patrick, RC

Ship	Hebe, 1823
Origin	Clogheen, Tipperary
Location	W lot 17, con 8, Ramsay
Family	Ellen (wife) nee McCrae
Catharine	14

This home was one of the stations where Mass was said in pioneer days.

In 1834, this family was said to be "doing well." By 1835 they had three daughters and two sons at home.

In the 1830s this farm was shared with a Mr and Mrs William Slattery and their two children who were not Robinson settlers. William may have been a brother of Patrick's who came out later. Patrick later went to Pakenham Township.

Catherine Slattery married another Peter Robinson settler, George Hanover, in 1832. His parents were Joseph Hanover and Catherine Daley.

Sliney/Slaney, John, 37

Ship	Fortitude, 1825
Origin	Kilworth, Cork
Location	S lot 23, con 5, Emily
Family	Mary, 34
Johanna	16
Mary	15
John	13
Edmond	11
William	9
Margaret	6
Thomas	5
Patrick	4
James	2
Michael	1

(Infant "born since ticket dated).

John Sliney Sr., died in Emily Township on March 24, 1826. Small Michael died in Emily "on St.John's Day." On arrival in Emily, daughter Mary "departed; married Michael Flaherty." Michael was a son of John Flaherty, of a family which had travelled on the Fortitude with the Slineys. However, this was not necessarily a shipboard romance because the two families came from the same parish in Ireland.

Smithwick, Robert D, Protestant

Ship	Hebe, 1823
Origin	Mitchelstown, Cork
Location	lot 13, con 12, Ramsay

For some reason, Robert Smithwick came out ahead of his family, possibly to get established first. He returned to Ireland in 1824, intending to sail again with the 1825 settlers, but he died in County Cork before he could do so.

Stack, James, 25

Ship	Amity, 1825
Origin	Listowel, Kerry
Location	S lot 7, con 6, Ennismore
Family	
Mary Pope	16

(Later m. Pat Twomey)
James Stack died in 1831.

Stack, John, 39

Ship	Amity, 1825
Origin	Listowel, Kerry
Location	S lot 5, con 7, Ennismore
Family	Peggy, 37
Robert	19 (S lot 6, con 6)
Peggy	16 (m. Dan O'Donoghue)
Thomas	15
Mary	12
Catherine	9 (m. John Pope)

Ship's notes: has a very good family; himself improvident.

Stack/Stark, Thomas, 40

Ship	Albion, 1825
Origin	Doneraile, Cork
Location	S lot 21, con 12, Emily
Family	Mary, 44
Honora	20
Richard	16
Maurice	13
Thomas	10
Mary	6
Johanna	4

Ship's notes: "a good, industrious man."
Little Johanna died May 30, 1826.

Stevenson, Thomas Protestant

Ship	Stakesby, 1823
Origin	Sixmilebridge, Clare
Location	lot 23, con 9, Ramsay
Family	Susanna (nee Nolan.)
Walter	18 (lot 23, con 9)
Anne	16
Margaret	14
Anthony	10
Susanna	8
Mary	6
Bett	3 months

Thomas and Walter Stevenson drew lots on opposite sides of the Mississippi, in what is now the Blakeney district. This family was often recorded as Stinson, Stanson or Stephenson.

Two deaths occurred before 1826; one was Thomas

Stevenson and the other an unspecified son, possibly Anthony. "This caused the family, who were very young, to disperse," wrote F.W.K. Jessop in 1834, while inspecting the settlement.

Walter Stevenson went as a hired man to the home of another Robinson settler, Gerrard Nagle. His sister Margaret later converted to Catholicism to marry Gerrard. She died while still a young woman, and he subsequently married her sister Mary, who remained a Protestant.

St. Leger, Thomas, 30
Ship	Stakesby, 1823
Origin	Sixmilebridge, Clare.

St. Leger, Margaret, 30
Ship	Brunswick, 1825
Origin	Sixmilebridge, Clare

Ship's notes: "wife of Thomas, taken out in 1823."

Letter, April, 1825
I am acquainted with the bearer, Margaret St.Leger, alias Markaham, from her infancy, and intimately in my parish these eight years past, and from my knowledge of her I consider her to be an honest, virtuous and well conducted woman, who is respectably connected in the County of Clare. She is now determined to go to her husband in Canada in America, where he is there two years past. I recommend her most earnestly to the care of Captain Robertson and the passengers of the vessel in which she is to sail."

This is one of the mysteries of the Peter Robinson settlement. Thomas disappeared; so did she. Did she know where he was? There is no sign of his having settled anywhere under Robinson's charge. Margaret may have been one of half a dozen women from the 1825 sailing who "met with friends in Montreal and remained there." Possibly this is where her husband went?

Sullivan, Bartholomew, 43
Ship	Amity, 1825
Origin	Churchtown, Cork
Location	N lot 8, con 4, Ennismore
Family	Mary, 34
John	21 (N lot 9, con 4, Emily)
Thomas	16 (N lot 7, con 4, Emily
Cornelius	13
Jeremiah	7
Ellen	2

Bartholomew born March 25, 1826 in Ennismore.

Sullivan, Charles, RC
Ship	Hebe, 1823
Origin	Kilworth, Cork
Location	lot 27, con 12, Huntley
Family	Honora, wife

Margaret Stevenson, who was a teenager when she travelled from Ireland on the Stakesby in 1823. She became the wife of Gerrard Nagle.

In 1826, this man was listed as being single. This was probably a mistake for he would have been classed as a widower had his wife died. For some reason he had not been located on his Huntley farm until October, 1824. Prior to that they had lived in Ramsay.

"Carrol O'Sullivan, in his letter dated Ramsay, Upper Canada, 19th February, 1824, writes to his friends in Ireland expressing his great satisfaction with his situation, how happy it has been for him to come to Canada. Invites his uncle and his two sisters to come out, and thankfully acknowledges that government has most faithfully and generously fulfilled its promises. John Mara, James Carty, John and Patrick Quinn write in the same way, as indeed do all the emigrants."

144

Sullivan, Cornelius, 44

Ship	John Barry, 1825
Origin	Dingle, Kerry
Location	S lot 1, con 7, Ennismore
Family	
Patrick	20 (N lot 7, con 5)
John	18 (N lot 8, con 5)
Mary	16
Elizabeth	14
Bridget	12

Ship's notes: "a very good and willing family, chiefly grown up. Behaved well on passage."

Sullivan, Jeremiah, 52 ("Darby")

Ship	Regulus, 1825	
Origin	Brigown, Cork	
Location	E lot 2, con 6, Douro	
Family	Alice, 50 (nee Kelly)	
Timothy	28	
Mary	26	(m. Anthony Allen)
Catherine	24	(m. Michael Mahoney)
Michael	22	(m. Mary Allen)
Kitty	20	(m. Timothy Leahy)
John	18	went to Otonabee
Denis	16	(m. Mary Condon)
Jeremiah	14	(m. Mary Walsh)
Johanna	12	
Alice	10	

Michael Sullivan, born in Ireland in 1803, came to Upper Canada in 1825. He married another Robinson settler, Mary Allen. Shown beside him is his daughter, who was married to James McCliggott.

Many of the Irish immigrants were taken ill during the voyage to Canada, and some died. Family tradition says that Darby Sullivan died two days before the ship docked, and Alice hid the death from ship's officers because she did not want him to be buried at sea. She succeeded in having him buried on land, but the location of the grave is unknown.

Alice had friends at Cobourg, a community where the immigrants stayed for a time, and she left her younger daughters, Johanna and Alice with them, promising to collect them the following spring. Perhaps she feared that they were not strong enough to face the arduous journey to the country via boat and wagon.

With several sons who were old enough to receive land, Alice settled in Douro Township. Timothy settled the East half lot 2, concession 2, but he was killed by a falling tree, a not uncommon fate among the settlers, who were unused to bush work. His brother Michael took the adjoining lot, while John was given land in Otonabee but resided with his mother for the first few years. Life must have been hard, for Alice never did get back to collect the two little girls, although this story has an interesting sequel.

Johanna Sullivan grew up in Cobourg, and married George Towns. He was a son of Samuel and Lydia Towns who had come to the area in 1820 from Jefferson County, New York State. The young couple took up farming, and in due course three children were born, whom they named Mary Eliza, Jeremiah and John.

In 1846 they moved to Douro, settling on lot 11, concession 5, where a new baby, George, soon made his appearance. Frances Towns Lynch, a descendant of Johanna, says that the mother and children arrived by sleigh, leaving George Sr. to follow on with the livestock and household furnishings.

It was just as well that Johanna was reunited with her family at this time, for tragedy struck soon after. Her husband fell from his horse, and after lingering for some months, he died. After his death Johanna gave birth to a daughter, Hannah.

Johanna Towns was made of good stuff. Left a widow with five small children, she nevertheless managed to finish clearing the land, and she raised her family to be good citizens. This woman who had left Ireland as a girl lived to be 82 years of age. Had she lived another five years, she would have seen the twentieth century.

It is impossible to mention all the interesting descendants of Darby and Alice Sullivan, but a few are of special interest. **Reverend Monsignor John Thomas Pearson** of Peterborough is a descendant of the Michael Sullivan- Mary Allen branch.

In the Kitty Sullivan- Timothy Leahy branch there was **William Leahy, the Irish Flash.** He was a runner who earned this nickname in the United States because of his great speed over short distances. His father, Patrick, was said to have been one of the best long distance runners in Canada at one time. William represented the United States in Pan American competition at the Buffalo Exposition, winning gold medals for the 100 yard dash and the 220 yards.

Bill Towns, another of Johanna's descendants, is a man whose name will live on in Douro. He was known, far and wide, as the township historian. His hobby was genealogical research, and before his death he received the Ontario Bicentennial Medal for his work in the preservation of history. The story of Towns' store at Douro is told elsewhere in this book.

Sullivan, John, 31

Ship	Stakesby, 1823
Origin	Watersgrasshill, Cork
Location	W lot 2, con 3, Darling

Sullivan, John

Ship	Hebe, 1823
Origin	Doneraile, Cork
Location	E lot 6, con 7, Goulbourn
Family	Mary (wife)
Bess	22
John	19 (lot 7, con 7)
Mary	
Margaret	

The birthplace for John Jr. is given as Ballyshannon, Donegal, which is surprising in a family from the south. John Sr. died in 1827, leaving a son and a daughter. There is no mention of his wife and second daughter in the 1834 report which documented this.

However, a report on the younger John indicates that Mary had died. "Absent from his lot since the death of his parents" noted agent Jessop. I learn that he is married and residing with his wife on the Rideau. The sister is married to a man named Nicholson in the neighbourhood."

Sullivan, John.

An 1834 report for Goulbourn Township says that an 1825 Robinson settler of this name was living on East lot 2, concession 10, where he had cleared 20 acres.

In 1826 there were two in the family, and one death had occurred. This is the same John Sullivan who was listed in the "return of improvements made by Irish Emigrant Settlers printed in 1827, which referred to the 1825 group.

Sullivan, John, 36

Ship	Brunswick, 1825
Origin	Doneraile, Cork
Location	lot 12, con 12, Emily
Family	Margaret, 32
Jeremiah	7
Denis	5
James	2

Sullivan, John, 41

Ship	John Barry, 1825
Origin	St. Mary's, Cork
Location	lot 10, con 3, Smith
Family	Ellen, 36
Ellen	20
Julia	15
Eugene	14

Ship's notes: "a very good family of kind and industrious daughters. Fully satisfied with their behaviour.

Sullivan, John, 30

Ship	Brunswick, 1825
Origin	Killarney, Kerry
Location	S lot 8, con 6, Ennismore
Family	Catherine, 30
Ellen	12
John	1

One death in 1826, and John was "sick all summer."

Sullivan, John, 21

Ship	Regulus, 1825
Origin	Mourn Abbey, Cork
Location	N lot 21, con 12, Emily
Family	Margaret 20
Timothy	1

One member of this family died in 1826.

<u>Mystery</u>
I am unable to identify which John Sullivan it might be, but a later report says that a John Sullivan, a Peter Robinson settler living on lot 16, concession 7, Pakenham Township was "murdered in Huntley in 1828 and leaves no heir"

Sullivan, Michael

Ship	Hebe, 1823
Origin	Croom, Limerick
Location	lot 10, con 4, Ramsay

1826: "working as a carpenter at Perth."
The location book says that a Michael Sullivan from Killarney? Cork was settled on the west half of lot 24, concession 10, Huntley Township. I cannot say whether this is the Michael listed above, or a different man. The ship's list doesn't show anyone answering to the latter description.

The John Sullivan house at lot 21, con 12, Emily, built c. 1850. Now owned by descendant Stephen Sullivan, it was once a stage coach stop on the Peterborough to Bobcaygeon run, where fresh horses were picked up, and the traveller could buy refreshments.

D.W.McCuaig photo.

Sullivan, Michael, 28
Ship	Albion, 1825
Origin	Doneraile, Cork
Location	W lot 19, con 7, Asphodel
Family	Judith, 26
Catherine	7
Michael	5
Mary	2

Ship's notes: "Judith Sullivan understands midwifery."

Sullivan, Patrick, 32, RC
Ship	Stakesby, 1823
Origin	Mallow, Cork
Location	lot 22, con 4, Pakenham
Family	Mary, 30
Mary	8

Patrick Sullivan went to the United States in 1824-1825, then returned, and worked in Montreal in 1826.

Sullivan, Patrick C., 24
Ship	Amity, 1825
Location	S lot 6, con 4, Ennismore

This man went to work on the Welland Canal when he was first in Canada, but by 1827 he managed to get "five acres chopped."

Sullivan, Richard
Ship	John Barry, 1825
Origin	St.Anne Shandon, Cork
Location	W lot 2, con 6, Emily
Family	Ellen, 38
Michael	19 (E lot 2, con 6)
Honora	17
Thomas	14
Catherine	12
James	9
Michael	6

Ship's notes: "a very good, quiet, willing and industrious family, deserving every attention and encouragement."
There was a new birth in 1826.

The family of Tobias Switzer, Jr. He came on the Star in 1825. His wife, Hannah Cunningham, is shown seated on the right of the picture.

Sullivan, William

Ship	Brunswick, 1825
Origin	Kilworth, Cork
Location	lot 23, con 7, Emily
Family	Judith, 40
Edmond	19 (S lot 23, con 7)
Mary	17
Elizabeth	15
Denis	12
Ellen	9
Johanna	6
John	3

On arrival, Judith was listed as "the widow Sullivan."

Sweeney, Denis, RC

Ship:	Hebe, 1823
Origin	Buttevant, Cork
Location	E lot 26, con 3, Ramsay Twp.
Family:	Norah, wife
Margaret	23
Catherine	19
Ellen	17
Joanna	16
Patrick	15

Cornelius	13
Denis	4

1826: Denis Sweeney, a nailor by trade, was "supposed to be in the United States."

Sweeney, Michael, 37

Ship:	Albion, 1825
Origin	Kilworth, Cork
Location:	E lot 9, con 9, Douro Twp
Family	Margaret 32
John	16
Richard	13
Mary	9
Catherine	5 (died)
Denis	1
Bridget	baby

Ship's notes : "a very decent, good family."
The ship's list also said that Michael Sweeney used the alias **Michael Sullivan.**

Sweeney, Timothy, 34

Ship	Albion, 1825
Origin	Buttevant, Cork
Location	lot 2, con 6, Douro Twp

Family	Johanna, 30
Honora	11
Mary	9
Catherine	4

Johanna Sweeney, died at the Peterborough depot, December 31, 1825. Catherine Sweeney died June 7, 1826. There was one new birth in this family after they arrived in Canada, so perhaps Johanna died in childbirth.

Swytzer/Switzer, Tobias, 38
Ship   Star, 1825
Origin: Adare, Limerick
Location   S lot 18, con 5, Emily Twp
Family: Eliza, 36
Jane   18   (m. Edward Fitzgerald,PR)
Christopher   16   (m. Ann McColl.)
Theresa   15   (m. John Fitzgerald, PR)
John   13   (m. Margaret Kerr)
Eliza   11
Tobias   10   (m. Hannah Cunningham)
Amos   2
<u>Born in Canada:</u>
Anna Mary   June 2, 1826. Died at 2 months.
                      Ann, born 1828.
                      (m. Christopher St. John.)

Tobias Switzer Sr. was listed as a reduced farmer, but soon after his arrival he was working as a wheelwright, so he must have had training in this skill. He also worked as a carpenter at a later date.

Little Amos died soon after the family reached Upper Canada. The Fitgerald men who married into this family were sons of Thomas and Margaret Fitzgerald, Peter Robinson settlers in Smith Township.

Tobias Switzer Jr. moved to Peel Township, Wellington County in the 1850s. Ann, her husband and her unmarried sister Elizabeth lived in Brock Township, Ontario County, where Tobias senior later joined them.

Three Clergymen.

Three clergymen were descended from Tobias Switzer Jr. The first of these was his son **Reverend James Cunningham Switzer.** Born in 1869, the ninth and youngest child of Tobias Switzer and Hannah Cunningham, Mr Switzer was ordained in the Methodist Church in 1896, following studies in theology at Wesley College, Winnipeg.   His appointments included charges at Sarnia, Brandon, Kelowna, Victoria, New Westminster and Vancouver. At one time he served as president of the Manitoba and Northwest Conference, and he was a delegate to the Ecumenical Conference of   the Methodist Churches.

Mr Switzer was one of the clergymen who presided at inaugural ceremonies of the United Church

Belinda Switzer at the age of sixteen. She was a daughter of Tobias Switzer Jr, who travelled on the Star in 1825.

of Canada in 1925. He continued in the United Church for another eight years, until retirement in 1933.

His son, **Reverend Gerald Breen Switzer** was also a United Church minister. Born at Holland, Manitoba, he earned degrees from the University of British Columbia, Columbia University and the University of Chicago. He also received an honorary degree from St.Stephen's College, Edmonton. In 1925 he was the first United Church minister to receive ordination in British Columbia.

Dr. Switzer's career was different from that of many clergymen; he had a radio ministry for the United Church over a 21 year period. He broadcast from Calgary, Vancouver and New Westminster. He also taught for ten years at Union College, later to become the Vancouver School of Theology. He also

A happy moment shared by Rev. John Wesley Miller and his wife, the former Lucinda Patrick. Mr Miller first sought out his future wife because of her beautiful voice; he came from a musical family himself. One of their sons has perfect pitch, and a grandson is a pianist and piano tuner.

served the church in the mission fields of northern British Columbia.

Another Methodist and United Church minister was Dr. Switzer's cousin, **Reverend John Wesley Miller.** Mr Miller was born in Brock Township, Ontario, a son of Samuel Miller and his wife, Belinda Switzer. (A daughter of Tobias Switzer Jr.) Born in 1883, he was the eldest of the couple's eight children.

Mr Miller received a Master's degree from the University of Toronto; he then studied theology at Victoria College and in Scotland. He first went to Salt Spring Island as a student minister in 1907 and he was ordained the following year. He served the Church until his retirement in 1946.

During his career he served at many different churches in BC. However, one of his proudest moments came in 1912 when the Methodist church at Port Alberni was opened; he had headed the fund raising

drive for the building. He was prominent in the ministerial association, serving in various offices for the United Church's BC Conference, as well as the Presbytery in Kamloops and in Vancouver.

He was a charter member of the University of British Columbia, and a member of the senate of the Union College. In private life, Mr Miller was fond of music; in fact, he met his future wife through that medium. His son, Frank, recalls that his father "sought out my Mother because of her beautiful voice."

The girl with the fine voice was Lucinda Patrick (Cynda within the family) and she was a member of the famous hockey family. Her brothers, Frank and Lester Patrick, were hockey stars of the twenties.

Mr Miller's parents had also met through music. His mother was a talented singer and pianist. Her father, Tobias Switzer Jr. made a horse and buggy available to her so that she could become a travelling music teacher. The day came when cousins in Brock Township invited her for a visit. A musical evening was arranged as part of her entertainment, and a young man named Samuel Miller, known to have a good voice, was one of the invited guests. Cupid was also present that night.

Frank Miller.

Another distinguished descendant of Tobias Switzer is Francis Patrick Miller, the eldest child of Rev. John Wesley Miller and his wife. A graduate of the University of British Columbia, Frank served with the Canadian Army during the Second World War, achieving the rank of Captain. In civilian life, he worked in the field of criminal justice.

For this work he has received several awards, including the John Howard Society Award in 1973 for distinguished humanitarian services; the J. Alex Edmison Award in 1980 for outstanding contribution to the field of corrections and criminology in Canada, and a citation for Meritorious Service in 1983 by the Correctional Service of Canada.

During his 37 years of service, he worked in several posts. He was Classification Officer at the Kingston Penitentiary; Executive Director of the Parole Service; Canadian Co-ordinator of the fifth United Nations Congress on Prevention of Crime.

Frank Miller has been a member of many groups and committees associated with crime prevention and criminal justice. He has been an advisor to government bodies in this field, and he has served as a member of the task force inquiry into the role of the private sector in criminal justice. He is a past president of the Church Council on Justice and Corrections, and the Canadian Association for the Prevention of Crime.

Teskey, John, Protestant
Ship:	Hebe, 1823
Origin	Rathkeale, Limerick.
	(Signed on at Buttevant, Cork)
Location	W lot 7, con 11, Ramsay Twp
Family	Anne (wife)
Joseph	24 (E lot 8, con 11)
Robert	22 (W lot 8, con 11)
John	20 (E lot 7, con 11)
Edmond	14
Eliza	12
Albert	9
Luke	6
Thomas	3

These people were a Palatine family from County Limerick. It is said that Anne Teskey and Sarah Dulmage, whose family came on the same ship, were half sisters.

The Teskeys, possibly because they had so many grown sons to help them, quickly became prosperous. The fact that they drew lots close to the Mississippi River meant that they were able to utilize the water power to start small industries. They were located at what is now Appleton, once known as Teskeyville.

This young man is Albert E. Teskey, a son of John Adam Teskey and his wife, Sarah Giles. Albert's great grandfather, John Teskey Sr. came on the ship Hebe in 1823.

The 1834 inspection report had much to say about the achievements of this family. John Sr. had "a a handsome dwelling house" which was far superior to the accomodation that the average settler could afford. This house is still in use, complete with an annexe which was once used as a dormitory for workers at the Teskey woollen mill. However, at that time the woollen mill was still some years in the future.

In 1834, John Jr was "working at his trade" while his brother Robert was working the west half of lot 2, concession 11, which had been purchased for him by his father. There was a large barn on the property but "bad soil." "He has built a stone grist mill," noted agent Jessop, "but most of the lot is under water, and what remains above it is rock."
"This family is worthy of encouragement for their conduct, and great exertions on the land."

In due course, Robert Teskey had a saw mill, Albert ran a store and post office, and Robert's sons, John Adam and William Rufus had a woollen mill. The Teskeys also operated a custom carding mill. In the 1880s, Wilton Teskey was proprietor of the

Appleton Flour Mills, and Rufus Teskey was a Ramsay Township Councillor.

In the early days the Teskeys were at first alarmed by the presence of Indians, who had a summer camp beside the Mississippi. They soon learned that there was nothing to fear, and a friendship grew up between the Teskeys and the Indians, to the point where two little native people were given the names Caroline and Amanda, after two Teskey daughters.

John Teskey Sr. died in March, 1854, at the age of 86, and his wife Anne two years later, age 78.

Thomson, John, 22, Protestant
Ship: Stakesby, 1823
Origin   Fermoy, Cork
Location: E lot 12, con 11, Ramsay Twp
Family   Margaret, 22 (wife)
Matthew   8 months.

By 1826 there had been another birth, and one death.

1834: "by trade a plasterer, but residing on his land. Doing very well."

Thornhill, Robert H, 21
Ship: John Barry, 1825
Origin: Mitchelstown, Cork
Location: N lot 6, "East Side Road",
                 Smith Twp

1827 report: "employed as a clerk in the establishment." This man remained in Peterborough for his first year in Canada, working at the depot for Robinson.

This is Robert Teskey, a Ramsay Township man who went to the Canadian West.

This is the Teskey house which was mentioned in the 1834 report. The addition on the right was originally built as living quarters for some of the mill workers.

Tierney, Matthew
Ship	Hebe, 1823
Origin	Rathkeale, Limerick
Location:	E lot 3, con 11, Ramsay Twp
	Alias **Matthew Teskey.**

Tierney left the district in 1826, never having occupied his lot. It went to Richard Dulmage, another Robinson settler.

Tobin, John, 52.

Ship:	Fortitude, 1825
Origin:	Brigown, Cork
Location	Douro Twp.
Family:	Ellen, 50
Thomas	30 E lot 10, con 3, Douro
Mary	28
Ellen	26
Johanna	24 (m. John Leahy)
Ellen	1

John Tobin died April 10, 1826.

Tobin, John, 28
Ship	Regulus, 1825
Origin:	Brigown, Cork
Location:	W lot 10, Con 2, Douro Twp
Family:	Johanna 27 (nee Lane)
Mary	21 *
Edmond	5
Maurice	3
Catherine	2

John Tobin was a son of John Tobin Sr. John Jr died in 1830.
* This Mary may have been a sister of Johanna

Torpey, William, 54
Ship:	Resolution, 1825
Origin:	Brigown, Cork
Location:	W lot 10, con 4, Douro Twp
Family:	Mary, 40 (nee Fitzgibbons)
Thomas	22 (E lot 10, con 4)
Michael	21 (m. Margaret Ryan)
Mary	19
Kitty	18
Honora	15
John	13 (m. Ellen McCarthy)
Elizabeth	10
Bridget	6

Thomas Torpey was an accountant. Michael Torpey was a school teacher.
William Torpey died in Douro August 20, 1826. In that year the family cleared ten acres of land, and produced 400 bushels of potatoes, 300 bushels of turnips, and 40 lbs of maple sugar. They also owned a cow.

John Torpey married Ellen McCarthy, and their children included William, Ellen, Bridget, Mary Anne, Johannah, Thomas, Eugene, Patrick and Catherine.

Toughal, James, 36
Ship:	Hebe, 1823
Origin	Doneraile, Cork
Location	W lot 19, con 11, Huntley Twp
Family	Ellen (wife)
Betty	(died at sea)

1826: three in the family at this point. Very soon after the birth of a new daughter, James Toughal died, and his widow remarried. There was probably some discussion about the future of his land, as these farms usually went only to men. Some years later, William Hickey attempted to obtain this lot, "if it is not to go to Toughall's daughter."

Trihy, Patrick, 34
Ship:	Elizabeth, 1825
Origin	Kilbolane, Cork
Location:	N lot 1, con 4, Ennismore Twp
Family	Anne, 34
Mary	18
Ellen	16
John	14
Anne	8
Michael	4

This family was first given land in Douro. By 1826 there were six in the family, one death having taken place.

Twomey/Toomey, James
Ship:	Stakesby, 1823
Origin	Cork
Location:	"left the boat on the way to Prescott."

Twomy, John,
Ship	Amity, 1825
Origin	not given
Location:	N lot 5, con 7, Douro Twp

Ship"s notes: "an honest, well disposed fellow." 1826: "at work on the canal."
A half brother, Maurice, came to the township at a later date.

Twomy, Patrick, 33
Ship:	John Barry, 1825
Origin	Glounthane, Cork
Location	S lot 8, con 4, Ennismore Twp
Family	Mary, 32
Patrick	9
Hannah	8

Ellen   7
Mary   2
Ellen   30

Ship's notes: "a willing, hard working, good man. In 1825 the family was joined by a woman who had "already been considered a settler up to that period." This may have been Ellen, listed above. She may have been a sister of Mary or Patrick.
1826: "recovering from illness."

Twomey/Toomey, Timothy.
Ship:	? 1823
Origin	Cork
Location:	W lot 26, con 5, Pakenham Twp

Wall, William, 48, mason
Ship	Resolution, 1825
Origin	Mitchelstown, Cork
Location	E lot 3, con 1, Marmora Twp
Family	Mary, 36
Anne	19
Mary	16
William	14
Thomas	12

The Walls had two acres cleared by 1826, on which they grew 200 bushels of potatoes and 23 bushels of corn in their first year on the land. They owned a pig and a team of oxen.

Walsh, Bryan, 35
Ship:	Resolution, 1825
Origin:	Templetenny, Tipperary
Family:	Mary, 32
Edmond	6
Mary	3
Patrick	2

One of the Walsh children died at sea, and Bryan Walsh died at Cobourg. His widow, left with two young children to support, married another settler. His name is difficult to make out. It looks something like Maurinnert.

Walsh, John, 36
Ship:	John Barry, 1825
Origin:	St Mary's, Cork
Location:	E lot 23, con 12, Smith Twp
Family:	Mary, 35
Thomas	15
John	12
Margaret	10
Michael	7
Bartholomew	3

Ship's notes: "an excellent family. Acquainted with gardening. Has behaved himself well and deserves every encouragement and recommendation. Wrought hard at the pumps."

Walsh/Welsh, Patrick, 40
Ship	Fortitude, 1825
Origin	Kilworth, Cork
Location:	N lot 12, con 9, Emily Twp
Family:	Ellen, 30
John	14
Peggy	11
Mary	9
Catherine	7
Ellen	5
Michael	1

Walsh, Richard, 33
Ship	John Barry, 1825
Origin	Inniscarra, Cork
Location:	W lot 11, con 6, Asphodel Twp
Family	Elizabeth, 24
Mary	3

Born in Canada:
William
Redmond
Richard
Patrick
John
Catherine
Two more daughters.

In 1826, this family made 50 lbs of maple sugar, and grew 300 bushels of potatoes, 100 bushels of turnips and 60 bushels of corn.

John Walsh served as a township councillor in Asphodel and this included several terms as Reeve. His great granddaughter, Rosemary (Walsh) Towns, has some interesting stories to tell of this family. She explains that Richard Walsh Sr. was a Canadian militiaman who helped to quell the rebellion of 1837, perpetrated in Upper Canada by William Lyon Mackenzie. In 1840, Richard and his brother soldiers each conributed a day's pay to assist with the building of General Brock's monument at Queenston Heights.

Redmond Walsh later went to the United States, where he fought in the Civil War . His sister, Kate, married Cornelius Sweet, a blacksmith and carriage maker. They eventually went to Trenton. The Walsh children attended S.S.# 6 school (later known as the Daisy D) and "it appears that Kate taught in the first school in Hastings, around 1855."

"Another of Richard Walsh's daughters married James Fife; one was Mrs D.Kellsy of Dummer, and another went to Pennsylvania."
Rosemary's great grandfather, John Walsh, married a Miss Kelly, and among their children was Rosemary's grandpa, known as "Drover Dick." Mrs John Walsh died at the birth of her twins, Elizabeth and William, in 1870. Elizabeth became **Sister Fidelity.** Says

Rosemary Towns: " William died at the age of 19; Sister was raised by her aunt, Kitty Kelly."

Rosemary Walsh Towns and her husband, Michael, operate the P.G.Towns grocery store at Douro, and in 1986 they received a heritage award as "Grocer of the Year." This story is told in a different section of the book.

Walsh/Welsh, Robin, 38

Ship	Resolution, 1825
Origin	Brigown, Cork
Location:	W lot 2, con 10, Douro Twp
Family:	Mary, 38
John	17
Thomas	15
Judith	14
Johanna	9
Robert	4
Michael	3

"one child born".

The 1827 report indicated that Robin Walsh was "farming on shares with T.A.Stewart" in Douro.

Walsh, widow, 50

Ship	Brunswick, 1825
Location	E lot 12, con 5, Douro Twp
Family:	
John	26
Margaret	23 (sister)
Mary	20
Johanna	18
Edmond	16

These people were sick during the summer of 1826. Widow Walsh's husband died in 1825.

Walsh, William, RC

Ship	Hebe, 1823
Origin:	Mallow, Cork
Location:	lot 20, con 11, Huntley Twp
Family:	Honora, (wife)

By 1826, the couple had a baby.
1834: "resides on his lot, and is doing well".

The 1851 census shows William and Honora, with two children: William 7
Michael 5

Ward, David, RC, 40

Ship:	Hebe, 1823
Origin	Newmarket, Cork
Location	lot 7, con 4, Ramsay Twp
Family:	Ally (wife)
Mary	9
Nora	14
Bess	5
Thomas	(born 1823 at Morphy's Falls.)

David Ward's birthplace was Ashford, County Limerick. By 1826 there were seven in this family, including a new birth. Twelve acres of land had been cleared.

David Ward died in 1826, and his son Thomas was named heir to the land. Alice then married Cornelius Ryan.

Welsh, Richard

Ship:	Hebe, 1823
Origin:	Clogheen, Tipperary
Location:	not given
Family:	Frances (wife)
Anne	
Mary	

A monument at St.Michael's graveyard, Corkery, to a couple who came to the Ottawa Valley with their families in 1823.

White, Joan, 40

Ship:	Fortitude, 1825
Origin:	Clogheen, Tipperary
Location	"went to Ottawa to join her husband."
Family:	
Patrick	16
Cornelius	14
Michael	12
Thomas	10
David	6
Abby	2

White, Michael, RC

Ship:	Hebe, 1823
Origin	Clogheen, Tipperary
Location	W lot 3, con 11, Goulbourn Twp
Family:	James (left at Morphy's Falls.)
	(Morphy's Falls is now Carleton Place. James soon settled in Huntley Twp.)

Another very old house in Emily Township, built by the Winn family, this has some fine beams under the floor which can be seen in the cellar. Today it is the home of Mr and Mrs Joe T.O'Neill.   D.W.McCuaig photo.

Here we do a little detective work. Michael came out in 1823 with James White, who was probably a son. Joan gave birth to a child in 1823 which probably explains why she remained in Ireland with her children. She came out at the next opportunity, i.e. with the 1825 sailing.

Their son Patrick obtained lot 1, concession 12, Huntley, but he died unmarried in 1827 and the land was reserved for his younger brothers, "David and Michael, who are unprovided for."

White, James, 38, (alias **Brunswick.**)
Ship: Hebe, 1823
Origin   Clogheen, Tipperary
Location: lot 17, con 10, Huntley Twp
Family   Nora (nee Hanora Mahoney)
William   (over 14)
Mary   (under 14)
James   2

This family travelled under the name Brunswick so were probably using the ticket of some other family. William White settled on the adjoining farm, but lived with his parents for some years.

Another child was born to this family in Canada, and one death was also reported. The Whites cleared fifty acres of their land, and then they sold this lot, purchasing in its place lot 22, concession 11 from the Canada Company.

James White Jr. m. 1. Alice Lindsay; 2. Catherine Sheehan.

William's wife was named Johanna. Mary married Edmund O'Keefe of Huntley, a son of William Keefe of Conna, County Cork. William was one of four brothers who came to Huntley Township in the 1840s, but it is believed that they were related to the O'Keefes who came with Peter Robinson in 1823.

Williams, George, 27
Ship: Stakesby, 1823
Origin: Glanmile, Cork
Location: unknown.

He may have been one of the young bachelors who worked at the depot and did not settle until 1824. Later, a **Jeremiah Williams,** not in the ship's lists, settled on lot 13, con 10, Ramsay Twp. His age was 38, and he hailed from Ballyghiblin, Cork.

Williams, William, 20

Ship	Resolution, 1825
Family	Michael 19 (E lot 5, con 5)
Eliza	22

Ship's notes: "one woman dead. This was probably Eliza as the group was reduced to two persons in a report compiled in 1826, when the two brothers were still living together.

Wynne, Richard, 27

Ship:	Stakesby, 1823
Origin:	Kanturk, Cork
Location:	lot 14, con 6, Ramsay Twp

1826 notes: "a carpenter, working at Perth". His neighbours apparently lost track of him, for in 1835 the parish priest noted that he was "away, or dead."

Wynne, Richard

Ship	Brunswick, 1825
Origin	Mallow, Cork
Location	S lot 1, con 8, Emily Twp
Family:	Elizabeth, 46
Henry	26 (N lot 2, con 8, Emily)
Robert	24
Richard	22
Anne	18
Elizabeth	16
George	13

Young, Francis, 44

Ship:	John Barry, 1825	
Origin	Newport, Tipperary	
Location:	lot 35, con 12, Smith Twp	
Family:		
William	24	W lot 37, con 13
Eliza	22	
John	20	W lot 35, con 12
Samuel	18	E lot 37, con 13
Honora	16	
Patrick	14	
Francis	12	
Robert	10	
Matthew	8	

Ship's notes: "a very excellent family. Willing, independent and obliging in every respect. Have behaved in the most exemplary manner , and deserve every attention and encouragement. Instrumental in saving the ship."

Francis Young was an engineer from County Tipperary. When he applied to come to Canada, the assistant priest at Newport wrote the following recommendation:
"I certify that I have long known Francis Young. He is a man of most industrious sober habits and great mechanical ability, and having a numerous family, consisting of seven sons from the age of 7 to 20 - and two daughters - I think him a person fully deserving of any encouragement which the Government may wish to offer to emigrants."

Born into a Protestant family, Francis Young was a convert to Catholicism as a young man, and as a result he was disinherited by his family. This happened in an era when some of the Penal laws were still in effect, so Francis must have held strong convictions in order to withstand the pressure under which he must have been placed.

He married Lady Elizabeth Blackall, the daughter of a wealthy Protestant family; she, too, was disinherited when she converted to her husband's faith. Having given birth to nine children, poor Elizabeth died. Francis subsequently led his family to Canada, carrying with him the tools of his trade.

The district where the Youngs settled became known as Young's Point. Francis looked forward to harnessing the water power there, and by 1827 he had built a grist mill and he constructed a saw mill the following year. He also built the first dam at Young's Point.

The family had a strong religious faith. The first Mass said in the district was held in their home. A priest travelled from Peterborough on horseback, and the dining table, covered with a red cloth, was pressed into service for the occasion.

The men of the family were great hunters, and they sometimes took a boat to the head of Stoney Lake in order to hunt. This was fifteen miles from home, yet they always went back on the weekend for Mass, later returning to the hunt camp.

Young's Point soon became a flourishing settlement. Timber drives came down the river, and at one time there were three hotels there.

A grandson of Francis, P.P. Young, began the steamboat line which has made the family famous in the area. The Stoney Lake Navigation Company operated for 62 years, and in that period eight boats were owned by the family.

These boats opened up the Kawarthas to tourists, and they also facilitated the movement of timber down river. Mighty logs, destined to become masts for British naval ships, were towed behind the steam boats. Granite from Stoney Lake was brought down also; some was used to build Sacred Heart Church in Peterborough and some formed the bed for Toronto street car tracks.

P.P.Young's granddaughter, Aileen Young, recalls that his boat, the Stoney Lake, "was the first boat over the Peterborough liftlock on opening day, July 9, 1904. It was a triumphant day for the Youngs. All the family were on board. The boys crewed the boat, except for Harold, the youngest, who sat in the bow."

The Stoney Lake, flagship of a fleet of eight steamboats owned by P.P.Young of Young's Point from 1883 to 1945. "P.P." is in the derby hat, his hand on his knee and his wife Ellen is beside him, at the right door of the wheelhouse.
This boat is fondly remembered for moonlight excursions and Sunday School picnics, and there was almost always a band on board. Bill Scollard was its only captain in all of its forty years from 1904 to 1944.
Courtesy of Aileen Young.

At the helm was the captain, William Scollard, a cousin of the family, and the boat's sole captain in forty years of operation.

"My Father, Fred Young, was at the engine that day, " Mrs Young recalls, "just as he was forty years later when the Stoney took her farewell journey over the liftlock en route for Kingston, where it had been sold to the Thousand Islands Steamship Lines. That day in 1944 was a sad occasion for the Youngs."

Aileen Young, a great great granddaughter of Francis and Lady Elizabeth Young, is married to Charles Young, whose family is not otherwise related. Those who wish to learn more about the family and about the interesting history of Young's Point, may purchase her book, Yesteryear at Young's Point, which is available at outlets in the Peterborough area. Mrs Young used the pen-name "Nathaway Nan" when she produced the book.

The Young family is also mentioned in Roughing it in the Bush by Susanna Moodie, and in By the Sound of Her Whistle by John Craig.

Young, John, 41, Protestant.
Ship: Stakesby, 1823
Origin: Adare, Limerick
Location: E lot 1, con 10, Ramsay Twp
Family: Katharine, 39 (wife)
Rachel   19
Margaret   18

The P.P.Young family of Young's Point. Back row:
wife Ellen; Fred, Pat, Jerry. Centre: Bobby, Molly.
Front: Harold, Irene, P.P.Young.

Courtesy of Aileen Young.

Letitia	17
Dorothy	15 ("Dorah")
Katharine	13
Maryanne	5
Harriet	3
Henry	(born at sea.)

Henry Young was born at sea in 1823. His tombstone in the St.James' cemetery, Carleton Place, reads:

"In memory of Henry Stakesby Young, born on board HMS Stakesby August 10, 1823, died September 7, 1894."

The ship's surgeon noted in his report that the birth took place on the second of the month. Whichever it was, the birth must have been greeted with delight, for the baby was the first living boy following a family of seven girls. Most of these girls were in their teens, so Henry must have received plenty of motherly care.

The Young family settled on a farm near the border between the townships of Ramsay and Beckwith, but unfortunately John Young died in 1828. After that the land was "let on shares" but held in trust for John's heir, little Henry.

The boy grew up to marry Rachel Docherty, the daughter of a neighbour, and the couple had seven children before her untimely death at the age of 42. More children were born after Henry married Henrietta Price, a girl from County Wicklow.
The children were Abraham Isaac, Hiram, Elizabeth, Charles Wesley, Easton, Elijah, Anne (Mrs Klemm), Edwin, Egerton Ryerson, John James, William Henry and Louise.

The obituary of one of these children, Charles Wesley Young, who died in 1911 at the age of 52, gives us a glimpse of what this family was like. Charles had gone to Michigan as a young man, but he came home when he inherited the farm from his father, Henry.

"While a hard worker, he took time off for many of life's pleasures, " wrote the editor of a Carleton Place paper of the day. "No man was fonder of his home, which was his land of pure delight. Humour had a big vein cut through his system and he could tingle from head to foot when the genuine streams got flowing in this aqueduct, a flow in him of kindness and good humour which made even dullness itself agreeable. He was a Trustee of the Methodist church and a member of the Quarterly Board, a faithful, fervent man there, with fertility in suggestion and a mind to swing into action when deeds were to be done. There were few people in the town or townships who did not know this quiet, plodding, honest, good-natured man, who would not trample on a worm."

Not all of this man's brothers could attend his funeral, for they lived in various parts of the United

Miss Edith Young, Reg. Nurse. Miss Young's ancestor was born on the ship Stakesby during the voyage to Canada, and christened Henry Stakesby Young.

States. However, one of them was able to be present to help Mrs Young (the former Isabella F.Virtue) through her husband's illness. The newspaper reported that "Elijah came from Saginaw three weeks ago and remained to the end, priceless as a pilot in the great emergency."

The funeral service was conducted at the Methodist church, and the size of the crowd in attendance was a tribute to Mr Young's popularity in the district. "The carriages covered a mile - a striking pageant of force and beautiful solemnity."

Children of this family included the late Harry Young, a well known farmer in the district; John V.Young, a retired high school principal, and the Misses Rachel and Edith Young.

Rachel F. Young , now retired, served as a social worker at Peterborough for many years. Edith G. Young, Reg. N., retired, has had a distinguished nursing career. She was Director of Nursing at the Almonte Hospital, and later became Director of Nursing at the Peterborough Civic Hospital. She completed her career as Director of Nursing Service and Nursing Education at the Ottawa Civic Hospital.

Grab bag.

The study of genealogy is an on-going thing. This was underlined when new information arrived after the foregoing section of the book had been put into print. Rather than leave out this material, which may prove useful to readers, we are inserting it here. The information came from the Bathurst District, and concerns marriages performed by Father John MacDonald, the pioneer priest at Perth. Although this material can be found in the records of St. John the Baptist, Perth, please note that most of the marriages here were probably not performed at Perth. Father MacDonald was an itinerant missionary priest who often married people in their homes. This fact is noted in his own diary with regard to Pat Corkery's wedding.

Thomas Collins and Helen Buckley were married Oct. 28, 1825. Their parents were Richard Collins and Catherine Donovan; James Buckley and Mary Ruddock.

Patrick Corkery and Mary Donohoe were married June 23, 1835. Parents: Michael Corkery, Mary Sheehan; Philip Donohoe and Bridget McDermit. The Donohoes were not Robinson settlers.

Thomas Coghlan and Jane Ballantine were married October 26, 1854. Parents: John Coghlan and Mary Magher; Duncan Ballantine, Mary Hannah. The latter were not Robinson settlers.

Patrick Dahill and Nancy Doolin were married Feb. 26, 1827. Parents: William Dahill, Mary Sheehan; James Doolin, Alice Ready. The latter were not Robinson settlers.

Edward Dowling and Mary Leahy were married Nov. 22, 1836. Parents: David Dowling, Mary Mahoney; Patrick Leahy, Joanna Fahey.

William Drake and Julia Bresnehan were married Feb. 4, 1824. Parents: Esmond Drake, Catherine Casey; Thomas Bresnehan, Honora Heffron.

William Flynn and Anne Dowling were married April 17, 1842. Parents: James Flynn, Margaret Harrigan; David Dowling, Mary Mahoney.

John Foley and Joanna O'Brien were married April 18, 1836. Parents: Thomas Foley, Catherine Nowlan; Timothy O'Brien, Catherine O'Leary.

This couple became the parents of the millionaire railroad men. It has now been discovered that another Timothy Foley, who married Ellen Hennessey in 1849 and a James Foley, who married Mary Cadogan in 1832, were brothers of this John Foley. Accordingly, I believe this to be the man who arrived in 1825, the brother of Patrick Foley who came to Upper Canada in 1823.

It has now been proved that George, William and Abigail Green were in fact brothers and sister: **Abigail married Denis Shanahan** Jan 18, 1824. Parents: William Green, Mary Connor; Denis Shanahan, Mary Riordan.

William Green and Elizabeth Connor were married Feb 5, 1826; parents: William Green, Mary Connor; Timothy Connor, Elizabeth Gregg.

George Green married **Elizabeth Green** Nov 4, 1827. Parents: William Green, Mary Connor; John Green, Margaret Tarrant.

Bridget O'Meara and Michael Dwyer married Oct 5, 1841. Parents, John O'Meara and Johanna Foley; John Dwyer, Catherine Fenton. The latter were not Robinson settlers.

Daniel Regan and Johanna Curran married Feb 11, 1839. Parents: Daniel Regan, Julia Greer; John Curran, Sarah Butler.

William Riordan and Sarah Butler married Nov 1, 1825. Parents: Timothy Riordan, Catherine Connell; William Butler, Margaret O'Brien.

Elizabeth Ward and Robert Baily married March 3, 1840. Her parents were David Ward and Alice Riley who travelled with her on the ship Hebe in 1823.

Michael Dominic Nagle of Huntley Township with his second wife, Ellen Burke. A son of Garrett Nagle, this man was a small boy when he came to Upper Canada in 1823. The photo dates from 1875.

The Palatine settlers

In Canada, there are many families who are descended from the Palatine settlers of County Limerick. Their ancestors had been forced to leave the Palatinate province of the Rhine because of religious persecution; many of these Protestant people fled to the United States, but about 800 went to Ireland, arriving there in 1709. A few settled in the northern part of County Kerry, but most relocated in County Limerick, in such places as Rathkeale, Adare, Kilfinane and Ballingrane.

Some Palatine surnames which are known to us in Canada include Dulmage, Lowes, Miller, Switzer and Teskey; Fitzelle, Glazier, Hartwick, Heck, Piper, Ruttle, Shier and Sparling. The first five names on this list are found among the Peter Robinson settlers; all were from County Limerick.

Examples: the family of Garret Dulmage went from Croom to Ramsay Township in 1823. The families of George and Michael Lowes went from Nantinant to Emily Township in 1825. The George Miller and Tobias Swytzer families moved from Adare to Emily in 1825, and a large family of Teskeys travelled from Rathkeale to Ramsay in 1823.

In Ireland, the Palatine families had been comparatively privileged people. For the first twenty years after their arrival as refugees they were allowed to rent five acres of land for every man, woman and child, at a rent of five shillings per acre, with the British government underwriting the cost. Their Protestant faith gave them preferred status in that era of Irish history, so soon after the War of the Two Kings.

In 1760, John Wesley visited the Palatine community in County Limerick, recording in his journal his favourable impressions of these German-Irish people. "There is no cursing or swearing, no Sabbath-breaking, no drunkenness," he wrote.

By the 1780s the settlers had begun the process of assimilation into Irish society. One historian noted that the German language was dying out among them, and that they had "left off their sour kraut" in favour of potatoes and wheaten bread. Most of these folk were by now industrious tenant farmers.

In 1907, a twenty-five year old Canadian Methodist clergyman, Reverend John Wesley Miller, followed in the footsteps of his great namesake, John Wesley, by visiting the Palatines of County Limerick. He was of Palatine descent himself. His paternal grandfather, John Miller, had left Ireland in 1842, settling in Brock Township, Ontario County. His maternal grandfather and great grandfather, Tobias Swytzer junior and senior, had settled in Emily Township in 1825 with the Peter Robinson settlers.

Delighted with his trip to Ireland, Mr Miller recorded his impressions in a journal, and he also wrote an article for The North Ontario Times at Uxbridge, Ontario.

"The first Palatine I met was at Limerick, his name was George Miller. On the way to Ballingrane I met a Mr Teskey whose mother was a Switzer. At Ballingrane I was fortunate in being in time to attend an annual meeting of Palatines at the Barbara Heck Memorial church on St.Stephen's Day, December 26, where I met a church full of Palatines. They received the Palatine 'from across the water' very heartily and I felt right at home."

He was invited to speak at the service, and it was later reported in The Christian Advocate that *"Mr John Wesley Miller of Victoria College, Toronto"* was called upon. *"Pleasantly and simply Mr Miller tells us of his Palatine ancestry and of his desire to see the spot about which he has heard so much in his far-away home. The fact that he arrived on Ballingrane's big day was simply what we call chance. Evidently he finds himself quite at home amid the unusual surroundings of an Irish country Methodist service."*

Later, the young minister was entertained to a turkey dinner at the home of Miss Barbara Ruttle, a grand-niece of Barbara Heck. There he was shown an ancient pear tree at the door, under which John Wesley himself had preached during a visit to the Palatines. In turn, Mr Miller was able to respond by saying that Barbara Heck and Philip Embury, who were born nearby, were well known figures in Canada, where they were held in high esteem. At the time of this meeting in 1907, Miss Ruttle was 82 years of age. She had been born in the year when Mr Miller's ancestors left the district with Peter Robinson.

Later, Mr Miller visited families whose surnames were similar to those in his family tree. He found that many of the local people maintained ties with family and friends in Ontario, and some had copies of Toronto papers to display.

"One of the men told me that he had seen my name before, and proved it by showing me The Christian Guardian which contained it several times."

Visiting the Rathkeale district, he noted that *"the 400 or 500 Palatines are living in the stone cottages built by the original settlers. They have been a small community of Protestants surrounded by a country full of Roman Catholics. They have had the hardship of the landlord and are now glad of the condition of things improved by the new Irish Land Act."*

"The Palatines have always been friendly with the Catholics. They were Protestants of Calvinistic and Moravian persuasion. A great number

emigrated to America in 1760; it was about this time also that John Wesley visited this part of Ireland. He was greatly pleased with the Palatines and found them ready to receive the gospel of repentance and faith. He visited the people four different times, and preached in 1789 at Ballingrane. As a result of this preaching, Canada got her Methodism. Barbara Heck went to Ontario and raised the money for the first Methodist church built in Canada."

Mr Miller concluded his report by suggesting that " there are no people that Canada has been prouder to assimilate into her blood than the Palatines because of their force of character, strong moral principles, energy, careful economy, a devotion to church and family, and loyalty to the state. I am sure that all of us with Palatine blood in our veins will stand by the traditions of the past and help to make Canada a truly great nation."

Women's work

Teenie Mayhew kept a diary. From her observations of life we can learn much about women's work in years gone by. Mrs Mayhew was a descendant of the Boyles of Pakenham, through her mother, Elizabeth Boyle, who was Mrs George Davis. Elizabeth's sister, Tomisini, was one of the first women teachers in Haggarty & Richards School # 3. Her diploma, dated 1879, is one of the family treasures today.

When Teenie Alice Davis was born in Wicklow Township in 1889, the women there were still practising the pioneer skills which their forebears had used. Her granddaughter, Mary Lou Quehl, has shared some memories with the author.

"Teenie's mother, like the other women of the area, made the family clothing from start to finish. This included shearing the sheep, spinning the wool and knitting the socks, toques and mitts. Webs of flannel were dyed with Diamond dye and taken to a mill in Carlow. The weaver would be shown the pattern desired and the webs would become material. For Teenie's mother it was usually checkered. With this material, shirts for the men and dresses or skirts for the girls were produced."

The men spent all winter at the lumber camp, earning some much needed money to augment the family income. This meant a lonely and anxious time for the women, left on the farm. When the spring break-up began, Teenie would see her mother sitting at an upstairs window, watching for the first glimpse of her returning husband.

During the long winter evenings, the women had time for handicrafts. Teenie made her first quilt when she was ten years old, in 1899. She was almost 90 when she completed the last quilt that she made. As each grandchild got married, Teenie would present a beautiful quilt to the bridal pair. However, that was far in the future.

Young Teenie was needed at home, so her schooling was sparse. She attended school for "21 days before Christmas and then from Christmas until Easter." However, she learned the three R's, which stood her in good stead throughout her life.

"Teenie used to make shingles by hand with her father. They used a splitting wedge on a block, hit it with a maul, and a thin shingle would come off. Grandma would work the shingle horse. She would have to scrape it as smooth as she could and taper it to one end. They made shingles for barns."

"They also had a graining horse on which they made all their own mitts and moccasins from deer hide. To do this they would soak the hides in water until the hair came off, then put them on a pole. Using a special knife, they had to take the grain off. This is a layer between the hair and the hide."

"The hide was then put into a solution like soft soap and it was turned and mixed until suitable. When it was removed from this mixture it had to be pulled. Two people would pull on each end until the hide was dry, and very soft. From this the hide was taken to the smokehouse and hung over poles, and a fire lit and left to smoke. This would turn the hide from almost white to a dark brown. This also made the hide softer yet."

"The mitts were made by cutting two pieces, minus the thumb. These were sewn together and then the thumb piece was cut and sewn in. It was sewn with babish, which is hide cut very thin and soaked in water, and pulled to about the size of string. The mitts were not very good if they got wet, but were very comfortable when dry."

Teenie was just seventeen when she married Edward Mayhew, and she began married life at Burgess Mines, where her husband earned $1.25 a day. When the Depression came they moved back to Wicklow, where once again the old pioneer skills were called into play. They farmed, and preserved their own produce, and they hunted game which was salted and smoked, and they collected wild berries.

Like others of her generation, Teenie had to overcome many ups and downs. Her home burned to the ground in 1938, and little was saved. Her husband and three sons were at the lumber camp when this took place. Fortunately, friends and neighbours pitched in to build temporary accomodation until a new house could be built.

Then came the Second World War, and three of Teenie's boys were called upon to serve their country. More anxiety for a mother! Luckily, Teenie had learned to enjoy the simple things of life, and there was always something to lift her spirits. "In her later years," Mary Lou recounts, " Teenie loved to play cards and would never miss a card play at the church halls at Combermere and Maple Leaf. She loved birds, flowers, crocheting, knitting and, of course, making quilts."

Teenie Mayhew died in 1979, and her funeral service was conducted from the church in which she had been married. Now she lies in the nearby graveyard, after a full and happy life. She did not achieve fame or fortune in her lifetime, but she is an example of all those women who have quietly made a worthwhile contribution to Canadian life, by being hard working wives and mothers, and responsible members of a rural community.

The new pioneers

When we think about our Canadian ancestors, we usually associate the greatest hardships with the early days, when they first came out from the old country to hack a living out of the bush. We should also remember that when their children and grandchildren later moved to the United States or to the Canadian west, they, too, underwent a homesteading experience.

The following notes are reproduced from memoirs written for his family by the late Eugene Leahy of Nebraska, and reprinted with the permission of his daughter, Marie J. Knudtson of Colorado.

"Suddenly I am inspired to record my life happenings as I remember them. Grandfather Michael Leahy and my Dad, Francis Patrick Leahy, were born in Peterborough,Ont. (Editor's note: Michael was a son of Patrick Leahy of Douro.) Grandfather Leahy married Bridget Torpey and my father was one of ten children born to this union. In 1869 the Leahy family moved to a farm near Lost Nation, Iowa. In 1883 they moved to a farm near Wisner, Nebraska. This Leahy family produced a priest, three pharmacists, a doctor and a dietician, plus two tavern owners, my Father, Frank Leahy, and his brother Joe.

Mom and Dad settled on a farm north of Wisner where brother Jack and I were born. When I was about three years old, Dad's hogs died with cholera, and corn was but nine cents a bushel, so Dad quit the farm.

After a period operating a tavern in Nebraska,and then Montana, the family tried South Dakota. In 1909 we moved to the new town of Lamro, SD, where we farmed a section of land belonging to the Lamoureux (Lamro) family. When we landed in Lamro in February,1909, there was a foot of snow and that winter was very severe. We lived in a tent until Dad got our house built. The tent had a wooden floor and sides, but the roof was canvas, not much of a place for my Mother and sisters, but to we boys it was a lark! My bedroom, along with the hired man, was a stall in the new barn.

After the hard winter, cattle belonging to the

These Leahy brothers were all outstanding athletes in their day. Left to right: Frank Leahy, football coach of Notre Dame University; Eugene Leahy; Tom Leahy. They were descendants of Patrick Leahy of Douro Township, an 1825 settler.

U-Cross outfit were thin and weak. They died along the creek, and in it,too weak to get out after going for water. We used to back a wagon up to the creek, attach a chain to the horns of the critters, and pull them on to the bank, where some of them would eventually gain strength to move off, but many died.

One day, one of them was down near our barn, and Frank, then but two years old, walked out to where the critter was and tried to get on its back, when we discovered it all and got him away from there. The critter was too weak to harm him or he might have been killed. Maybe, had we let him go, it would have been Frank's first steer ride, starting him on a career as a rodeo performer.

Lets go back to my school days at Wayne. I was 14 when in the eighth grade there. I'd been out of school when at Roundup,Montana; much to my joy there was no school while we were there. I had a horse to ride, a .22 rifle to shoot, the Musselshell River to swim in, and I thought to myself, Tom Sawyer never had it so good! It was a tough assignment at Wayne to get caught up to my fellow students and my first report card resulted in the school being short in red ink.

Having had boxing gloves at home since I was five years old, I became rather good at boxing and whipped every kid in Wayne, until I incurred their emnity. They framed me one day, brought a man over to fight me, and me but sixteen. Del McDermott was his name, an actor with the Walter Savage carnival. He really tried to whip me but I held my own, and spectators said I had the best of the three rounds we fought. It resulted in a nice friendship between Dell and me. I last saw him in 1918 in Winnipeg.

When I was 17 years old I was propositioned to go to Stuart, Nebraska and box a preliminary for the Sullivan-Buckels fight. I was accepted, and won by a k.o. in the first round. I'll never forget what Buckels said to me as I left the ring. "My God, kid, that is the first time I ever saw anyone knocked out with pillows!" We had on 14 ounce gloves and they used five ounce gloves in regular fights.

About a month later I was watching a wrestling match in Stuart, and they called me out of the crowd to fight a man who was there, boasting, so again I accepted. As I stepped into the ring a gambler showed me a $20 bill and said "this is yours if you will k.o. him- I don't like him." So I'm in there, hands not taped, swinging from the floor, to get that twenty, and I broke my right hand, badly. But even so I would have knocked him out as I had him against the ropes, but the promotor yelled "stop it!" and the referee pinned me from behind, and my Uncle Jim Kane jumped into the ring and punched the referee, and we had a wild minute or so before order was restored. That tin horn gambler never gave me the twenty, and I had a ruined right hand. The doctor had no x-ray and as my hand was so swollen that each knuckle was a dimple, he told me to come back when the swelling went down. By then it didn't hurt me, so I never went back.

My only time to fight as professional was in 1922 in Omaha when I had the first preliminary for the Britton-Padgett fight, when Britton was champion welterweight of the world. I won with a k.o. in the third round. There was a huge sum of $75 in it for me. I had intended to box about every two weeks to make expenses while in pharmacy college, even if I used an assumed name, but I ruined my back at Sioux Falls playing baseball, so that idea went out the window."

Being a sportsman, Gene Leahy in later years loved to tell a story about Father Steve McNamara, the priest who married Gene and his wife,Florence.
"Father Mc had been a school mate of my uncle, Bill Leahy, also a Jesuit. Father Mc was well known and liked by everyone. He was a wonderful man,with a great sense of humour to go with his Irish face. He had been stationed at Riverton, Wyoming at one time and soon after his arrival a woman of the parish said "Father, they are violating the Sabbath here every Sunday, playing baseball, and I wish you would give them a good lecture from the altar this Sunday."

Father Mc said he would,and he did. After the sermon he said to the parishioners, "I understand Riverton has a baseball team and that they are going to play a game this Sunday. I want all of you to be there, for I am going to umpire." Needless to say, the woman never bothered him again."

Gene Leahy did become a pharmacist, and he eventually gave up boxing. He played football for Creighton College, and he was called the "greatest football player the Missouri Valley has ever known." He was fullback and team captain in 1918 when his team was undefeated, and was named All American Player. He played baseball for his college, and also played in a semi-professional league in four states.

He was also the university light-heavyweight boxing champion. Had he attended a better known university, he might have become a household name in the United States, as his brother Frank did. As an adult, Gene coached many football and baseball teams, and he put his town of Rushville,Nebraska on the map in 1952 when he was instrumental in getting the Milwaukee Braves to hold a baseball school in the town. It became an annual event, with the Yankees at the school in 1963 and the California Angels in 1965.

Eugene Leahy received many honours in his life, including being inducted into the baseball Hall of Fame in 1980.

PR PR PR PR PR PR PR PR PR PR PR

Ed Nagle, buffalo hunter

When Peter Robinson visited Ireland in 1823, he had to reassure the prospective emigrants on the subject of Indians and wild animals, which they expected to find surrounding them in Canada. While many were afraid, it seems that others relished the thought of new experiences. Edmund Nagle, a son of two Peter Robinson settlers, Gerrard Nagle and Margaret Stevenson, was a man with a first hand knowledge of Canada's native people and also of Canadian wildlife.

Edmund was born at Ste.Hyacinthe, Quebec. He had a trapline in the the Quebec forests as a boy, and although he attended St.Lawrence College, near Montreal, he was expected to work during the summer, and so became adept at working in the bush. He also learned the millwright's craft.

Leaving home at the age of 19, he went to Minneapolis for a year, but he missed the Canadian wilderness and so went north to Manitoba. He travelled the Red River to Winnipeg with a winter's provisions in his boat; this was before the railway was built and water travel was the fast way to go.

He went buffalo hunting on the plains, travelling with parties of Salteaux and Cree Indians. This was the start of a lifelong interest in the culture of these people, and years later The Edmonton Daily Capital reported that his "collection of Indian curios and relics and handicrafts has long been noted for its completeness."

Ed Nagle and his brother decided to farm near Dauphin, and they travelled there by ox-cart to the farms of their choice. However, farming was too dull for Ed's liking, even though he tried to break the monotony by working occasionally as a millwright. As the Daily Capital was later to record, "the wander-fever was again in his blood, and he could not settle down."

In 1883 he moved to Edmonton, where he easily found work at a mill belonging to the Hudson's Bay Company. In the wintertime he went to the bush to work a trapline. Four years later he took a trip to the north and in due course set up in the fur trade business, in partnership with a Mr Hislop. They purchased an existing business from a Mr Secord, and it is said that "the final agreement ... was signed at midnight, by the light of a campfire, and in the midst of a smudge which Mr Nagle had lighted in order to secure a few minutes' grace from the virulent attacks of myriads of mosquitoes."

This smacks of a romantic old story in the Boys' Own Paper, and the names of the places in Hislop & Nagle's territory make equally evocative reading. . Posts were established at Forts Smith, Resolution, Rae, Providence and Simpson, at Hay River, at Forts Liard, Nelson, Wrigley, Norman and Good Hope, and at

Edmund Nagle, a buffalo hunter and fur trader in the nineteenth century.

Arctic Red River. All this expansion was not without opposition from the Hudson's Bay Company, but "Mr Nagle and his partner used great tact, keeping their plans to themselves and watching their opportunities carefully... after they had their own line of steamships their progress was very rapid. One catch alone, brought to Edmonton in the early days, consisting of 109 silver and black fox skins, was worth over $123,000."

At each post, business was carried on by several men, including an interpreter. People from many Indian tribes traded with Nagle, including Yellow Knives, Dog ribs, Chippewas and Slaves, as did the Inuit. This business continued until 1912 when the partners sold their interests to the Northern Trading Company, and Ed Nagle went into real estate in Edmonton.

Edmund Nagle took part in the Riel Rebellion. Unlike many of the militiamen who were pressed into action at the time, he was given a fair amount of leeway in carrying out his service. Again, we quote The Daily Capital:

"Having had many disagreeable experiences owing to the mismanagement of discipline which prevailed, so that orders were issued by anyone who wore a stripe, Mr Nagle made the stipulation in 1885 that he received his orders from General Strange personally. He acted as captain of the scouts, and his training as a seaman was tested when he undertook to pilot the advance boats down the river. This was a highly perilous undertaking, as many of the rebels were concealed along the banks, and Mr Nagle and his party afforded splendid targets. He placed his boats along a stretch of six miles, at intervals of one mile apart, ahead of the big boat with the soldiers on board, and any danger was semaphored from the leading boat back."

This "seaman's training" referred to the fact that Nagle had once obtained a first-class certificate as a captain of inland water vessels, when he and Hislop were operating their own steam boats.

This tireless adventurer was in his forties when he married Eva Klapstein, a Polish girl some twenty years his junior. One wonders whether Eva's honeymoon was a grand adventure or a nasty shock, for it was fraught with danger. The pair were married in Edmonton, but they returned to the wilderness on their wedding trip. Much later they recalled the events of the journey for the benefit of The Capital's reporter, who wrote:

"One of the prized pictures in the family collection shows Athabasca Landing as it was in 1895 and Mr and Mrs Nagle pushing off the boat in which they began their romantic honeymoon. Dropping down the river with the beautiful scenery of a northern fall around them, they could well understand the love of the first settler for this country. But after some days they were faced with a difficulty - the river had begun to put on its winter fetters and there was ice ahead. There was nothing for it but to change to dog teams. And so they journeyed for some time longer, when they met open water again, and then took to skiffs. Many other incidents occurred which might have daunted a less courageous bride, starting to the northern country for a stay which was to last over many years."

The couple had five children, all but one of them born in the north. Their eldest son, **Ted Nagle**, worked for Cominco as a mining engineer, and during the 1920s he spent four years in the Fort Smith area, prospecting and claim staking for the company.

PR PR PR PR PR PR PR PR PR PR PR PR

The Prospector from Peterborough

Mike O'Grady was a prospector-turned-resort owner. In common with many Canadians in the gold rush era, Michael had a dream. He headed west to British Columbia, hoping to find a fortune in gold. He worked in the Upper Arrow and South Slocan area, hoping to find a mining claim to make him rich; instead, he located some hot springs.

While bathing in the water, where the temperature was 120 degrees, he thought of Ponce de Leon, the Spanish explorer who searched Florida for the Fountain of Youth. Accordingly, Mike O'Grady called his find the St.Leon Springs.

In 1896, Mike obtained a grant for 470 acres of land which included not only the hot springs but lakeshore and mountain scenery as well. He wanted to build a resort hotel, but capital was a problem. He approached the CPR company for backing but was turned down because they were already developing the springs at Banff.

A lesser man might have gone home to Peterborough, but Mike O'Grady went back to panning for gold, and his luck turned. He found a claim which he sold for $35,000, a tidy sum in those days, and he used the money to build his hotel. He brought in the finest lumber from Vancouver and built a magnificent three-storey structure with 28 rooms, an enormous dining hall, and a mahogany-lined bar.

People flocked to the hotel, brought there by a twice-weekly steam boat service which, ironically, was run by the CPR. The only blot on the horizon was the location of the hot springs. Patrons did not want to climb up the mountainside to reach this water; they preferred to sun themselves by the lake.

Mike wanted the hot springs to be the major attraction at the resort. He figured that if the guests would not go to the springs, then the springs must come to them. He installed a large wooden pump, and a pipeline to bring the water down. He was chagrined to find that the water had cooled by the time it reached the bottom. Undeterred, he put in a boiler and attempted to heat the water in a large tank behind the hotel, which rather defeated the purpose of the hot springs.

Progress dealt the hotel a death blow. The boat schedules were changed, a new railway line took patrons farther afield, and a rival concern, Halcyon Hot Springs, built another hotel. When Mike's bar was closed, due to the fact that he had forgotten to renew his liquor license, it was the beginning of the end. There was no highway into the resort, and without the boats it was difficult for tourists to reach the Irishmen's paradise.

At ease with nature and the wildlife which abounded near the hotel, Mike stayed on, prospecting for gold, and trapping in winter. In the end the hotel was sold, but the new owner permitted him to remain on the premises, until at last he entered a home for the aged.

There are many tales about Mike O'Grady. Once, he was visited by some escaped convicts who gave him a rough time. Although it was never proved, legend said that he had discovered a lucrative mine, and the crooks tried unsuccessfully to make Mike lead them to the site. They were later captured.

Another unwelcome visitor was a police officer who tried to arrest Mike for keeping a wild animal in captivity. Mike had earlier rescued an abandoned grizzly bear cub, which he kept as a pet. When the animal became too large for comfort he kept it in a cage. He soon realised that the beast might be better off in a zoo, so he wrote away to try to find one that would take it. The policeman's visit was the result.

Making an excuse, Mike slipped outside and released the bear. Without evidence, an arrest could not be made. The bear went back to the wild, and Mike looked around for a smaller pet. He became foster parent to two little black bear cubs, which wore collars like any household pet.

Later in life he must have projected the image of a backwoods St.Francis, going for his mail accompanied by a pair of collie dogs and a couple of deer. He was capable of taming wild birds and it is said that an osprey, a fish -eating hawk, would perch on his shoulder and accept snacks from his hand.

After Mike's time, the hotel was run by a man who catered for the bush-clearing crews and local hydro workers, as well as the few tourists who ventured along the logging road. The hotel eventually closed in 1965.

Not long afterwards The Peterborough Examiner noted that the Gates of St.Leon Hotel, built by a native son, now deceased, was about to be destroyed. "Next year the torch will be put to the three-storey building on the shores of the Arrow Lakes. Then flood waters from the Columbia River hydro project will roll over the sandy beach."

So ended the dream of Michael O'Grady, the prospector from Peterborough.

Ray Madden

The ponds and creeks of Ramsay Township were an early training ground for Raymond Madden, a high school teacher who has won many awards for his coaching skills and for his own athletic achievements. The youngest of ten children, he had six older brothers who taught him to skate and to play ball at an early age.

Later on, teacher training at McArthur College, Queen's University, qualified him to teach history and physical education; before that he earned a BA in history at St.Patrick's College, Ottawa, and he also studied history at Carleton University. He now teaches at the Smiths Falls & District Collegiate Institute.

While he has a keen interest in history, Ray Madden has a gift for coaching.
"After many years of playing, I began coaching in high school and minor hockey programmes since I felt that it was time to give something back to the sports and activities that I had enjoyed as a result of the efforts of many other dedicated people over the years," he says.

As a youngster, he competed in track and field meets as a pole vaulter, representing the Almonte High School at events in Lanark County and beyond. In the 1960s he played junior hockey for the Almonte and Arnprior clubs; he played for the St.Pat's College Shamrocks and in 1970 was a member of the Almonte Packers Intermediate Championship club. He received a number of trophy for his skills.

In the summer, Ray played baseball and softball at Kingston, Almonte and Smiths Falls, playing on championship teams in the two latter places.

His life as a coach is hardly less busy. He has coached junior football, minor hockey and junior fastball for about 15 years. In 1976 he started a high school fastball team which was later developed into a team apart from the school, known as the Smiths Falls Junior Redmen. The Redmen were Ontario Champions in 1981,1983 and 1986, and Ontario finalists in 1978 and 1982. They also participate in inter-provincial competition. Ray is quick to give part of the credit to several assistant coaches who have helped him over the years.

"I have been fortunate to win a few personal awards, trophies etc for coaching in softball and hockey over the years," he says, *"but the real reward lies in being able to provide an activity for today's young people where they can enjoy themselves and gain a sense of accomplishment."*

He helped to establish the Smiths Falls Minor Softball Association in 1979, and he served as its president in 1983-1984. He was president of the South Rideau Softball League from 1982-1985.

Ray Madden is married to the former Shirley Boal of Almonte. They and their grown children are avid downhill skiers.

Graduates of the Almonte High School have had a hard act to follow. Dr James Naismith, inventor of Basketball, and Dr.R.Tait McKenzie, sculptor, who was Director of Physical Education at the University of Pennsylvania, both attended that school. It appears that Ray Madden is doing his best to follow in a tradition which was established by that distinguished pair.

Coach of Notre Dame

Frank Leahy has gone down in American history as "the coach of Notre Dame." Even in Canada, his name is well known, although he never lived in this country. He coached winning football teams at three different American universities and this included an outstanding career as football coach at Notre Dame. He served a term as general manager of the Los Angeles Chargers in the American Football League. He and two of his brothers had outstanding athletic ability. They were descendants of the Patrick Leahy and Torpey families of Douro Township.

The Leahy boys came naturally by their athletic ability. Their father, Francis P.Leahy, was one of the old-time strong men. His speciality was stick-pulling, where two men sat facing each other with their hands on a pole, as each attempted to pull the other off the ground. Francis was a boxing promoter, who managed Montana Jack Sullivan.

Francis was born in the Peterborough area, a son of Michael Leahy and Bridget Torpey. He married Mary Kane in Omaha. Her people had come from County Mayo, Ireland, years before. Her father, the police chief at O'Neill, Nebraska, was a keen baseball player, while her mother, Cecelia O'Boyle Kane, was a dab hand with a shotgun. Two of Mary's brothers, Matt and Jim Kane, were well known boxers in the American west.

Francis and Mary had a large family. The story of their second son, Eugene, is told elsewhere. Frank Leahy was one of their younger children, and when he graduated from high school in 1925, they permitted him to go to stay with Gene in Rushville,Nebraska, where he worked for a time before entering Notre Dame University. It was Frank's ambition to play football under the great coach, Knute Rockne, and to prepare himself for a coaching career in the future.

Frank eventually became the coach of that school, with a winning percentage that was only a few points behind Rockne's own.Gene Keahy later noted

"I believe it to be a greater record for, in Rockne's years, through no fault of his own, he had to schedule a weaker team some years to fill a schedule, whereas Frank's Notre Dame teams never had a breather, but took on the best of the nation. One year they beat five of the top ten teams in the nation, losing to none of them; one year his Notre Dame team beat both teams which eventually played in the Rose Bowl.."

"As coach of Notre Dame, Frank brought them back to the great glory known only under Rockne, as no coach had been able to do after Rockne was killed in a plane accident. Frank also had a great record as coach at Boston College, where his teams lost but two games in 1939-40 and beat Tennessee in the Sugar Bowl game, New Years's Day 1941. They lost the Cotton Bowl game, 1940, to Clemson, 6-3. When they beat Tennessee 19-13, it was perhaps the greatest game I ever saw."

Frank Leahy's combined record as head coach at Boston and Notre Dame was 197 wins, 19 ties, 13 losses. During his years at Notre Dame there were 107 wins, 9 ties, 13 losses. This put him at .005 of a percentage point behind Rockne as the best ever in major college football circles. Rockne's score was 105 wins, 5 ties, 12 losses.

Players coached by Leahy left their mark on football, both professional and collegiate. Thirty-six of his players won All American honours. A friend once asked: "Frank, your reputation as a coach is that you are a severe disciplinarian and you demand extra effort from your players, with very hard workouts; do they like you?" His answer: "I do not care too much whether or not they like me; the question I am concerned with is do they respect me?"

Mr and Mrs Frank Leahy had a close family life. A niece recalls that "Uncle Frank was a strict disciplinarian. He demanded certain standards of behaviour from his football team and also from his family.: His eight children addressed him as "sir" and everyone was expected to be washed and neatly dressed before appearing at the meal table.

The Leahys lived at one time in a lovely house which had formerly belonged to the gangster, Al Capone. The children were thrilled by the fact that the house had a secret passage in it, and although this was strictly off limits to them, they could not resist showing it to visitors.

Even more thrilling was the fact that an unopened safe was hidden inside the passage, possibly the property of Al Capone!

"As I remember the story, Uncle Frank said that the safe was there when they moved in and they never tried to open it for fear that it might be booby-trapped and would blow up the house with all their belongings. I really don't know if it was ever opened."

Eventually, Frank Leahy was enshrined in the Football Hall of Fame. To his sorrow, his elder brother Gene was too ill to attend the ceremony. Frank wrote to Gene, saying "If it was not for you, I wouldn't be here, either." Gene had helped to pay Frank's way through college, knowing that his young brother would have a better chance of success in his chosen career if he was able to play for a "big name" university.

Some people say that if Gene himself had attended such a school, his career might have surpassed that of the famous Frank, so talented was he in athletics. He was unselfish enough to further his brother's career instead. The American sports world owes much to the Leahy brothers, whose ancestors left Ireland with Peter Robinson in 1825.

A scene from the film The Prisoner of Zenda, set decoration by Edward G.Boyle.
Photo courtesy of Universal Studios.

Edward G Boyle

Edward G.Boyle is the only descendant of Peter Robinson settlers who is known to have to won a Hollywood Oscar.

Descended from the Boyles of Pakenham, Edward Boyle was born at Cobden, near Renfrew, and at the time of the First World War he served with the Princess Patricia's Light Infantry. He was badly wounded in action, and after the war he headed for California, believing that the climate might be better for his health.

He wound up in Hollywood, where in due course he became an interior set designer for the movies. In 1966 he received an Oscar for his work on the film "The Apartment." Before receiving this coveted award he had previously been nominated seven times.

Earlier movies on which he had worked also received Oscars for design, "Gone With the Wind" being one of the most famous, but Edward Boyle did not climb the stage to receive them. R.Andrew Lee, Head of Research at Universal Studios, explains that set designers were not recognized in a separate awards category in those days, so the film's artistic director actually accepted the statuette.

When Boyle finally received his Oscar, relatives in the Ottawa Valley, watching the award ceremonies on television, were surprised and proud to recognize one of their own.

Some other films for which he designed the sets were : A Star is Born; Irma La Douce; Son of Monte Cristo; Some Like it Hot; The Children's Hour; Seven Days in May; The Fortune Cookie; Gaily,Gaily; The Prisoner of Zenda; Arch of Triumph; The Private Affairs of Bel Ami.

Mr Lee, a member of the motion picture academy, and one of those involved in selecting award winning films to receive Oscars, says that Edward Boyle always worked on "quality films."

David Boyle

Young David Boyle is following in the tradition of the great Irish orators, Daniel O'Connell and Charles Stewart Parnell, delighting audiences with his ability to speak in public. Just as Irishman Thomas D'Arcy McGee once travelled through the Ottawa Valley to address crowds of people, so David has also reached a wide audience, although his performance had been on television, something undreamed of in McGee's time.

Young David Boyle, a public speaking champion.

David began his public speaking career as a grade five student, three years ago. With his discourse on "The Human Brain" he was selected as the top speaker in his school,and then went on to compete in the South Carleton Family of Schools public speaking contest. He not only came out on top on that occasion, but he also swept the Westernn Area finals.

This success qualified him to participate in the Carleton Board of Education's Oral Communications Finals, an event which was broadcast on Ottawa Cablevision. Here again the young orator was successful, placing third in a most talented field. Needless to say, his parents and friends were delighted with his achievements.

David Boyle is a great great great great grandson of Henry Boyle of Pakenham, and is therefore a member of the seventh generation of Boyles to have lived in Canada.

Senator Will McGuire

One of Peterborough's most distinguished sons was Senator William Henry McGuire, who was born in that city on May 31, 1875. An entry in a copy of the Parliamentary Guide states that his parents were descended from some of the earliest settlers of the Newcastle District.

This was indeed true. His paternal grandfather, Lawrence McGuire, migrated from County Fermanagh to Otonabee Township in 1828. On his mother's side , the senator was descended from Michael Lehane, who moved from Charleville, County Cork, to Emily Township in 1821.It is interesting to note that Michael's wife, Deborah, was closely related to Patrick Sarsfield, Earl of Lucan, who was the defender of Limerick and one of the commanders of King James" forces against William of Orange.

Senator McGuire's paternal grandmother, Elizabeth Power McGuire, was among the Peter Robinson settlers.in Otonabee in 1825, as were her parents.

Will McGuire was one of 14 children. Several of these eventually moved to the United States. One brother was Father Michael McGuire and a sister, Margaret, became Sister St. Gertrude. Yet another brother was named Sarsfield, in honour of the Earl of Lucan.

The McGuires were a close family. They were not wealthy, but the parents inspired their children to become high achievers. Will trained as a lawyer, studying at the University of Toronto and Osgoode Hall. His brother, Father Michael, helped to finance this education, just as he had previously been helped by a cousin, Archbishop McEvoy. In turn, Will was later able to help his sister to study for a teaching career.

A story is told in connection with his parents' Golden Wedding celebration, held in 1903, which illustrates the rather different way in which family life was experienced when families were large, and young people began their working life early.

All the McGuire children were present for the anniversary, with the exception of one son who had died young, and when they sat down to eat, they realized that it was the first meal that they had ever eaten when everyone was present. The eldest son, R.P.McGuire, had left home before the youngest child was born. As things turned out, the experience was never repeated. R.P. had to leave for home that day, and his father died not long afterwards. So, only one meal was ever shared by the whole family at one time.

A barrister, Will McGuire was a member of the Toronto law firm of McGuire, Boles & McGuire. He was appointed King's Counsel in 1933. His wife was the former Miss Anna MacNevin of Ottawa, whom he married in 1911.

In politics, Will McGuire was a Liberal. He was one of the founders of the Toronto Men's Liberal Club, and was at one time the president of <u>The Liberal,</u> a weekly newspaper at Richmond Hill. He was summoned to the Canadian Senate in 1926.

PR PR PR PR PR PR PR PR PR PR

R.B.Manion, a former leader of the Conservative Party in Canada. His maternal ancestors travelled on the Stakesby in 1823.

R B Manion

Soldier, doctor, politician, author. It sounds something like the rhyme that children used to recite in their school yard games, but in this case the string of professions applies to one man, the illustrious Robert Manion.

Through his mother, Mary Anne O'Brien, he was a descendant of Peter Robinson settlers Timothy O'Brien and his son, Patrick. On his father's side he was descended from the Manions of Huntley, a prominent family who had entered the township even before Robinson's immigrants arrived. When Mary Anne O'Brien married Patrick J. Manion, they had this in common; the homes of their respective ancestors had been used as "stations" where Mass was celebrated, well before their parish churches were built.

Robert decided to become a medical doctor. He graduated with honours from the University of Toronto and then went with his new bride, Yvonne, to practice medicine at Fort William. His skills were sought after when the first world war broke out, and he served in Europe as a medical officer, winning the Military Cross at Vimy Ridge.

Later, he was recall those days in a book, "A Surgeon in Arms." This volume was well received, as was another book, entitled "Life is an Adventure."

After the war he was elected Member of Parliament for Fort William. He then embarked on a distinguished political career. In the Meighen government he served as Minister of Soldiers' Re-establishment, and also as Postmaster General. Under R.B.Bennett he was Minister of Railways and Canals. Manion served as Leader of the Conservative party from 1938 to 1940. He died in 1943.

His family meant a lot to him, so it was only natural that one of his close friendships was with his cousin, Dr. John. R.O'Brien of Ottawa.

Dr.O'Brien's daughter, Dorothy, recalls that the Manions were often entertained in her family home. One of her treasures is a copy of Dr.Manion's book, "Life is an Adventure", which was autographed by the author and presented to her father.

Alex Edmison, Q C

We have seen that Thomas Fitzgerald had "very orderly habits" and displayed a "strict moral example." It appears that some of these characteristics were passed down to his great great grandson, the late Alexander Edmison, Q.C.

Alex Edmison not only had a distinguished career in the legal profession, but he also made a worthwhile contribution to the adminsitration of Canada's penal system. He was also a university professor and an author.

J. Alexander Edmison was born at Cheltenham, Ontario in 1903, a son of Rev. John Hall Edmison and his wife, the former Elizabeth Agnes Fitzgerald. The little boy was descended from two of the oldest families in the Peterborough area. His mother was the granddaughter and great granddaughter of Gerald and Thomas Fitzgerald respectively. John Edmison, his paternal ancestor, was one of the earliest settlers of Smith Township, having arrived there in 1819.

Members of the Fitzgerald family served their country well. Gerald Fitzgerald saw active duty during the Fenian Raids. His grandson, H.G.Fitzgerald, was Reeve of Lakefield.

Alex Edmison fought for his country during the Second World War. He received a commission in the Black Watch (Royal Highland Regiment of Canada), and had reached the rank of Major by the time of his discharge in 1945. He then assumed the post of senior liaison officer with UNRRA to Supreme Headquarters, Allied Expeditionary Force, For his work at that time he subsequently received citations from General Eisenhower and General de Gaulle. This post war work included the harrowing experience of touring Europe's refugee and concentration camps.

Alex Edmison received his education at Queen's and McGill Universities. He was called to the Quebec Bar in 1932 and created KC in 1944. All his life he had been interested in penology, and before the outbreak of war he had served as a director and as legal counsel to the Prisoners' Aid and Welfare Association at Montreal. Later he was to become associated with the John Howard Society in Ontario. He served as a member of the National Parole Board of Canada from 1959-1969.

Alex Edmison's name is well known in Canadian university circles. He was Assistant to the Principal at Queen's throughout the 1950s. He was a professor in the Department of Criminology at the UnIversity of Ottawa from 1969 to 1973. He was a member of the Board of Governors of Queen's Theological College, and of Trent University.

His influence on Canadian life was felt on a broad scale. Despite all these achievements, he maintained a keen interest in his roots. When a history of Douro Township was produced in Centennial year under the auspices of a special committee, he was editor of the publication, and he also contributed some of the written material, as did other local historians. He said in the preface to this book that his visits to Douro were among his "earliest boyhood recollections." They were also among his treasured memories.

Judge James Newton

The Honourable Judge C. James Newton did not have a career in the law in mind when he graduated from the Almonte High School in 1938. His plan was to become a pharmacist, but world events reshaped his destiny. As he says, "I was six months' apprenticeship and one year of university away from completing my pharmacy degree when war was declared."

The war altered the course of his life. He joined the RCAF in 1940, and graduated as a pilot at Camp Borden in 1941. Next came a flying instructor's course, after which he trained other pilots for the war. He was pleased to receive an overseas posting in 1943, but before it went into effect he was involved in a mid-air collison while teaching flying at Trois Rivieres, Quebec. As a result he spent the next few months in hospital, having sustained permanent leg injuries.

His Honour Judge C.James Newton.

After the war, he gave up his plan to become a pharmacist, but was determined to complete his education in another field. He attended Osgoode Hall law school and graduated in 1948, He then returned to Almonte to set up a law practice, where he was to remain for two decades.

Judge Newton recalls several important milestones in his career. In 1960 he took in a partner, P.J.Dadson, and their firm became known as Newton & Dadson. James Newton was appointed a Queen's Counsel in 1961. In 1968 he became Crown Attorney for the County of Lanark, a full time position which he held until 1978, when he was appointed a County Court Judge at Brockville. In the summer of 1984 he was appointed to Lanark County as County Court Judge. At the time of writing he is a District Court Judge at Perth, Ontario, for the County of Lanark.

Between 1968 and 1978, in addition to his work as Crown Attorney for the County of Lanark, James Newton travelled extensively throughout Ontario for the Attorney General, doing special prosecution work in prominent trials and retrials.

Judge Newton is a great great grandson of Thomas and Ellen Madden, who left County Cork on the ship Stakesby in 1823, settling in Ramsay Township. This distinguished descendant of theirs was born in Huntley Township, not many miles from the original Madden homestead. His parents were Charles Newton and his wife, the former Laura Madden.

Judge Newton is married to the former Bettie Campbell of Toronto, and they have four grown children.

An Irish teacher

Many of the descendants of the Peter Robinson settlers have worked as teachers, farmers and nurses, and they never did achieve fame and fortune. However, it is people such as these who, working away quietly from year to year, have been the backbone of Canada. Farmers keep us alive with the food they produce, nurses help to heal our bodies when our health breaks down, and teachers have an even more awesome responsibility. They hold in their hands the future of our society.

Kevin Leahy of Douro has been selected to represent the teachers here, although he modestly claims to have done nothing out of the ordinary. His neighbours think otherwise. Teacher, farmer, musician, local historian and preserver of Irish tradition, he has been aided and abetted in his many endeavours by his wife, Bernice, who is also a teacher.

"For any success I may claim as principal/teacher in St.Joseph's school, or as a member of the community at large," he explains, " a large share of the credit goes to my wife Bunny, who was able to help me very greatly, both professionally and musically."

Kevin, who retired from teaching in 1982, is a descendant of Dennis Leahy of Douro and his wife, Mary Moher. Dennis came out on the ship Fortitude in 1825 with members of his family, including his parents and maternal grandmother. Kevin, a son of Mr and Mrs F.D.Leahy, believes that his family and his environment had much to do with moulding his character. As one of eight boys, he had a happy childhood on the farm, dividing his time between the Leahy and Moher households.

Kevin grew up to be a teacher. He feels that teaching was a vocation for him, and he always believed that he had a knack for communicating with young people. He says that he enjoyed helping pupils to find themselves.

He began his career at the age of 18, teaching at S.S.# 4 Galway, in a township at the top of Peterborough County. He enjoyed this, but returned to Douro after a year when he was needed on the farm. He went back to teaching after the Second World War, when teachers were scarce, and he spent the next four years at S.S.# 4, Douro. Then he got married,and returned to the farm once more, but he was soon roped in to teach at S.S.# 5.

It was in 1955 that life changed, both for the Leahys and for the students of Douro. This was the year in which St.Joseph's,a new four-roomed school was built in the township, and Kevin was invited to become principal there. He accepted the challenge, and spent more than a quarter of a century at "the four corners", leaving an indelible impression upon the school.

Former parents and students say that he dispensed more than the three r's at St.Joseph's. They feel that he moulded character. Kevin's response to this is to say that his career as a teacher

"hinged as much on a set of favourable circumstances and the contribution of many people as on any strengths of my own."

An excellent staff and supportive parents were of great help, as was the late Monsignor McCarthy, a man whom Kevin Leahy credits with inspiring staff and pupils alike to aspire to high ideals.

St.Joseph's school was an institution where "high priority was given to recognizing children's strengths and weaknesses in learning, and giving appropriate guidance and help," Kevin explains, believing that his staff " tried hard to help children discover their personal talents and abilities, and thus realize their self worth." He goes on to say that " children were encouraged to have a high respect for any work done well; that the world needs everyone's talents and skills, no matter how humble these may be. Our chosen school motto was "age quod agis" -what you do,do well."

In a district where most of the children were of Irish descent, part of this voyage of self discovery came through the celebration of many facets of their Irish heritage. Music was,of course, an important part of the curriculum. Students made up the main choir at St.Joseph's church, next door to the school. Many successes came as a result of entering the Kiwanis music festival. Any student above the third grade could study the violin at school; a qualified teacher was hired from Toronto, and shared with the Peterborough Symphony.

Kevin Leahy, himself an accomplished violinist, helped to coach these pupils.

"Music, especially the violin, has been part of my life. Playing the violin offers a continuous challenge. I know it has enriched my life,and I hope that some of this enrichment was passed on to the youngsters it was my great privilege to know and to teach."

Life at the school was not all serious study. "True to Irish tradition, we seldom missed an opportunity for a party or a celebration. Always a Christmas concert, a Valentine party, a Hallowe'en party, and of course St.Patrick's Day always was recognized in some form; a Mass, Irish music, sometimes a community event."

Senior students also had the chance to investigate and take pride in their heritage. For a number of years the eight graders each wrote their own family history, This work was assisted by the late Bill Towns, himself descended from Peter Robinson settlers, who knew the history and the genealogical connections of the township.

In retirement, Kevin Leahy continues to

promote the Irish heritage of his township. As this book goes to press, he is working with others to promote an Irish festival in Douro, which will include the annual Rose of Tralee competition. In 1967 he headed a committee which produced a volume of township history, and his interest in the heritage of the area is on-going.

He has grown up with a very Irish respect for the land.

"I grew up being involved in farm life," he says, *"and somehow I just could not separate myself from it. All during my years of teaching I kept the farm operating with my own work, that of family members, and sometimes hired help. Rather than interfering with my teaching, I think that the farm has made me a better teacher."*

He is now a full-time farmer,and he derives great satisfaction from working with his Simmental cattle and Belgian horses. On St.Patrick's Day, 1987, Kevin noted that the family census included 13 calves, with more to come, and twin filly foals, with two mares due to foal later.

Kevin and Bunny have seven children to share their interests. One source of family pride is that they now own the lot where their ancestor Michael Leahy (father of Dennis) settled in 1825. They purchased it some years ago. For over twenty years, this lot has been the scene of the annual St.Joseph's school sleigh ride, with eight or nine teams of horses present. This is a link with the past which is much appreciated by all the participants.

Father William Irwin

What happens when a man has a vocation for the priesthood, but at the same time has a gift for business management? If you happen to be Father William Irwin of Edmonton there is no conflict of interest at all; you use all your talents to serve God and your fellow man.

At the time of writing, Father Irwin is president and chief executive officer of Catholic Social Services in Edmonton. In 1977 he received the Queen's Silver Jubilee Medal; in 1986 he was named Citizen of the Year by the Edmonton Junior Chamber of Commerce. These bare facts do not come close to explaining the achievements of this man, who has spent much of his life helping people in need.

Father Irwin was the founding executive director of Catholic Charities, Archdiocese of Edmonton(now Catholic Social Services) a body which celebrated its silver jubilee in 1986. This is a multi-function social service agency, aimed at improving the quality of life for people in Edmonton and Central Alberta.

The agency "affirms the dignity and worth of human beings, irrespective of race,sex,age, national origin, religion, colour and creed and recognizes their right to individual differences. People are viewed, not as dependents who must be supported, but as brothers and sisters who have their right to equal opportunities, to be fully themselves, and to freedom of opinion and belief." (Taken from the Employee Handbook.)

Today, the agency offers counselling services to families and children; settlement services for immigrants and refugees; training for the disabled. Treatment, training and residential care is available to mentally handicapped adults, as well as to young people who are mentally retarded or emotionally disturbed. People who are addicted to alcohol or drugs are not forgotten, and young offenders and "street people" are also helped.

Today, Catholic Social Services employs more than 300 people. Although the staff have the necessary academic qualifications, Father Irwin picks people on the basis of their ability for the job, sometimes going out to recruit people whom he believes would fit comfortably into a certain slot. As a co-worker puts it: "he sees different gifts in each one of us, and tries to cultivate them."

Father Irwin believes in teamwork. He says that "decisions come to management through the democratic process." It is just as well that he has a talent for delegating authority, for he is frequently called away from his duties at the agency, to attend a meeting of one of the many committees or advisory boards on which he serves, or to give a paper at an international conference.

His participation in such work cannot be listed here in full, but the list includes being a member of a committee for the United Nations' World Food Organization; serving on the National Parole Board, and being a member of the Senate of the University of Alberta.

He has delivered papers dealing with the care of emotionally disturbed children, at conferences in many parts of Canada and the United States and in Dublin, Ireland, and he has spoken in New Delhi, India, on services for the developmentally delayed.

Although his social work has received this international recognition, Father Irwin is, first and foremost, a Roman Catholic priest. Every morning, he celebrates Mass before beginning his duties as head of Social Services. On the weekends he celebrates Mass at various parishes in Edmonton, and he often officiates at weddings.

His priestly assignments, which have been mostly in Edmonton, have provided a further opportunity for the Church to put his administrative skills to good use. Under his leadership, new churches were built at St.Matthew's,Edmonton; Sacred Heart, Gibbons; St.Clare's, Redwater. Chapels were also constructed at the St.Hilda and St.Clement schools in Edmonton.

One might well ask how this energetic man manages to cram so much activity into his day. The answer is that he manages on less than the usual amount of sleep. A typical day begins at 5.30 a.m. and does not end until 11.p.m. His evenings are filled with priestly duties, report writing, wedding rehearsals, etc. He does manage to squeeze in a few recreational activities such as skiing, cycling and attending concerts.

Father Irwin's preparation for the life he now leads called for similar dedication. Born in Peterborough, Ontario, he attended schools in Edmonton before entering St.Joseph's Minor and Major Seminary. He was ordained on June 6, 1954 at St. Joseph's Cathedral, Edmonton, by Most Reverend Anthony Jordan, O.M.I. His first assisgnment was that of Assistant to the Cathedral.

In 1961 he received a Master's Degree in Social Science from Fordham University, School of Social Services, New York, with a major in psychiatric social work, planning and administration. In due course he was admitted to the Academy of Certified Social Workers, and granted certificates of registration by the British Columbia Association of Social Workers and the Alberta Association of Social Workers.

In two rather different fields, he was made a Fellow of the Royal Society of Health (London,England) in 1977 and a Fellow of the Royal Society for the Encouragement of Arts and Commerce (London,England) in 1980.

Father Irwin is a descendant of David Conroy and his wife, Catherine Sullivan, who came on the ship Amity in 1825, They were his great,great, great grandparents. He is also descended from Edmond and Bridget Allen who travelled on the Resolution, and from the O'Briens of Douro, and from Timothy and Catherine Curtin who came on the Star.

He believes that, in helping to provide social services to the community, he is carrying out Christ's direction to care for the poor and hungry, outlined in Matthew 25: 35-40. This ideal is in keeping with the outreach philosophy of the Church of the 1980s.

He doesn't say much about himself. Family members are equally modest, saying simply that Father Irwin began Edmonton's Catholic Social Services with just himself and a secretary, "and it has now burgeoned into one of the largest social services in the country." It is obvious that this success did not come about without a great deal of help and dedication. As a co-worker says: "men like Father Irwin don't come your way very often."

Sister Chrysostom Doran

"She was endowed with a commanding personality, a beautiful contralto voice, and a forthright disposition." So stated an account of the achievements of Sister Chrysostom Doran, following her five year term as Reverend Mother of the Villa St.Scholastica Community in Duluth, Minnesota, from 1919 to 1924.

The girl with the forthright manner was Margaret Doran, born in Wisconsin in 1875 to Daniel Doran and his wife, Kate Allen. Daniel was a grandson of an Emily Township settler, Martin Doran.

Margaret was a girl with a goal. She planned to get an education, and then to enter the convent. As soon as she could, she accepted teaching positions at rural schools, saving her salary to pay for her future education, and that of a younger sister. She attended the sacred Heart Institute at Duluth and then the St.Cloud Normal School.

Her parents, who had moved to Grand Rapids when she was young, managed a hotel there. Her father was mayor of the community and also ran as a Democratic candidate for the Minnesota State Legislature. His untimely death in 1901 left his widow with young children to care for (the youngest of her brood of thirteen was only five years old), so Margaret, the eldest girl, set aside her plans for entering the convent to help at home. She was thirty years of age before she was free to pursue her vocation.

She entered the Villa St.Scholastica community, making her profession of vows in 1908. She served as a teacher, and later as principal, of several parochial schools. She became Reverend Mother of the community in 1919.

During her term as administrator, many things were achieved. Thirty-five permanent members were added to the community.

"The most notable accomplishment, from the point of view of Benedictism, was the partial adoption of the Divine Office," noted one writer.

Later, Sister Chrysostom Doran attended the Catholic University of America in Washington, DC, and after graduation she became supervisor of parochial elementary schools. She also served as directress of Sisters in the triennial vows for some years, before retiring in 1949. She died ten years later.

Father Lawrence McAuliffe, 1912-1962.

Father P L McAuliffe

When Martin and Catherine McAuliffe left County Cork for Upper Canada in 1825, they probably felt that they were going to the ends of the earth. How amazed they would have been if they could have foreseen that one of their descendants would live in China! This man was Father P. Lawrence McAuliffe, a son of Patrick McAuliffe of Emily Township.

After ordination to the priesthood, Father McAuliffe volunteered for the China mission with the Scarborough Foreign Mission Society. The young priest's journey to his new home was far longer than the distance between Ireland and Canada. He travelled to Shanghai via the Pacific and Japan, and then journeyed three hundred miles south to the Diocese of Lishui, in the province of Chekiang. His daily round consisted of parish duties, and in studying the Mandarin language and a number of local dialects.

All went well until the spring of 1941, when the Japanese invaded the area. Continuing air raids destroyed the churches, schools and hospitals administered by the Church. The missionaries and their flock were forced to evacuate the area.

This meant an exhausting trek of several months' duration, with the fear of capture by the enemy always with them. The refugees were attacked by enemy aircraft, and even when things were relatively quiet there was still the scourge of illness and the difficulty of finding food. Even so, the travellers had a better chance than those who had stayed behind; the entire area was overrun by hostile troops, and many of the inhabitants were killed, or died of starvation.

Finally, Father McAuliffe was picked up by a British army truck. His long walk ended at Hengyang in Hunan province, on September first. He had been almost four months on the road.

Once again he resumed his priestly duties, this time as assistant to an Italian bishop who was in charge of the mission there. The Japanese air raid on Pearl Harbour brought American air force servicemen to the district and because Father McAuliffe was an English-speaking Canadian priest who could identify with these young men, he volunteered to servce as their chaplain.

In 1944 he was transferred with them to Calcutta, India. He returned to Canada, via the United States, in 1945. He was able to spend a furlough in the Peterborough area with his family.

Before long, it was back to the mission field, but, sadly, he only lived to the age of 49. He died suddenly, of a heart attack, in the Dominican Republic, where he had served for nine years. It may be that his wartime experiences undermined his health.

Being aware that his health was poor, Father McAuliffe had expressed a wish that, should he die, he should be buried with his parishioners at Esperalvillo, a village that he loved. In those days, in the tropics, funerals were held on the day of death. The priest lay in the chapel, dressed in his vestments, as word went out into the district that he was gone.

Sixteen Scarborough priests arrived from all over the region, including the Regional Superior who preached the sermon. Five Grey Nuns and nine American Dominicans gathered to sing the Mass. Many of the people from the district crowded into the chapel that evening; some had been walking all day in order to attend the funeral. Representatives of the Canadian Embassy were also present.

The burial took place by moonlight, augmented by the glow of candles carried by the sisters. Father McAuliffe was the first Scarborough priest to be buried in the region. He had spent much of his life there in travelling by mule from one remote place to another, reaching the people in the isolated country districts. Those who worked with him remembered him as a man who was completly devoted to his work as a missionary priest.

The Famous Foleys

If Peter Robinson had lived to see what became of his settlers in Ramsay Township, he would have been delighted to learn of the success of the Foley brothers, the sons of two members of his group. These men eventually went to Minnesota, where they became railroad millionaires. They built thousands of miles of track in both Canada and the United States, including much of what later became the Canadian National Railway and the Canadian Pacific Railway.

The Foley brothers were Timothy, Michael, Thomas and John. Their father was John Foley from Castlelyons, County Cork; we are not sure at this stage whether he was the son of Patrick, who settled with his parents near Clayton in 1823, or Pat's young brother, John, who settled in the same neighbourhood.

Johanna, John's wife, came from Liscarrol, County Cork. She travelled on the Stakesby with her parents in 1823; she was a daughter of Timothy O'Brien. In all, John and Hannah, as she was known, had twelve children.

The future railroad men were among the eldest of the twelve. Timothy was born in 1838, Thomas in 1840, John in 1842 and Michael in 1845. A sister, Catherine, later to become Mrs J. Sheehan, was born between John and Michael. Timothy married Mary Louise Guthrie, Thomas married Jessie Craig, Michael married Helena White and John did not marry.

The Foley boys were raised in Lanark Township, and at an early age Timothy and another brother went into the sawmill and lumber business, operating concerns at Pakenham and Almonte.

In 1879 the brothers went to Minnesota, where they again went into the lumber business. In time, Timothy and Michael turned to railroad contracting, while Timothy and John operated extensive lumber interests, with mills at St. Cloud, Cold Springs, Milaca and Foley. Needless to say, Foley, Minnesota was named for them.

Some of the railway lines built by the Foleys were the Great Northern and the Northern Pacific; the Soo; the St. Paul, Milwaukee, Burlington & Northwestern; the Grand Trunk Pacific between Saskatoon and Prince Rupert; the Canadian Northern through Sudbury and Port Arthur; the five- mile Connaught tunnel at Glacier, British Columbia, and more! In all, about 25,000 miles of line. Timothy Foley was at one time president of the Duluth & Winnipeg Railway.

Timothy Foley was not a proud man. It is said that in his early days as a railroad contractor he spent a great deal of time with the construction crews, often taking part in their actual work, just as he had participated in rafting operations on the Ottawa and Madawaska Rivers in his own country. He had come all the way from supervising a handful of river drivers to running an operation which often saw fifty thousand men working at one time.

Back home in Ramsay Township, their friends kept track of their achievements via The Almonte Gazette, which printed stories such as this one, which appeared about eight years after they left the district.

Foley Brothers Get a Big Contract.
The St.Cloud (Minnesota) Times says:
"Yesterday the contract for building the St.Paul and

Timothy Foley, millionaire railway contractor, was a native of Lanark County.

Minneapolis line of road from Hinckley to West Superior was awarded to Messrs Foley Brothers of this city. The cost of completing the road, ready for the rolling stock, will be one million dollars. The distance to be built is 70 miles, and work will be commenced as soon as the sub-contracts are let.

Mr Timothy Foley goes to Duluth tomorrow to sub-let contracts and make necessary arrangements for the immediate prosecution of the work. Two thousand men will be put at work. With such a number employed, more of less of them sick at all times, doctors are necessary. Dr Ramsay of this city has been appointed surgeon-in-charge and will establish a hospital corps along the line of operations. He will place one or more doctors with the working forces and will bring to this city any who may be injured by accident, or are seriously ill."

The threat of illness or accident was a serious one. Living under primitive conditions, the "navvies" might succumb to illnesses which are virtually unknown today. Accidents to both men and horses were quite common; the dualine used for blasting rock was dangerous, and death or dismemberment was unfortunately part of the railroad scene. Incidentally, this Dr. Ramsay was a brother-in-law of the Foley men. He practised medicine at St.Cloud, and was president of the Northern Minnesota Medical Association.

There came a time when it seemed as though everything those Foley men touched turned to gold. They built tunnels, bridges, dams and office buildings, highways and airfields. There was the George Washington bridge in New York City, mighty dams in California, aviation plants and highways in Alaska. Holdings included the Foley Bros. Wholesale Grocers, and the Flour State Baking Company.

American magazine writers have used such words as "saga" and "dynasty" writing about the Foley family. One journalist said "these brothers were largely responsible for changing the northwest country from a wilderness, to blossom as a rose."

The Foleys were staunch supporters of the Roman Catholic Church. In later life Timothy Foley was honoured by the Vatican for his charitable works at St.Paul, and in 1918 the knighthood of the order of St. Gregory the Great was conferred upon him. This order, founded by Pope Gregory XVI in 1831, is conferred upon members of the laity in recognition of special services to Church and state.

Timothy Foley and his wife, Mary Louise, hosted many dignitaries from Rome who were visiting the United States. Mary Louise was a daughter of a Scottish couple, James Guthrie and Margaret Reid of Middleville in Lanark County. They were staunch Presbyterians and possibly neither they nor the senior Foleys approved of this mixed marriage at first, for Timothy and his bride were married at Almonte without their parents' knowledge.

Timothy Foley died in 1920, leaving an estate of more than four million dollars. Many of his relatives in Lanark County received bequests under the will.

The Foley brothers had travelled a long way from the farms assigned to their ancestors by Peter Robinson in 1823.

Monsignor Pearson

Reverend Monsignor John T.Pearson is the present rector at the Cathedral of St-Peter-in-Chains at Peterborough. This seems particularly appropriate, for the parish was established to look after the spiritual needs of the Peter Robinson settlers and other immigrants of that era, and Monsignor Pearson is descended from two of those families.

"When the emigrants arrived here in 1825 the only Roman Catholic Diocese in Canada was that of Quebec," says Monsignor Pearson. *'although there was an English-speaking Auxiliary Bishop to the Bishop of Quebec. In the year 1826 the Kingston Diocese was established, as the second diocese in Canada and the first English-speaking one. The Auxiliary Bishop to Quebec, Bishop Alexander McDonald, became the first Bishop of Kingston. In that very year, 1826, he established the parish of St. Peter-in-Chains to look after the spiritual needs of the*

Monsignor J.T.Pearson of Peterborough is descended from several of the old families of the Peterborough area.

large number of Irish immigrants."

"The first church was of log and, following a gift of land from King William IV of England, the present large stone edifice was erected in 1837-38 from stone taken from the local Jackson's Creek. This has been a Cathedral Church since 1882."

Monsignor Pearson is descended from the Allen and Sullivan families of Douro Township. (The Pearsons came at an even earlier date.) In actual fact, he can claim descent from seven people who came from Ireland with Peter Robinson. The Allens came on the ship Resolution in 1825. Edmond Allen and his wife, Bridget Fleming, were the ancestors of Monsignor Pearson; they were accompanied by a daughter, Mary, who later married Michael Sullivan, and by Bridget's father, John Fleming.

Jeremiah Sullivan and his wife, Alice Kelly, travelled on the Regulus with their family, including a son Michael, mentioned above. Mary and Michael later had a daughter, Catherine, who became Mrs Daniel Pearson.

Most Rev J M Sherlock

Most Reverend John Sherlock, Bishop of London.

Official host to Pope John Paul II. That,in effect, was the role played by the Most Reverend John Sherlock, Bishop of London, Ontario, when His Holiness visited Canada in 1984. At that time, Bishop Sherlock was president of the Canadian Council of Bishops, the body which issued the invitation to the Pope to come to this country. As president of the Conference, Bishop Sherlock was responsible for the national planning which was necessary for the visit.

Although he was born in Regina, Saskatchewan, the Bishop is a descendant of several old Ottawa Valley Irish families, including the Sherlocks and the Tierneys. His great grandmother, Mary Corkery, arrived as a young girl in 1823 with the Peter Robinson immigrants, travelling with her parents, Michael and Mary Corkery. She grew up to marry Michael Tierney. The bishop is also a descendant of the O'Brien family; his mother was the former Catherine O'Brien, Mrs Joseph Sherlock.

John Sherlock was educated at schools in Brantford, Ontario, at St. Jerome's College, Kitchener, and at the University of Toronto. After university he entered St.Augustine's Seminary, where he earned his Doctor of Divinity degree. Ordination to the priesthood followed in 1950. He took post-graduate studies in Canon Law at the Catholic University of America in Washington,D.C., graduating in 1952 with a licentiate in Canon Law.

Pastoral duties followed. From 1952 until 1963, Father Sherlock served at St.Eugene's Parish, Hamilton and at St.Augustine's,Dundas. From 1963 until 1974 he was pastor of St.Charles Garnier parish, Hamilton, where he was responsible for the construction of a new parish church.

During that period he also served as Advocate Judge for the Regional Marriage Tribunal. Between 1963 and 1966 he was chaplain of McMaster University's Newman Club, and national chaplain of the Newman Clubs of Canada.

In the area of community service, he took part in the establishing of co-operative housing groups in the Hamilton area; he was chairman of the Wentworth County Roman Catholic Separate School Board; vice-chairman of the board of St.Joseph's Hospital, Hamilton; chaplain of the Catholic Hospital Conference of Ontario.

On August 28,1974, he was consecrated Auxiliary Bishop of London, and on May 6,1978 was elected Vicar-Capitular of the diocese when Archbishop Carter was transferred to the Archdiocese of Toronto. John Sherlock was named ninth Bishop of London on July 8,1978, and installed on August 21 of that year.

He served as president of the Canadian Conference of Bishops from 1983 to 1985, and naturally the highlight of those years, and indeed of his life in the Church, was the Pope's visit. At the time of writing, he is liaison Bishop for the Canadian Conference of Bishops with the Catholic University Chaplains of Canada and the presidents of Catholic Colleges and Universities.

In 1985, Bishop Sherlock received a Doctor of Law degree, Honoris Causa, from the University of Windsor, and in 1986 a Doctor of Divinity Degree, Honoris Causa, from Huron College, London.

His ancestors, Michael and Mary Corkery, were devout Catholics whose pioneer home was one of the early stations where Mass was celebrated by the missionary priest from Perth. A large number of their descendants have served the Church as priests or nuns. Two of Bishop Sherlock's brothers have also been ordained to the priesthood. Father Philip Sherlock is pastor of St. Mary Margaret parish, Hamilton, and the late Father William Sherlock was pastor of St.Boniface parish, Maryhill.

Other members of this family have distinguished themselves in their chosen fields. One brother is a dealer in rare books and an expert in Canadiana. Another brother and one sister are social workers with Master's degrees. A second sister has an honours degree from the University of Toronto, and is a graduate librarian. She is married to a former president of Laurentian University who is now

Executive Director of the Ontario Association of Universities and Colleges. A sixth brother is Business Administrator of the Roman Catholic Episcopal Corporation of the Diocese of Hamilton, who serves as president of the Ontario Separate School Trustees' Association at the time of writing.

Grocer of the Year

When the Towns family of Douro received the coveted title, "Grocer of the Year" in 1986, they were up against some some tough competition. Twenty-two stores from across Canada were considered for the honour of winning the Arnold Rands Heritage Store Award, sponsored by the Canadian Federation of Independent Grocers, based in Peterborough. The award is open to stores anywhere in Canada that have a long history, are still operating out of their original building, and are managed by at least a second generation of the founding family.

At the Towns store, operated now by Michael Towns and his wife Rosemary, three generations of the family can be seen at work, as well as a number of other employees. When the award was made in 1986, family members on the job included Michael and Rosemary, his mother and uncle, Mrs Bill Towns and Mr Joe Towns, and, as part-timers, the four children of Michael and Rosemary. Their family has a long history of serving the public.

George Towns, whose wife was Peter Robinson settler Joanna Sullivan, ran the Douro post office in his home in the 1890s also stocking a few items such as tea and tobacco. In 1892, his son, P.G.Towns, ran a store in Peterborough, but he soon decided that he preferred rural life, so he opened a store in a Douro house two years later. He soon began to build the store which is in use today. It has since been enlarged, to provide for a greatly expanded business.

P.G.Towns was 75 when he died in 1948; he had worked at the store and operated a post office there until the week before his death. His sons, Joe and Bill, ran the store until the 1960s, when Bill and his wife Mary became the owners. Mary is also a descendant of Peter Robinson settlers, the Torpeys and the Condons.

Michael and Rosemary purchased the store in 1973, although Bill (who died in 1985) and Mary, a popular postmistress, continued to work there. It is interesting to note that Rosemary is descended from

Three generations of the Towns family receive the coveted Grocer of the Year award.

In front of the Douro post office, postmaster Michael Towns and his wife, the former Rosemary Walsh.

Richard and Elizabeth Walsh, who travelled on the ship John Barry with the Robinson settlers of 1825.

Years ago, every hamlet had at least one store, but the advent of the motor car dealt a death blow to many of these small businesses. Customers were able to travel to the towns, where a better selection and lower prices were an attraction. Paradoxically, the Towns store has simply become bigger and better. They buy in volume, which keeps prices competitive, and they have a bright, attractive store with an excellent selection of groceries and meats. What hasn't changed is the old-fashioned service and the friendly reception given to neighbours and strangers alike.

As participants in the competition, the Towns family were visited three times by judges in the summer of 1986. In October they learned that they were one of three finalists, stores in Quebec and Saskatchewan being the others. Along with over 1000 grocers, the Douro group attended a convention at the Metropolitan Convention Centre in Toronto, where they learned that P.G.Towns and Sons had won the 1986 Heritage Store Award.

A medal presented to William George Towns on the occasion of Ontario's Bicentennial, for services to the community in the field of history.

The Bathurst District

Location tickets.

The location tickets given to settlers who came out in 1823 under the supervision of Peter Robinson looked like this:

Whereas ....born at of the age of ...years has been conveyed to this country at the Public Charge under the superintendence of the Hon.Peter Robinson,, and has produced a certificate of his being accepted as an Emigrant Settler to receive land in Upper Canada, and has taken the Oath of Allegiance,
We do assign to him seventy acres of land, being the ...part of lot... in the... concession of the Township of..................in the District of Bathurst, for which having cleared half the width of the Concession Road bounding the said seventy acres and having cleared and fenced three acres and a half within the said Location, and erected a dwelling house thereon, of at least sixteen feet by twenty, within two years from the date hereof, he will be entitled to receive a Grant free from any other expense than the usual fee of .... for Patent.
An additional tract of thirty acres adjoining the said seventy acres will be reserved for the space of ten years, to commence from this date which the said............ will be entitled to receive a Grant for, upon paying the sum of ten pounds sterling. The said several tracts of land to be liable to a Quit Rent of two pence per acre, payable at such time, and in such manner, as set forth in the Memorandum published by the authority of the British Government for the information of the said emigrants.

I have not seen a copy of the Oath of Allegiance mentioned above, but quite obviously it would have been different from the oath which was administered during the penal days. The majority of the Peter Robinson settlers were of the Roman Catholic faith and it is certain that they did not give up their religion.

Centenary celebration.

In 1923 the congregation of St.Mary's Church, Almonte, held special celebrations to commemorate the centenary of Irish settlement in Ramsay Township, which was also the centenary of their parish. While no reference was made to Peter Robinson at that time, we know that his group was in the minds of the organizers, for The Almonte Gazette reported (inaccurately, as it turned out) that
" there were over five hundred of these early Irish settlers. They were evicted tenants from County Cork."
Robinson's settlers located in several townships and became members of various churches, which is the most likely reason that no mention was made of him in the press at that time. In actual fact the events paid tribute only to those who had settled

St. Mary's church, Almonte. The original congregation was mainly composed of Peter Robinson settler. The present church replaced one that was destroyed by fire in 1869.

in Ramsay. However, those people were certainly the founders of St. Mary's parish, and we know that Mass was celebrated in private homes from 1823 on. The Gazette noted that the people were first visited by Father John MacDonald, a priest from Glengarry County who was appointed to Perth as pastor there.

"Father MacDonald tramped through the woods from Perth with his vestments and other necessaries strapped on his back."

Father MacDonald had a huge parish, which included many townships, including Beckwith, Ramsay, Drummond, Lanark, Fitzroy, Pakenham, Burgess, Bathurst etc. It is good to know that he soon acquired a horse for his travels. Mr Duncan MacDonald of Brockville has recently published extracts from this priest's diary, which he has translated from the Gaelic. A few notes from this work have been included in the genealogical section, by permission of Mr. MacDonald.

The 1923 celebrations included an entertainment in the Almonte Town Hall, and of course special services at the church. Among the visiting priests on that occasion was Monsignor MacDonald of the Diocese of Alexandria, an interesting link with the past as his namesake returned to Glengarry in the 1830s.

The priests' plot in St.Mary's cemetery, Almonte. Canon Patrick Corkery, Rev. Francis Corkery and Canon John Burke were descendants of Peter Robinson settlers.

When interviewed by the press after the celebrations, Canon Cavanagh made several remarks which are of interest to us today.

"This splendid event could not have come off more satisfactorily than it did. We had not expected to have His Grace, the Archbishop honour us with a Pontifical Mass, but he did so. For this act of generosity on the part of a man of his age, and taking into account the distance he came,,,and in addition to all this his very able address after the Mass, I say we one and all owe him a debt of gratitude. He gave the real finish to this grand religious demonstration."

He noted that Father Brownrigg and then Mr C.J.Foy of Perth also spoke to the congregation and

"those people of our parish who are descended from the old families should feel grateful for the excellent vindication they made of the good name and reputation of their good old grandparents. We all know that they have been slandered and badly used and yet after hearing all the truth concerning those early times in these parts, who among you would not be proud to call yourselves their children?"

This of course refers to the fact that the Irish people of the district had smarted under verbal and written abuse for many years, in connection with the Ballyghiblin riots, mentioned earlier.

All was apparently forgiven by the time of the centenary for Canon Cavanagh gave a public vote of thanks to a group of men, referred to by him as "our separated brethren" who assisted in the entertainment, and their families who turned out in large numbers to swell the audience.

A large number of the Peter Robinson families went to Huntley Township in Carleton County, and they, along with even earlier Irish settlers, founded the parish of St.Michael's, Corkery. Their centenary was celebrated in 1924, and an excellent historical booklet was published at that time by the late Dr.Dunn.

The Great Fire.

The summer of 1870 was a nightmare for the people of the Ottawa Valley. It is remembered as the year of the big fire. That summer had been extremely dry; no rain had fallen for weeks and the creeks and swamps were completely dried out. Fires were burning out of control in many parts of Eastern Ontario.

In August, an enormous fire raged through the townships of Pakenham, Fitzroy, Goulbourn, Huntley, March and Nepean, the first four being country where there were many Robinson settlers. Hull and Ottawa were both affected; Ottawa was saved only because the dam at Dow's Lake was cut, allowing the water to flood part of the city. Refugees crowded into Ottawa from the surrounding countryside.

At one point, The Ottawa Times reported: "in Nepean and March, only three houses stand this morning in fifteen miles. Fences, telegraph posts and crops in this district are all destroyed. The townships of Huntley and Fitzroy are actually in a blaze. A distance of ten miles above the Carp is in flame.

The Carleton Place Herald reported at the end of August that the fire had burned a swath through "Huntley, Goulbourn, March and Nepean, sweeping all before it for a distance of about seven miles wide and sixteen miles in length. One hundred families are left without food or shelter."

The communities of Stittsville and Bell's Corners were wiped out. In the country, houses and barns were razed. Livestock were caught in the flames, or had to be destroyed because there was no food for them.

Many of the families who had come out with Robinson in 1823 had to undergo this terrible experience. Even Ramsay Township, which was bypassed by the main fire, had many bush fires in the country, and people lived in a state of fear for some weeks, not knowing where fire might break out next.

Some people hid valuables in their wells, or buried them underground in the hope that they could be retrieved later. Stories of this 'buried treasure' still survive in some localities, where it is believed that money or silver may still exist.

People drove their horses and cattle into lakes in the hope of saving both themselves and their animals. Others tried to hide in wells and ditches. Mrs James Allen was one of those who perished in Huntley.

Later, some attempt was made to assist those who had lost "everything, or nearly all," and those listed in Huntley included the Allens, Kennedys, Ryans and Whites. The O'Connells of Goulbourn also lost their home. These families had lived through one of the worst natural disasters the Ottawa Valley has ever known.

Cormac and Brudenell.

During the 1850s, a number of families from the Huntley-Ramsay area went north to Renfrew County. Their new locations included Cobden, Killaloe, Renfrew etc. Some of these were second generation Peter Robinson families who settled in the Brudenell-Cormac area; genealogists may wish to check the cemeteries and census records for their families. I have also included some non- "Robinson" names from Ramsay and Huntley.

Surnames in that district prior to 1870 include Manion, O'Keeffe, O'Brien, Mullins, Dwyer, O'Connor, Green, Meagher, Sullivan, Walsh, O'Neil, Hogan, Regan and Ryan.

Peterborough

The boat.

They don't do things by halves in Peterborough. When the area planned Homecoming '75, a celebration which lasted all year, displays, contests, church services and the sale of a souvenir booklet were only part of the great event. Knowing that 1975 was the 150th anniversary of the coming of the Peter Robinson settlers to the area, the Homecoming committee planned a re-enactment of the landing of the pioneers on the banks of the Otonabee River, in a spot which is now part of down town Peterborough.

The route was no problem; it is known that the settlers came up the Otonabee from Rice Lake. Costumes were easily provided, and the manpower for the boat during the weekly demonstrations at Little Lake was provided by the Peterborough Rowing Club. The difficulty was in providing a boat which resembled the flat-bottomed craft used by Robinson's settlers.

Using as much ingenuity as Robinson's men, a local man, Nick West, set to work in the fall of 1974 to build a replica. He had not built a boat prior to this, and historical records were few. No pictures or blueprints were available . Using materials supplied by the Peterborough Lumber Company, Nick relied on descriptions left by Robinson himself which indicated that the flat-bottomed boat was sixty feet long, twelve feet wide and eight feet high. There were eight long oars on each side, with two steering oars at each end.

Nick built the boat in his backyard, having first created a working model. The craft was made of spruce and pine and it was eight feet wide at the keel and ten and a half feet wide at the gunwale. The oars, also made from spruce, were thirteen and a half feet in length. The great project was finished in early July, 1975, just in time for the re-enactment.

The launching was facilitated by the use of a crane, a refinement not available to the pioneers. Like Robinson before him, Nick was worried about the safety of the boat, hoping that the joints wouldn't loosen as the wood dried. Robinson relied on Providence to assist him; West called in the fire department to stand by with a pump, in case the worst happened. Everything went according to plan.

In all, five pageants depicting the settlers' arrival were held, under the leadership of the Rowing Club. Residents of the different townships settled by the 1825 immigrants travelled in the boat each time. The voyages in Robinson's day were made with 35 passengers each time, along with 20 oarsmen and five tons of freight.

Nick West's project was a great success. The Peterborough Examiner called it "a behemoth of boats." Their reporter explained that the craft would have cost $4,500 to build, excluding the labour of Mr West and his volunteer assistants, but that the Homecoming committee had only had to find a little more than $2,000, thanks to the generosity of local suppliers.

At a later date, the committee was offered $10,000 for the boat by representatives of an American museum. They were gratified by the offer, but naturally chose to keep their replica in the Peterborough area. It came to rest in the Lang Century Village. The working model went to the Peterborough museum.

At the re-enactment of the first landing at Little Lake, there was a special touch when Lady Robinson, whose husband was a descendant of Sir John Beverley Robinson, Peter's brother, was presented with a bouquet by little Maureen Anglesey. She is a descendant of John O'Grady, one of the settlers of 1825. It was truly a day to remember.

The Irish monument on the bank of the Otonabee River, at Peterborough. Performing the unveiling in 1975 were Irish Ambassador, James O. Flavin and Fred O'Grady of Peterborough. Fred was the chairman of the Homecoming '75 committee, and he is a direct descendant of the O'Grady family who came with Peter Robinson in 1825.

The monument.

Peterborough is named after Peter Robinson, and his name is perpetuated in the district in several ways. One of the most tangible reminders is a three ton monument which stands on the banks of the Otonabee River, near the Red Oak Inn, in the heart of Peterborough.

This monument was unveiled in 1975 by Mr James Flavin, who was at that time the Irish Ambassador to Canada. It is a green marble stone which stands close to seven feet high. A bronze plaque is attached to it, which describes coming of the Peter Robinson settlers in 1825.

The committee in charge of the project were careful to word the information in such a way that it not only praised the leadership of Robinson, but also commemorated the life and work of his Irish settlers.

Conclusion

It is now more than 164 years since the first of Peter Robinson's settlers set foot on Canadian soil. There are a number of questions which we can ask ourselves with regard to their survival as a group.

1. Were they a cohesive group, or did they quickly become assimilated into Canadian society?

I find that people in what was then the Newcastle District (Peterborough County and part of Victoria) often have a good working knowledge of the settlement of 1825 and the part which their ancestors played in it. This is partly because of the magnificent celebrations which took place at the time of the 150th anniversary of the arrival of these settlers, and partly because chapters on the Robinson emigration of 1825 can be seen in several excellent local histories.

The 1825 settlers came in large numbers and usually managed to get land near to that of relatives or old neighbours. Social life centred around the various churches, and because in those days of poor transportation most people chose to marry neighbours, many of the pioneer families intermarried with others who had come with Robinson.

In some cases, people in the Peterborough area can show a large number of Peter Robinson family names in their family trees. This book cannot show the extent of this connection because in most cases I have documented little after the first or second generation. I do not mean to imply that there are cases of "I'm my own Grandpa." However, many of the families have interlocking connections by marriage, and my advice to the genealogist is, don't overlook anything!

In the case of the 1823 settlement, they have become assimilated to some extent, outside of the townships of Ramsay and Huntley, where kinship ties are still close. Robinson was unable to settle all his people in one spot and many took up land in districts where Scottish settlers abounded. Although in the early days ethnic and religious boundaries were seldom crossed, the people in the more remote areas tended to lose their connection with the Robinson group as a whole.

One thing is common to descendants of these settlers of both the 1823 and 1825 groups; they are very much aware of their Irish heritage, and great pride is taken in it.

2. Was there a connection between the 1823 and 1825 groups? Were there any common factors, apart from the fact that Robinson was their superintendent?

The answer is yes . I have found a direct connection between a number of the families. Some of these are spelled out in the families section of the book. It appears that other members of some families also came out in the 1830s and 1840s, although not under government auspices. It is certainly true that in 1825 Robinson brought out more people from the parishes from which the 1823 settlers had come. Some were neighbours and relatives, as we know; others were probably not connected at all.

3. What of the people who left Canada for the United States? Did they maintain ties with Ontario?

From the mid nineteenth century on, many of these people moved to the United States, with the Dakotas and Minnesota a popular destination. It appears that people from both the Bathurst and the Newcastle Districts did this, often settling in some new area which abounded in the names of Robinson's families! Here again the families intermarried, and in some cases the tradition has been handed down that their people came out from Ireland with Peter Robinson, settling first in Canada.

4. Peter Robinson: concerned leader or careless official?

I hope that I have succeeded in exploding some of the myths surrounding Peter Robinson as a leader. While he was no more a saint than the rest of us, he emerges through his voluminous correspondence as a man who genuinely cared for the welfare of his charges, and who genuinely wanted the experiment to succeed. This is corroborated by contemporary letters, written by the settlers themselves, in which they praise Robinson's work.

Too many people nowadays try to rewrite history in the light of our modern values and capabilities. I should like to see them try to do better as leaders of such an expedition, given the lack of facilities afforded the people in the 1820s.

I have attempted to give readers an overview of the Peter Robinson settlers, approaching the topic in three ways. Firstly, background material is essential if we are to understand why Robinson brought these people out here at all.

I have highlighted each family because I wanted to know something about these people as individuals, human beings with the same hopes and dreams as ourselves. I have given what genealogical information I have for the sake of researchers. I have faithfully tried to piece together as much as possible from all the official papers, as well as information given to me by descendants. The latter is being passed on in good faith, just as it was given to me, and I take no responsibility for errors that may have occurred in other people's research.

I have not checked church records as I feel that it would be an invasion of privacy for me to print certain information without the permission of the families concerned.

While it is impossible to track down all the families of the settlers - and I advertised extensively and wrote hundreds of letters - I have featured a few of them in various categories to show their fields of achievement. I should be delighted if readers would share with me any stories which I have not uncovered to date.

Most of all, I hope that this book will lay to rest the myth that the Peter Robinson settlements were a failure! How can this be so? In this book I have given examples of some who have achieved greatness in the eyes of the world. We must also be careful to pay tribute to those who have quietly worked away in their own small corners. Farmers, municipal politicians, school teachers and stay-at-home mothers; when all is said and done, these are the people who make the greatest contribution to the community with their selfless service, day after day, year after year. While such work is not confined to the ranks of the Robinson settlers, there must be many thousands of descendants of the original 2500 or so, so their influence must have spread far and wide.

Then there are those who served the Church! For some reason, the Robinson settlers seem to have been an unusually devout group. When I first began my research I decided to keep a record of all those who had answered a religious vocation. Very soon, my head began to spin, as I found family after family who had given their young people to the service of God and humanity, as priests, nuns or as Protestant clergy. The task of recording them all is impossible.

Think of the influence of these people, not only in Canada but in many countries around the world. The priests who braved the rigours of pioneer travel to minister to their flocks. The missionaries, who faced possible death in foreign lands. The teaching and nursing sisters who have helped thousands of people who have passed through their care. Although only a few can be mentioned in this book, I hope that readers will remember the contribution made by all.

I have found that the descendants of the Robinson settlers - those who are aware of the connection - have an immense pride in their heritage, as well they might. I hope that this book has done something to further their knowledge of those who went before.

Acknowledgements.

An old Welsh greeting goes like this: "Hail, Guest! We ask not what thou art: if friend, we greet thee hand and heart; if stranger, such no longer be: if foe, our love shall conquer thee."

It appears to me that this sentiment has been extended to other Celts, for I have been overwhelmed by the welcome, the trust and the assistance which have been given to me by a great number of descendants of the Peter Robinson settlers.

People have been truly "flaithiuil" with their hospitality, their time, their family documents and their family photographs. This Irish Gaelic word, meaning "generous" has been retained among the older people of Douro Township, who pronounce it "flahool" and it is surely no accident that this word has gone into their English speaking vocabulary. Generosity for them is a way of life.

A special word of thanks must go to Sister St. Donald of Mount St. Joseph, Peterborough. This book is dedicated to her because of all that she did to get my research started at the Peterborough end. Her kind acts certainly got the ball rolling.

Mary Towns of Douro permitted me to see her late husband's papers, and we shared some laughter, too. Shirley and Fred O'Grady took time off from their work as North American Co-ordinators of the Rose of Tralee Festival to take me about to see people and places. Simon Connell of Emily Township accompanied my husband and me on a tour of his area, pointing out the places of " Peter Robinson" interest.

Then there are the people who, despite that the fact that they are authors in their own right, willingly shared information with me and sometimes gave permission for me to quote items from their work. They include Edgar Boland, Garvin Boyle, Simon Connell, Michael Diamond, Clare and Elizabeth Galvin, Robert Legget, Duncan MacDonald and Aileen Young.

Another special thank you goes to Marie J. Knudtsen who has allowed me to share with readers some of the experiences recorded by her late father, Eugene Leahy.

Others assisted in many different ways. Some of them have become friends or pen pals. Although this is my tenth book, I have seldom met with such help and kindness in going about my work. I hope that nobody has been overlooked in the following list, for everyone's assistance is much appreciated.

Joan Anderson; Adelaide Armstrong; Florence Bowes; Flora Campbell; Bob Conroy; Father David Corkery; John Dunn; Linda Fahey; Kathleen Fenton; Doris Fleming; Mary Gallagher; Wilhelmine Greene; James Guiry; Alison Hare; Marie Harris; J.J.Hogan; Reg Hunter; Father Bill Irwin; Elaine Kennedy; Marie Knudtsen; Bonnie Guthrie Kuehl; Kevin Leahy; Dawn Leduc; R.Andrew Lee; Clyde Lendrum; Edmund Lunney; Frances Towns Lynch; Ray Madden; Frank Martin; Dorothy McBride; Marianne McKenzie; Frances McLean; Essie and Reg McQuigge; Frank Miller; Judge C. James Newton; Marion O' Connell; Basil and Mary O'Keefe; Dorothy and Mary Oatway; Bert Owens; Joanne Packham; Monsignor J.T.Pearson; Thomas D. Pearson; Basil Phelan; Dorothy Pratt; Mary Lou Quehl; Mary Regan Rand; Viola Reid; Violet Richardson; Laura O'Brien Russell; Most Rev. John Sherlock; Marilyn Snedden; Madeleine and Howard Snow; Jean Steel; B. Wesley Switzer; Rosemary Walsh Towns; Margaret Wallace; Mr and Mrs James B. Walsh. There were also a number of people who, while they were unable to give direct information, were kind enough to write to suggest others who could help.

If I could give a prize for to the person who came up with the most information to share, it would have to go to Olive Doran. She produced an incredible number of photographs, as well as genealogical tables which enabled me to trace the relationship of the people in the pictures to the original settlers. Having seen this data I attempted to work out just how many "Peter Robinson" families she and her husband Elmer are both descended from, or related to by marriage. I gave up. The total is staggering.

Bibliography

Peterborough, Land of Shining Waters. Centennial Committee, City and County of Peterborough, 1967.

Bennett, Carol
Valley Irish Juniper Books, 1983.

Connell, Simon J.
Some Facts from St.Luke's Past, 1986.

Craig, John.
By the Sound of Her Whistle Peter Martin Associates, 1966.

Diamond, C. Michael.
The Children of the Settlers, 1985.

Dunn, Dr. J.F., Souvenir of the Centennial, St.Michael's Church, Huntley. 1924.

Edmison, J. Alex (ed)
Through the Years in Douro. Douro Centennial Committee, 1967

Galvin, Clare
The Holy Land. (History of Ennismore Township.)

Graham, Jean Lancaster.
Asphodel, A Tale of a Township. Township of Asphodel, 1978.

Haydon, Andrew.
Pioneer Sketches in the District of Bathurst. The Ryerson Press, 1925.

Kirkconnell, Watson.
County of Victoria Centennial History. 1921, 1967.

MacDonald, Rev. John.
Diary, 1823-1837. Translated by Duncan W. MacDonald, 1985

McGill, Jean.
A Pioneer History of the County of Lanark, 1968

Nelson, D.Gayle
Forest to Farm. Early Days in Otonabee. The Keene/Otonabee 150th Anniversary Committee, 1975.

Pammett, Howard. Lilies and Shamrocks. A History of Emily Township, County of Victoria. 1818-1873. Emily Township History Committee, 1974.

Poole, Dr.T.W. The Early Settlement of Peterborough County. 1867.

Young, Aileen:
Yesteryear at Young's Point.

Source material.
Crown land papers
Census records 1841, 1851, 1861, 1871
The Peter Robinson papers, PAC.
(Includes ships' lists, corresondence, location tickets, character references, location book.)
Reports of the Select Committee of the House of Commons on Emigration.
Upper Canada Land Patents, Ontario Archives.
Upper Canada Sundries, various volumes, PAC.

Newspapers.
Almonte Gazette etc
Bathurst Courier
Bytown Gazette
Carleton Place Herald
Ottawa Citizen
Ottawa Times
Peterborough Examiner
Renfrew Mercury
Toronto Globe.

Other information gleaned from Who's Who and the Parliamentary Guide; cemeteries and cemetery records; Tweedsmuir Histories; family histories; church histories; diaries; letters and interviews with descendants of Peter Robinson settlers.

I may as well say here that I am also glad to answer people's genealogical queries if they feel that I can give them any further assistance, but please do enclose a stamped, self addressed envelope for a reply. I can be contacted at R.R.2, Renfrew, Ontario. K7V 3Z5.

Copies of this book may be obtained by writing directly to the publisher:
Juniper Books,
R.R.2,
Renfrew, Ontario.
K7V 3Z5.
Groups or individuals purchasing three or more copies may buy them at 20% off the retail price. Please add one dollar per order for postage and handling.

Acknowledgements

I wish to extend my thanks to all those who permitted the use of their family photos in this book. I also wish to thank my husband, **D. W. McCuaig,** who took some of the modern photos in the book, and who also made copies of every heritage photo so that the originals could be returned at once to their owners.

St. Luke's Roman Catholic Church, Downeyville.
D.W.McCuaig photo

About the author

Carol Bennett is a Canadian writer, partly Irish by descent, who has a continuing interest in Canadian history. Her ancestors lived within sight of Ireland's holy mountain, Croagh Patrick in County Mayo, so she cannot claim to be a descendant of a Peter Robinson family. However, she has long been interested in finding out more about that group of settlers, and this book is the result.

She is a former weekly newspaper editor, and she is married to D.W. McCuaig, the former publisher of a group of newspapers in the Ottawa Valley. He has contributed a number of photographs to this book.

Other books by Carol Bennett include:
historical novels, written as Jane Barrett:

1976	Woman of Ireland (Simon & Schuster)
1977	Daughter of the Regiment (PaperJacks)
1979	The Bittersweet Tree (PaperJacks)

Non fiction, written as Carol Bennett, published by Juniper Books:

1980	In Search of Lanark
1981	In Search of the K & P
1982	In Search of Lanark, revised edition
1982	The Admaston Heritage Book
1983	Valley Irish
1984	The Story of Renfrew (ed.)
1985	In Search of the Red Dragon (The Welsh in Canada)
1987	Peter Robinson's Settlers.

Index

St. Michael's church, Corkery. The parish was founded in 1824 and many of the first members were Robinson settlers of 1823. This stone church replaced an earlier structure which was located in the present cemetery.